'Insightful, intelligent and thought-provoking, this study provides fascinating contexts within which new dimensions of both novels are brought to the fore, in light of each other.' – **Stephanie Smith**, *University of Florida*

The Great Gatsby and *Tender is the Night* are F. Scott Fitzgerald's best-known novels. They draw on Fitzgerald's own vivid experiences in the 1920s but transform them into art.

Part I of this indispensable study:
- provides interesting and informed close readings of key passages
- examines how each novel starts and ends
- discusses key themes of society, money, gender and trauma
- outlines the methods of analysis and offers suggestions for further work.

Part II supplies essential background material, including:
- an account of Fitzgerald's life
- a survey of historical, cultural and literary contexts
- samples of significant criticism.

Also featuring a helpful Further Reading section, this volume equips readers with the critical and analytical skills which will enable them to enjoy and explore both novels for themselves.

Nicolas Tredell is a freelance writer and formerly taught Literature, Film, Drama and Cultural Studies at the University of Sussex.

Analysing Texts is dedicated to one clear belief: that we can all enjoy, understand and analyse literature for ourselves, provided we know how to do it. Readers are guided in the skills and techniques of close textual analysis used to build an insight into a richer understanding of an author's individual style, themes and concerns. An additional section on the writer's life and work and a comparison of major critical views place them in their personal and literary context.

D0263046

ANALYSING TEXTS

General Editor: Nicholas Marsh

Published

Chaucer: The Canterbury Tales   *Gail Ashton*
Aphra Behn: The Comedies   *Kate Aughterson*
Webster: The Tragedies   *Kate Aughterson*
John Keats: *John Blades*
Shakespeare: The Sonnets   *John Blades*
Wordsworth and Coleridge: Lyrical Ballads   *John Blades*
Shakespeare: The Comedies   *R. P. Draper*
Charlotte Brontë: The Novels   *Mike Edwards*
George Eliot: The Novels   *Mike Edwards*
E. M. Forster: The Novels   *Mike Edwards*
Jane Austen: The Novels   *Nicholas Marsh*
William Blake: The Poems   *Nicholas Marsh*
Emily Brontë: Wuthering Heights   *Nicholas Marsh*
Daniel Defoe: The Novels   *Nicholas Marsh*
Philip Larkin: The Poems   *Nicholas Marsh*
D. H. Lawrence: The Novels   *Nicholas Marsh*
Shakespeare: The Tragedies   *Nicholas Marsh*
Mary Shelley: Frankenstein   *Nicholas Marsh*
Virginia Woolf: The Novels   *Nicholas Marsh*
John Donne: The Poems   *Joe Nutt*
Thomas Hardy: The Novels   *Norman Page*
Marlowe: The Plays   *Stevie Simkin*
F. Scott Fitzgerald: *The Great Gatsby / Tender is the Night*   *Nicolas Tredell*

Analysing Texts
Series Standing Order ISBN 0–333–73260–X
(*outside North America only*)

You can receive future titles in this series as they are published by placing a standing order. Please contact your bookseller or, in the case of difficulty, write to us at the address below with your name and address, the title of the series and the ISBN quoted above.

Customer Services Department, Palgrave Ltd
Houndmills, Basingstoke, Hampshire RG21 6XS, England

F. Scott Fitzgerald:
The Great Gatsby /
Tender is the Night

NICOLAS TREDELL

First published 2011 by
PALGRAVE MACMILLAN

Palgrave Macmillan in the UK is an imprint of Macmillan Publishers Limited, registered in England, company number 785998, of Houndmills, Basingstoke, Hampshire RG21 6XS.

Palgrave Macmillan in the US is a division of St Martin's Press LLC, 175 Fifth Avenue, New York, NY 10010.

Palgrave Macmillan is the global academic imprint of the above companies and has companies and representatives throughout the world.

Palgrave® and Macmillan® are registered trademarks in the United States, the United Kingdom, Europe and other countries.

ISBN 978–0–230–29221–5   hardback
ISBN 978–0–230–29222–2   paperback

This book is printed on paper suitable for recycling and made from fully managed and sustained forest sources. Logging, pulping and manufacturing processes are expected to conform to the environmental regulations of the country of origin.

A catalogue record for this book is available from the British Library.

A catalog record for this book is available from the Library of Congress.

10   9   8   7   6   5   4   3   2   1
20 19 18 17 16 15 14 13 12 11

Printed and bound in China

ONCE AGAIN
TO

ANGELA

Contents

General Editor's Preface   x

Acknowledgements   xi

Note on Quotations   xii

List of Abbreviations   xiii

Introduction   1

Part I   ANALYSING *THE GREAT GATSBY* AND *TENDER IS THE NIGHT*

1   Beginnings   5
　Gorgeous Gatsby: *The Great Gatsby*, pp. 7–8   5
　On the Edge: *Tender is the Night*, pp. 11–12   11
　Gatz into Gatsby: *The Great Gatsby*, pp. 94–6   14
　Lucky Dick: *Tender is the Night*, pp. 130–2   19
　Conclusions   25
　Methods of Analysis   27
　Suggested Work   28

2   Society   29
　The Fifth Guest: *The Great Gatsby*, pp. 19–21   29
　The Vanishing Hosts: *Tender is the Night*, pp. 43–6   34
　Gatsby's Guests: *The Great Gatsby*, pp. 60–2   40
　Quick Odyssey: *Tender is the Night*, pp. 88–9   48
　Conclusions   54
　Methods of Analysis   56
　Suggested Work   57

3 Money   **59**
  Buying Power: *The Great Gatsby*, pp. 29–30   59
  Shopping Spree: *Tender is the Night*, pp. 64–5   64
  Courtship and Money: *The Great Gatsby*, pp. 141–2   68
  Marriage and Money: *Tender is the Night*, pp. 175–8   74
  Conclusions   80
  Methods of Analysis   84
  Suggested Work   85

4 Gender   **87**
  Blocked Energies: *The Great Gatsby*, pp. 12–15   87
  Under Whose Sway?: *Tender is the Night*, pp. 313–15   94
  Lies and Driving: *The Great Gatsby*, pp. 58–9   100
  Dick's Debacle: *Tender is the Night*, pp. 303–5   104
  Conclusions   109
  Methods of Analysis   110
  Suggested Work   111

5 Trauma   **113**
  Blood in the Dust: *The Great Gatsby*, pp. 131–2   114
  Blood on the Bed: *Tender is the Night*, pp. 123–6   118
  Death of a Dream: *The Great Gatsby*, pp. 153–4   126
  Cutting the Cord: *Tender is the Night*, pp. 322–4   132
  Conclusions   138
  Methods of Analysis   139
  Suggested Work   140

6 Endings   **142**
  Dust in the Eyes: *The Great Gatsby*, pp. 169–70   142
  Blessing the Beach: *Tender is the Night*, pp. 335–7   146
  Beating On: *The Great Gatsby*, pp. 171–2   152
  Dying Fall: *Tender is the Night*, pp. 337–8   157
  Conclusions   160
    Beginnings   160
    Society   161
    Money   161
    Gender   162

Trauma 162
Endings 163

Part II   THE CONTEXT AND THE CRITICS

7   F. Scott Fitzgerald: Life and Works **167**

8   The Historical, Cultural and Literary Context **183**
The Historical Context 183
The Cultural and Literary Context 189

9   A Sample of Critical Views **195**
James E. Miller, Jr. 196
Richard D. Lehan 199
Sarah Beebe Fryer 201
Barbara Will 203
Susann Cokal 206
Conclusions 208

Further Reading 209

Index 213

General Editor's Preface

This series is dedicated to one clear belief: that we can all enjoy, understand and analyse literature for ourselves, provided we know how to do it. How can we build on close understanding of a short passage, and develop our insight into the whole work? What features do we expect to find in a text? Why do we study style in so much detail? In demystifying the study of literature, these are only some of the questions the *Analysing Texts* series addresses and answers.

The books in this series will not do all the work for you, but will provide you with the tools, and show you how to use them. Here, you will find samples of close, detailed analysis, with an explanation of the analytical techniques utilised.

At the end of each chapter there are useful suggestions for further work you can do to practise, develop and hone the skills demonstrated and build confidence in your own analytical ability.

An author's individuality shows in the way they write: every work they produce bears the hallmark of that writer's personal 'style'. In the main part of each book we concentrate therefore on analysing the particular flavour and concerns of one author's work, and explain the features of their writing in connection with major themes. In Part II, there are chapters about the author's life and work, assessing their contribution to developments in literature; and a sample of critics' views are summarised and discussed in comparison with each other.

Some suggestions for further reading provide a bridge towards further critical research.

Analysing Texts is designed to stimulate and encourage your critical and analytic faculty, to develop your personal insight into the author's work and individual style, and to provide you with the skills and techniques to enjoy at first hand the excitement of discovering the richness of the text.

Nicholas Marsh

Acknowledgements

As ever, my deepest gratitude is to my wife Angela; our discussions about Fitzgerald's work began when we first went to see the Robert Redford film of *Gatsby* in 1974 and have continued ever since.

I am also most grateful to Sonya Barker at Palgrave for her invitation to write this book and her support during its composition; to Nicholas Marsh, the Series Editor, for his encouraging and insightful comments on the original proposal and on the completed draft; to the anonymous external readers of the proposal and draft for their positive and constructive feedback; to Juanita Bullough for her thorough and thoughtful attention to the typescript; and to Felicity Noble at Palgrave for her characteristically prompt, efficient and helpful response to queries.

Note on Quotations

Quotations from *The Great Gatsby* and *Tender is the Night* are from the Penguin Classics 2000 editions. This edition of *Tender* follows the original order of the novel, which is widely preferred today, rather than the order of Malcolm Cowley's rearranged version (first published in 1951).

All quoted definitions of words are from the *Oxford English Dictionary*, unless otherwise stated.

All Shakespeare quotations are from the RSC/Macmillan *Complete Works* (2007).

List of Abbreviations

By F. Scott Fitzgerald

AA *Afternoon of an Author* (London: Bodley Head, 1958)
AM *All the Sad Young Men* (New York: Charles Scribner's Sons, 1926)
CU *The Crack-Up*, ed. Edmund Wilson (New York: New Directions, 1993)
GG *The Great Gatsby* (London: Penguin, 2000)
PH *The Price was High: The Last Uncollected Stories of F. Scott Fitzgerald*, ed. Matthew J. Bruccoli (London: Quartet, 1979)
TN *Tender is the Night: A Romance* (London: Penguin, 2000)
TP *This Side of Paradise* (London: Penguin, 1996)
TR *Taps at Reveille* (New York: Charles Scribner's Sons, 1971)

By F. Scott and Zelda Fitzgerald

RE *The Romantic Egoists*, ed. Matthew J. Bruccoli, Scottie Fitzgerald Smith and Joan P. Kerr (New York: Charles Scribner's Sons, 1974)

By other writers

FR Jackson R. Bryer (ed.), *F. Scott Fitzgerald: The Critical Reception* (New York: Burt Franklin, 1978)
FS Ernest Hemingway, *The First Forty-Nine Stories* (London: Arrow, 2004)
SG Matthew J. Bruccoli, *Some Sort of Epic Grandeur: The Life of F. Scott Fitzgerald* (London: Cardinal, 1991)

Introduction

The Great Gatsby (1925) and *Tender is the Night* (1934) are the most highly regarded of F. Scott Fitzgerald's four completed novels and remain widely read and much studied. *Gatsby* is the more famous of the two: it has been filmed four times, in 1926, 1949, 1974 and 2000, attracting key actors to the lead role – Warner Baxter, Alan Ladd, Robert Redford and Toby Stephens – and a fifth film is now in the making, starring Leonardo DiCaprio and directed by Baz Luhrmann (famed for his *William Shakespeare's Romeo + Juliet*). Through the novel and films, Jay Gatsby has become an iconic figure in American and perhaps global culture, a symbol of high aspiration, glamorous success and romantic defeat, like Fitzgerald himself. Very much a product of its time, *Gatsby* also seems to speak vividly to many readers today. But *Tender*, likewise engaging with aspiration, success and defeat, also continues to find many readers and interpreters and its concern with the traumas of sexual abuse and of war speaks to us perhaps more strongly than ever in the twenty-first century.

Both *Gatsby* and *Tender* exemplify Fitzgerald's achievement of a style which might be called 'romantic modernism', in which a sustained lyrical grace associated with Romantic poetry (Keats, Shelley) is combined with that unsparing engagement with the fragmentation and abrasiveness of modernity which characterises Modernist writing (Eliot, Joyce). Both novels are rich in complexities and ambiguities; but each is distinctive in terms of its structure and narrative technique. *Gatsby* is a concentrated first-person narrative which exemplifies Modernist compression and selection while remaining an accessible and compelling read; *Tender* is an episodic, extended chronicle with, for the most part, an omniscient narrator, more reminiscent in some respects of nineteenth-century fiction

1

than *Gatsby* but nonetheless fully engaged with the crises of modernity. Both novels represent societies in which the bonds of community and family have been loosened and in which other modes of human association – primarily the party – prevail. Both examine how money and consumerism can intimately shape relationships and behaviour. Both address questions of gender at a time when feminine and masculine roles and possibilities are especially in flux. Both unsparingly examine physical and psychological trauma (war, murder, manslaughter, suicide, incest, bereavement, disappointment, dissolution, disintegration) and move towards the status of modern tragedies. Both have memorable, haunting endings which reverberate in the reader's mind. Both raise many questions and have generated a huge amount of criticism and commentary. The aim of this book is to look closely at the style of the two novels and relate its distinctive features to their structures, themes and broader implications.

In *Part I*, Analysing *The Great Gatsby* and *Tender is the Night*, we select short extracts for close analysis, examining them in terms of the kinds of sentences of which they consist, their diction (their choice and use of words), their imagery, their handling of time, their use of point-of-view, and, where appropriate, their intratextual relations (the links between different parts of the same text) and their intertextual relations (the ways in which they allude to and invoke other literary and cultural texts). We shall consider how such elements contribute to the topics of each extract and relate those topics to the wider themes of the novels, steadily expanding our knowledge and understanding of them.

In *Part II*, The Context and the Critics, we shall explore the biographical, historical, cultural and critical contexts of the novels. There is a summary of Fitzgerald's life and works, a survey of the relevant aspects of the history and culture of Fitzgerald's times, a sample of key critical views, and suggestions for Further Reading to help readers navigate the vast and fascinating critical and cultural territory which now forms the hinterland of *Gatsby* and *Tender*.

PART I

ANALYSING *THE GREAT GATSBY* AND *TENDER IS THE NIGHT*

1

Beginnings

On a first reading, the beginning of a novel gives us an initial idea of the style, tone, narrative technique and themes of the whole work, initiates a relationship between reader and narrator, and raises expectations about the text, the reading experience, which is to come. These expectations will not necessarily be fulfilled; indeed, they are likely to be modified in significant ways. On second and subsequent readings, our knowledge of the novel as a whole inevitably influences how we read the beginning and we are likely to understand it differently – to grasp more clearly how it prepares us (sometimes by indirection or misdirection) for the rest of the work. In analysing the beginnings of *The Great Gatsby* and *Tender is the Night*, it will enrich our enjoyment and understanding to aim to develop a kind of double vision: to see the beginning both as it might appear to a first-time reader and as it might appear to someone rereading the book.

We shall look first of all at the beginning of *Gatsby* and consider how it might appear on a first and then on a subsequent reading.

Gorgeous Gatsby: *The Great Gatsby*, pp. 7–8

In my younger and more vulnerable years my father gave me some advice that I've been turning over in my mind ever since.

'Whenever you feel like criticizing anyone,' he told me, 'just remember that all the people in this world haven't had the advantages that you've had.'

He didn't say any more, but we've always been unusually communicative in a reserved way, and I understood that he meant a great deal more than that. In consequence, I'm inclined to reserve all judgements, a habit that has opened up many curious natures to me and also made me the victim of not a few veteran bores. The abnormal mind is quick to detect and attach itself to this quality when it appears in a normal person, and so it came about that in college I was unjustly accused of being a politician, because I was privy to the secret griefs of wild, unknown men. Most of the confidences were unsought – frequently I have feigned sleep, preoccupation, or a hostile levity when I realized by some unmistakable sign that an intimate revelation was quivering on the horizon; for the intimate revelations of young men, or at least the terms in which they express them, are usually plagiaristic and marred by obvious suppressions. Reserving judgements is a matter of infinite hope. I am still a little afraid of missing something if I forget that, as my father snobbishly suggested, and I snobbishly repeat, a sense of the fundamental decencies is parcelled out unequally at birth.

And, after boasting this way of my tolerance, I come to the admission that it has a limit. Conduct may be founded on the hard rock or the wet marshes, but after a certain point I don't care what it's founded on. When I came back from the East last autumn I felt that I wanted the world to be in uniform and at a sort of moral attention for ever; I wanted no more riotous excursions with privileged glimpses into the human heart. Only Gatsby, the man who gives his name to this book, was exempt from my reaction – Gatsby, who represented everything for which I have an unaffected scorn. If personality is an unbroken series of successful gestures, then there was something gorgeous about him, some heightened sensitivity to the promises of life, as if he were related to one of those intricate machines that register earthquakes ten thousand miles away. This responsiveness had nothing to do with that flabby impressionability which is dignified under the name of the 'creative temperament' – it was an extraordinary gift for hope, a romantic readiness such as I have never found in any other person and which it is not likely I shall ever find again. No – Gatsby turned out all right at the end; it is what preyed on Gatsby, what foul dust floated in the wake of his dreams that temporarily closed out my interest in the abortive sorrows and shortwinded elations of men.

If we imagine ourselves reading *Gatsby* for the first time, with little or no knowledge of its plot or characters, what might we say about this opening? It introduces a first-person narrator but does not tell us the narrator's name, gender, marital status, family background, financial situation or geographical location (except that he has come 'back' from 'the East'). The only details it gives for Gatsby are his surname and gender ('the man'). But a first-time reader could make some inferences. The opening use of comparative adjectives to describe the narrator's past self, his reference to 'my younger and more vulnerable years', sets the novel in the dimension of time and implies that he is hardened by experience, older and less easily wounded psychologically than was once the case. But the narrator then invokes his father's advice and stresses how he has continued to think about it, which could imply that he has not in fact quite acquired the mature adult identity which the opening of his sentence implies. His father's words, in direct speech, take up almost all the second paragraph, reinforcing the impression of a strong and persistent paternal influence.

After these two short paragraphs, two much longer ones follow. In the first sentence of the third paragraph, a multiple sentence in which three clauses are linked by conjunctions ('but', 'and'), the narrator affirms the deeper significance of his father's declaration that not everybody has had the advantages that his son has had. Our first assumption might be that his father is talking about material privileges. But the narrator indicates there is more to it, although he does not immediately say why. This increases the impression of evasiveness and indirection which the narrator's reticence about his personal details has already conveyed. Instead of explaining his father's deeper meaning, the narrator shifts to a statement of the effect of his father's declaration upon him; it has made him inclined to hold back judgements upon people. Coming in the first long paragraph of the novel, this seems an important statement about himself, and he goes on to elaborate it by saying that his non-judgemental attitude has made him into a person in whom other people confide – particularly those who have an 'abnormal mind'; the narrator is quick to distinguish himself from such people, however, identifying himself as 'a normal person'. We learn that he has been to college but that his openness to confidences led to accusations that he was a 'politician' – not in the most common modern sense of the word, where it refers to a person who practises politics as a career, but in the sense of someone who acts in a manipulative and devious way, typically to gain advancement. He makes it clear that he regards these accusations as unjust. But his choice of words makes his position as confidant seem intriguing and romantic: 'privy to', 'secret', 'unknown' suggest the thrill of sharing in concealed knowledge about someone's life; 'wild' is an adjective which indicates excess and freedom from constraint. To some extent, this romantic, thrilling vocabulary casts doubts on the narrator's claim that he did not seek out most of these confidences and often tried to avoid or discourage them – he seems to find them quite exciting.

The narrator then goes on to claim that reserving judgements is a matter of 'infinite hope' – the adjective 'infinite' suggests he has an unconstrained element – and he implies that he refrains from being judgemental because he might miss 'something' – some glimpse of human possibility, perhaps. He returns to his father's maxim but now makes it clear that the 'advantages' of which his father spoke were not (at least in his son's interpretation) the primarily material ones of wealth and social standing, but ethical and what we might today call genetic: 'a sense of the fundamental decencies is parcelled out unequally at birth'. He does not, however, specify the nature of the 'fundamental decencies'.

In the next paragraph, the narrator asserts the limit of his tolerance and suggests that proper conduct is important. But rather than putting this in an abstract way, he employs two metaphors: 'the hard rock' and 'the wet marshes'. This suggests a certain poetic quality in the narrator's utterance, a liking for imagery rather than plain statement. He then provides some more definite information about himself, though much is still vague. As in his opening statement, he starts a sentence with an adverb which indicates a definite, if undated time ('When') and a place, even if very loosely specified ('the East') where he has had a set of experiences of which he speaks only in general terms, again using a romantic vocabulary – 'riotous', 'privileged', 'the human heart' – which links up with 'secret griefs', 'wild' and 'unknown' in the previous paragraph. Just as the romantic diction in the previous paragraph made the confidences of 'wild, unknown men' seem attractive, so his vocabulary here endows the 'excursion' he mentions with appeal, even as he asserts that he wants no more such excursions and expresses a desire for moral discipline and alertness in military metaphors, 'in uniform' and 'at … attention'.

Beginnings   9

Much as he seems to react against his experience in the East, however, the narrator still admires Gatsby – this is the first proper name in the novel – and speaks highly of him, again using romantic terms: 'gorgeous', 'some heightened sensitivity to the promises of life'. But he then uses a technological image to suggest this sensitivity; it is as if Gatsby 'were related to one of those intricate machines that register earthquakes ten thousand miles away'. This is the first sign in the novel of the narrator's readiness to draw on technological imagery to describe a romantic sensibility. He defines this sensibility more precisely as 'an extraordinary gift for hope' and we can link this with his use of the word 'hope' in the previous paragraph; its repetition, in a different context, suggests that hope, of a limitless ('infinite') or unusual ('extraordinary') kind, is important to the narrator. He starts the next sentence with 'No', as if he were arguing with someone (perhaps himself), pre-empting an objection, and affirms his view that 'Gatsby turned out all right at the end'. The problem was 'what preyed on Gatsby'; again, he does not specify the nature of this but uses metaphors – 'preyed' (which suggests a predatory creature) and 'foul dust'. It is this which has, for a time, made the narrator lose interest in the fluctuating emotions of human beings. It seems, then, that the narrator has been through some extraordinary experience involving Gatsby which has left him chastened but which is also, in some ways, attractive and significant.

Rereading the beginning of *Gatsby* with an awareness of the novel as a whole, we know that the narrator is called Nick Carraway; that he is now in his early thirties and presumably still single; that he comes from a prosperous family in the US Midwest; and that he has gone back to his native city after trying, in the spring and summer of 1922, to make a career as a bond salesman in New York, in the American East, and undergoing a spectacular encounter with Jay Gatsby, who was in love with Daisy Buchanan (*née* Fay), Nick's second cousin once removed. We know of Gatsby's dream, of his extraordinary and doomed attempt to realize it, and of his violent death. How does this knowledge influence our rereading? It enables us to see more clearly how Nick's narrative voice, as established in these first four paragraphs, is characterized by features which will recur in the novel: by circumlocution – the use of many words where fewer would do; and by euphemism – the substitution of mild or less direct words for ones that are harsh or blunt when referring to something unpleasant or embarrassing; we can make an intratextual link – that is, a link between two parts of the same text – between the circumlocution and euphemism we find in the opening and its recurrence at other key points of the novel, for example in Nick's account of the discovery of Gatsby's body, which we shall consider in chapter 5 of this book. We can also make an intratextual link between the romantic vocabulary and imagery in the opening of *Gatsby* and the similar vocabulary we find later on in the novel, for instance in Nick's retailing of Gatsby's early courtship of Daisy, which we shall discuss in chapter 3. Nick does not say at the start of the novel that the events of the summer involved drunkenness, adultery, organized crime, manslaughter, murder and suicide.

When we reread the beginning of *Gatsby*, we may find we question the assertions that Nick makes about himself there. Is it true that he is 'inclined to reserve all judgements'? He seems, for example, to judge Jordan Baker quite harshly, condemning her as 'incurably dishonest' on scanty evidence (*GG* 58). Is it true that he is, as he implies, 'a normal person'? Although he hardly mentions his father again after the start of *Gatsby*, there is nonetheless a sense, which plays through the novel, that he has not quite acquired an autonomous masculine identity of his own and this might seem odd in a man who turns 30 in the summer of 1922. Moreover, he remains unmarried and apparently unable to form a stable bond with a woman (or a man); his relationships with the girl back home to whom he writes weekly letters signed 'Love, Nick' (*GG* 59), the girl who works in the accounting department of the Probity Trust (*GG* 57) and Jordan Baker all come to nothing. Is it true that he is not a 'politician', in the sense of someone who invites confidences in order to increase his own advantage, or has his encounter with Gatsby been advantageous, in a sense, in giving him a privileged glimpse into the human heart (or simply gratifying his voyeuristic impulses)? Is it true that he is a person who tries to avoid confidences, or does a part of him like learning the secrets of others, perhaps as a compensation for his own inhibited approach to life? Nick is not an unreliable narrator in the sense of a narrator who is definitely shown to be wrong in his interpretation of events and characters (including himself); but he cannot be seen as a wholly reliable one either.

The beginning of *Gatsby* raises many questions for a first-time reader. Reading the rest of the text answers some of these questions but, as we have seen, raises others. We shall now turn to the opening passage of *Tender*:

On the Edge: *Tender is the Night*, pp. 11–12

On the pleasant shore of the French Riviera, about half way between Marseilles and the Italian border, stands a large, proud, rose-colored hotel. Deferential palms cool its flushed façade, and before it stretches a short dazzling beach. Lately it has become a summer resort of notable and fashionable people; a decade ago it was almost deserted after its English clientele went north in April. Now, many bungalows cluster near it, but when this story begins only the cupolas of a dozen old villas rotted like water lilies among the massed pines between Gausse's Hôtel des Étrangers and Cannes, five miles away.

The hotel and its bright tan prayer rug of a beach were one. In the early morning the distant image of Cannes, the pink and cream of old fortifications, the purple Alp that bounded Italy, were cast across the water and lay quavering in the ripples and rings sent up by sea-plants through the clear shallows. Before eight a man came down to the beach in a blue bathrobe and with much preliminary application to his person of the chilly water, and much grunting and loud breathing, floundered a minute in the sea. When he had gone, beach and bay were quiet for an hour. Merchantmen crawled westward on the horizon; bus boys shouted in the hotel court; the dew dried upon the pines. In another hour the horns of motors began to blow down from the winding road along the low range of the Maures, which separates the littoral from true Provençal France.

A mile from the sea, where pines give way to dusty poplars, is an isolated railroad stop, whence one June morning in 1925 a victoria brought a woman and her daughter down to Gausse's Hôtel. The mother's face was of a fading prettiness that would soon be patted with broken veins; her expression was both tranquil and aware in a pleasant way. However, one's eye moved on quickly to her daughter, who had magic in her pink palms and her cheeks lit to a lovely flame, like the thrilling flush of children after their cold baths in the evening. Her fine high forehead sloped gently up to where her hair, bordering it like an armorial shield, burst into lovelocks and waves and curlicues of ash blonde and gold. Her eyes were bright, big, clear, wet, and shining, the color of her cheeks was real, breaking close to the surface from the strong young pump of her heart. Her body hovered delicately on the last edge of childhood – she was almost eighteen, nearly complete, but the dew was still on her.

Let us first approach the beginning of *Tender* as we did the start of *Gatsby* and ask what a first-time reader, with little or no knowledge of its plot or characters, might say about it. *Tender* begins with a third-person rather than first-person account, gives a definite sense of location in time and place (a June morning in 1925) and introduces two characters, though these are initially identified not by name but by their family relationship – a mother and daughter. The leisurely description of the hotel, beach and seascape, running across two paragraphs, could suggest that this location is going to play a significant part in the story. In the second paragraph, the beach is called, in a metaphor, a 'bright tan prayer rug', a mat used by Muslims for praying; to a first-time reader, this might be no more than a passing flourish, but it does introduce a religious reference.

In the third paragraph, in the description of the daughter, the imagery and diction become lyrical and romantic: 'magic in her pink palms'; 'cheeks lit to a lovely flame'. A simile introduces the idea of innocence: the daughter's cheeks are compared to 'the thrilling flush of children after their cold baths in the evening'. The daughter's forehead is described as 'fine' and 'high', and a further simile likens the appearance of her hair bordering her face to 'an armorial shield', that is, a shield bearing a coat of arms; this gives a hint of medieval romance, of courtly love, of the pure lady who inspires the chivalric knight's chaste devotion; but it also distantly invokes the idea of warfare, like the 'old fortifications' in the previous paragraph. This is followed by the vivid, energetic verb 'burst' and a triplet of nouns, 'lovelocks', 'waves', 'curlicues' (decorative curls or twists), which convey a sense of abundance and curvaceousness.

The next sentence elaborates the description of the daughter, applying no less than five adjectives to her eyes which convey their radiance, their size, their clarity, their moisture, and the emotion which they express. The sentence goes on to stress that the colour of her cheeks is 'real' – that is, not produced by make-up – and that it comes from within, from 'the strong young pump of her heart' – a mechanical image which goes back to ancient times. The statement that her 'body hovered delicately on the last

edge of childhood' develops the idea of childhood innocence invoked by
the simile of children after their baths. The verb 'hovered', like 'quavering'
in the previous paragraph, suggests a kind of in-between state, and 'the
last edge of childhood' indicates a threshold situation, brings in a sense of
danger – the 'last edge' of childhood could also be the edge of a cliff over
which the daughter, moving into adulthood, might fall. This sense of
approaching a hazardous threshold is continued in the adverbs 'almost'
and 'nearly' that precede 'eighteen' and 'complete'. The image of the 'dew'
still on her links up with one of the adjectives applied to her eyes in the
previous sentence, 'wet', and resonates with the literal use of the term
'dew' in the second paragraph. After such an elaborate description, the
first-time reader might expect that the daughter would play a significant
part in the novel, that she might, indeed, be the heroine.

Rereading the beginning of *Tender* with an awareness of the novel
as a whole, we know that the setting of the hotel, beach and seascape
does indeed figure prominently in the novel and will recur very near
the end; we can see that the religious allusion in the image of the
'bright tan prayer rug of a beach' links up with Dick's last gesture
on his Riviera stage when he blesses the beach 'with a papal cross'
(*TN* 292). We also know that the daughter, Rosemary Hoyt, is a movie
actress who will play a significant part in the story but she will not, as a
first-time reader might have expected, be the heroine or even the most
important female character – that role is reserved for Nicole Diver –
and she will fade out at some important points. But we can see more
vividly on rereading how she relates to the overall symbolic pattern
of *Tender*: the comparison of her face to 'an armorial shield' links up
with the references to warfare and wounding which resonate through
the novel and the simile which likens the natural colour of her cheeks
to 'the thrilling flush of children after their cold baths in the evening'
contributes to the crucial theme of innocence – and innocence violated.
And we can understand why she will prove so dangerously attractive to
the protagonist of *Tender*, who has not yet appeared: Dick Diver.

Both the beginnings we have analysed are indirect and to some
extent misleading. We will now look at passages which occur later in
each novel but which could also serve as beginnings. These introduce
the central character, and deliver information about him, in a more
straightforward way.

Gatz into Gatsby: *The Great Gatsby*, pp. 94–6

James Gatz – that was really, or at least legally, his name. He had changed it at the age of seventeen and at the specific moment that witnessed the beginning of his career – when he saw Dan Cody's yacht drop anchor over the most insidious flat on Lake Superior. It was James Gatz who had been loafing along the beach that afternoon in a torn green jersey and a pair of canvas pants, but it was already Jay Gatsby who borrowed a rowboat, pulled out to the *Tuolomee*, and informed Cody that a wind might catch him and break him up in half an hour.

I suppose he'd had the name ready for a long time, even then. His parents were shiftless and unsuccessful farm people – his imagination had never really accepted them as his parents at all. The truth was that Jay Gatsby of West Egg, Long Island, sprang from his Platonic conception of himself. He was a son of God – a phrase which, if it means anything, means just that – and he must be about His Father's business, the service of a vast, vulgar, and meretricious beauty. So he invented just the sort of Jay Gatsby that a seventeen-year-old boy would be likely to invent, and to this conception he was faithful to the end.

For over a year he had been beating his way along the south shore of Lake Superior as a clam-digger and a salmon-fisher or in any other capacity that brought him food and bed. His brown, hardening body lived naturally through the half-fierce, half-lazy work of the bracing days. He knew women early, and since they spoiled him he became contemptuous of them, of young virgins because they were ignorant, of the others because they were hysterical about things which in his overwhelming self-absorption he took for granted.

But his heart was in a constant, turbulent riot. The most grotesque and fantastic conceits haunted him in his bed at night. A universe of ineffable gaudiness spun itself out in his brain while the clock ticked on the washstand and the moon soaked with wet light his tangled clothes upon the floor. Each night he added to the pattern of his fancies until drowsiness closed down upon some vivid scene with an oblivious embrace. For a while these reveries provided an outlet for his imagination; they were a satisfactory hint of the unreality of reality, a promise that the rock of the world was founded securely on a fairy's wing.

An instinct toward his future glory had led him, some months before, to the small Lutheran College of St Olaf's in southern Minnesota. He stayed there two weeks, dismayed at its ferocious indifference to the drums of his destiny, to destiny itself, and despising the janitor's work

with which he was to pay his way through. Then he drifted back to Lake
Superior, and he was still searching for something to do on the day that
Dan Cody's yacht dropped anchor in the shallows alongshore.

Cody was fifty years old then, a product of the Nevada silver fields, of
the Yukon, of every rush for metal since seventy-five. The transactions
in Montana copper that made him many times a millionaire found him
physically robust but on the verge of soft-mindedness, and, suspecting
this, an infinite number of women tried to separate him from his money.
The none too savoury ramifications by which Ella Kaye, the newspaper
woman, played Madame de Maintenon to his weakness and sent him to
sea in a yacht, were common property of the turgid journalism in 1902.
He had been coasting along all too hospitable shores for five years when
he turned up as James Gatz's destiny in Little Girl Bay.

To young Gatz, resting on his oars and looking up at the railed deck,
that yacht represented all the beauty and glamour in the world. I suppose
he smiled at Cody – he had probably discovered that people liked him
when he smiled. At any rate Cody asked him a few questions (one of
them elicited the brand new name) and found that he was quick and
extravagantly ambitious. A few days later he took him to Duluth and
bought him a blue coat, six pair of white duck trousers, and a yachting
cap. And when the *Tuolomee* left for the West Indies and the Barbary
Coast, Gatsby left too.

In a more chronologically straightforward narrative than *Gatsby*,
this passage could serve as the start of the story. Compared with the
novel's actual opening, it is packed with information. Proper nouns
pepper the text: names of people, places, an institution and Cody's
yacht: James Gatz, Jay Gatsby, Dan Cody, Ella Kaye; Lake Superior,
Little Girl Bay, Minnesota, Duluth, Nevada, the Yukon, the West
Indies, the Barbary Coast; St Olaf's College; the *Tuolomee*. We learn
how Gatsby and Cody met, their respective ages (17 and 50) at the
time, and we discover the sources of Cody's wealth. As well as these
concrete details, the passage also provides us with less tangible facts
about Gatsby's youthful ambitions. Although *Gatsby* is a first-person
narrative, the pronoun 'I' is used only twice in this passage, in both
cases with 'suppose'. Apart from these brief signs of a first-person
narrator, and of the hypothetical quality of his suppositions, we could
be reading a third-person account. The passage exemplifies one of the
ways in which Fitzgerald overcomes the limitations of the first-person

narrator in *Gatsby*; Nick himself could not have observed the events he describes; but we can believe that he is retailing, in his own words, what Gatsby has told him. The absence of direct speech increases the sense of a slightly distanced narrative.

There are four timescales in the passage. The first is 'the specific moment' in which Gatz becomes Gatsby, when he sees Dan Cody's yacht anchor in a dangerous spot on Lake Superior; this seems virtually instantaneous, a life change concentrated into seconds. The second is Gatsby's rowing out to the yacht, his warning to Cody, and Cody's questioning of him. The third is the 'few days' which elapse between Gatsby's and Cody's first meeting and Cody's purchase of clothes for Gatsby. The fourth is the span of years before Gatsby and Cody first meet. But it should be stressed that, although this passage provides a more chronologically straightforward account of Gatsby's early life than we have had so far, its different timescales are not arranged in strict chronological order. The passage starts with the crucial moment of change from Gatz to Gatsby and proceeds to Gatsby's rowing out to the yacht and warning Cody, but then shifts back to Gatsby's earlier life; it takes this up to his dropping out of college and his return to Lake Superior but goes back in time again to summarize Cody's earlier life and his five years at sea before returning to the point just after Gatsby has warned Cody of his dangerous anchorage. The passage thus zigzags in time in a way that mirrors, in a microcosm, the chronological zigzagging of the whole novel.

In the third sentence of the passage, Gatsby's change of identity is skilfully and strikingly suggested in a double sentence where the proper name in the first clause changes into another proper name in the second, at points where the grammatical structures in each clause are almost parallel: 'It was James Gatz who ... it was already Jay Gatsby who'. This suggests both the continuity (in the structural similarity of the sentences) and the disjunction (in the change of proper name) between the two phases of Gatz/Gatsby's life. Three of the sentences include a dash (rather than a semi-colon or colon) to indicate a shift in the sense, and one sentence has an interpolated clause with a dash at either end. Fitzgerald is fond of dashes and, when they occur in his narrative prose, they tend to sharpen the reader's attention to meaning. For example, the sentence that starts 'He was a son of God' could simply have continued 'and must be about His Father's business', but the interpolation, highlighted by dashes at either end, of 'a phrase which if it means anything, means just that' prompts us to look back at the phrase 'a son of God' and consider its meaning more deeply.

The diction of the passage includes a range of terms which carry ambivalent connotations: 'riot' (echoing the adjective 'riotous' in the opening passage of the novel) means a violent disturbance of the peace by a crowd or, in a more archaic mode which is relevant here, rowdy behaviour (in chapter 3, Nick uses the term 'rioters' to mean those who behave rowdily (*GG*, 57)). But 'riot' can also mean an impressively varied and lavish display, as in the phrase 'a riot of colour', which is not actually used in the novel but seems highly appropriate to the spectacular parties Gatsby mounts and to the rich palette of colours in the text itself. 'Gaudiness' and 'glamour' suggest things which are attractive but cheap and superficial; 'grotesque' implies distortion; and 'fantastic' connotes both something which is the product of the imagination and something which is remote from reality. 'Conceits' has the primary meaning here of elaborate images – over-elaborate and artificial ones – but also carries a hint of its now more common sense, of excessive pride in oneself (in this respect, it links up with the reference to Gatsby's 'overwhelming self-absorption' in the previous sentence). 'Beauty' is twice employed, but its positive associations are undermined by some of the words which qualify it; the first time it is used, it is preceded by the adjectives 'vast, vulgar, and meretricious' and the last two adjectives both carry negative connotations: but the now-dated meaning of 'vulgar', 'characteristic of or belonging to ordinary people' is also relevant here; in a sense Gatsby is extraordinary but he does come from 'ordinary' people and in some sense embodies their dreams (as his father's pride in him, expressed in the last chapter of the novel, demonstrates). 'Meretricious' indicates something which is showily attractive but lacking real value; the archaic meaning of 'meretricious', characteristic of a prostitute, may also figure here, implying how much Gatsby's idea of beauty is bound up with a commodity which (like Daisy) can be bought and sold. When 'beauty' occurs a second time, it is coupled with, and preceded by, 'glamour', and we have already pointed out the negative significance of the latter term.

The imagery in this passage works both to evoke and evaluate the young Gatz/Gatsby. The image of his heart being in a 'riot' suggests disorder. The image of a 'universe of ineffable gaudiness' conveys the scale of James Gatz's fantasies but also, in the term 'gaudiness', their extravagant or tasteless brightness and showiness. Although the 'clock ticking on the washstand' is actually there, an audible, visible and tangible object in Gatz's room, it takes on a symbolic dimension; its ticking suggests that time is slipping by and that Gatz/Gatsby is subject to time and change. This symbolic aspect is enhanced when we link Gatz's timepiece with the two other key references to clocks in the novel, which occur during Gatsby's first reunion with Daisy: his inadvertent displacement of 'a defunct mantelpiece clock' in Nick's bungalow and the simile of Gatsby 'running down like an over-wound clock' when he shows Daisy round his house (*GG* 84, 89). The idea of moonlight as liquid conveyed by the verb 'soaked' and the adjective 'wet' relates to a range of references to moisture and liquidness in the text of *Gatsby*: for example, the 'wet ball' into which Daisy squeezes the letter the day before her wedding (*GG* 74) and the 'horribly black and wet' hearse which bears Gatsby's coffin to the cemetery (*GG* 165).

The metaphor of 'the rock of the world ... founded securely on a fairy's wing' suggests the combination of hardness and fragility which recurs in the novel; we can link it with Nick's simile in chapter 8, after Tom defeats Gatsby at the Plaza Hotel, that '"Jay Gatsby" had broken up like glass against Tom's hard malice' (*GG* 154). If this later image seems to confirm the primacy of hard reality, the 'rock/fairy's wing' metaphor implies the converse: that imagination – the 'fairy's wing' – may be the real foundation of the world. In this perspective, Gatsby comes to grief not because he believes in the primacy of the imagination but because his imagination is flawed – and this imagination, it is implied, is also that of a culture. Most of the evaluative terms used of Gatsby's youthful fantasies – 'gaudiness', 'glamour', 'grotesque', 'fantastic', 'conceits', 'vulgar', 'meretricious' – could also apply to shoddy works of art; they suggest that Gatsby's self-construction is a grandiose, overblown aesthetic project which cannot fulfil his best aspirations. It is because Gatsby's life is failed art that it breaks on the brute reality Tom represents; a better artist-in-life might have been able to incorporate and reshape that reality.

The extract contains several intertextual references – that is, references to other literary and cultural texts. The most important is the statement that James Gatz, as a boy, 'must be about His Father's business', which refers to the New Testament Gospel of St Luke in which Mary and Joseph find their missing 12-year-old son with the elders in the temple in Jerusalem; when Mary asks why he disappeared without telling his parents he replies: 'wist [know] ye not that I must be about my Father's business?' (2.42–52). The phrase 'a fairy's wing' contributes to that faint but fascinating strand of allusion in *Gatsby* to another drama of crossed loves and spectacular displays, Shakespeare's *A Midsummer Night's Dream*. The metaphor of 'the drums of [Gatz's] destiny' has a martial, military air, linking Gatsby's life with that of Americans who rose from obscure origins to success as soldiers, such as General Ulysses S. Grant (who figures significantly in *Tender*, as we will see). But it is an image which could also allude to the jungle drums of Joseph Conrad's *Heart of Darkness* (1902) and suggest an analogy between the fate of two degraded idealists – Conrad's Kurtz and Fitzgerald's Gatsby.

We now turn to the passage in *Tender* which describes Dick Diver's early life. In the original version of the novel, this occurs near the start of Part 2, but in the rearranged version it is very near the opening of *Tender*.

Lucky Dick: *Tender is the Night*, pp. 130–2

At the beginning of 1917, when it was becoming difficult to find coal, Dick burned for fuel almost a hundred textbooks that he had accumulated; but only, as he laid each one on the fire, with an assurance chuckling inside him that he was himself a digest of what was within the book, that he could brief it five years from now, if it deserved to be briefed. This went on at any odd hour, if necessary, with a floor rug over his shoulders, with the fine quiet of the scholar which is nearest of all things to heavenly peace – but which, as will presently be told, had to end.

For its temporary continuance he thanked his body that had done the flying rings at New Haven, and now swam in the winter Danube. With Elkins, second secretary at the Embassy, he shared an apartment, and there were two nice girl visitors – which was that, and not too much of it, nor too much of the Embassy either. His contact with Ed Elkins aroused in him a first faint doubt as to the quality of his mental processes; he could not feel that they were profoundly different from the thinking of Elkins – Elkins, who would name you all the quarterbacks at New Haven for thirty years.

' – And Lucky Dick can't be one of these clever men; he must be less intact, even faintly destroyed. If life won't do it for him it's not a substitute to get a disease, or a broken heart, or an inferiority complex, though it'd be nice to build out some broken side until it was better than the original structure.'

He mocked at his reasoning, calling it specious and 'American' – his criterion of uncerebral phrase-making was that it was American. He knew, though, that the price of his intactness was incompleteness.

'The best I can wish you, my child,' so said the Fairy Blackstick in Thackeray's *The Rose and the Ring*, 'is a little misfortune'.

In some moods he griped at his own reasoning: Could I help it that Pete Livingstone sat in the locker-room Tap Day when everybody looked all over hell for him? And I got an election when otherwise I wouldn't have got Elihu, knowing so few men. He was good and right and I ought to have sat in the locker-room instead. Maybe I would, if I'd thought I had a chance at an election. But Mercer kept coming to my room all those weeks. I guess I knew I had a chance all right, all right. But it would have served me right if I'd swallowed my pin in the shower and set up a conflict.

After the lectures at the university he used to argue this point with a young Rumanian intellectual who reassured him: 'There's no evidence that Goethe ever had a "conflict" in the modern sense, or a man like Jung, for instance. You're not a romantic philosopher – you're a scientist. Memory, force, character – especially good sense. That's going to be your trouble – judgment about yourself. Once I knew a man who worked for two years on the brain of an armadillo, with the idea that he would sooner or later know more about the brain of an armadillo than any one. I kept arguing with him that he was not really pushing out the extension of the human range – it was too arbitrary. And sure enough, when he sent his work to the medical journal they refused it – they had just accepted a thesis by another man on the same subject.'

Dick got up to Zurich on less Achilles' heels than would be required to equip a centipede, but with plenty – the illusions of eternal strength and health, and of the essential goodness of people; illusions of a nation, the lies of generations of frontier mothers who had to croon falsely that there were no wolves outside the cabin door. After he took his degree, he received his orders to join a neurological unit forming in Bar-sur-Aube.

In France, to his disgust, the work was executive rather than practical. In compensation he found time to complete the short textbook and assemble the material for his next venture. He returned to Zurich in the spring of 1919 discharged.

The foregoing has the ring of a biography, without the satisfaction of knowing that the hero, like Grant, lolling in his general store in Galena, is ready to be called to an intricate destiny. Moreover it is confusing to come across a youthful photograph of some one known in a rounded maturity and gaze with a shock upon a fiery, wiry, eagle-eyed stranger. Best to be reassuring – Dick Diver's moment now began.

This extract focuses on Dick Diver, the protagonist of *Tender*, and presents key aspects of his earlier life using a variety of techniques: we hear the third-person narrative voice of the novel, inclined to elaborate sentences, to mixing humour and seriousness, and to phrasing which reminds the reader that this is a story unfolding: 'as will presently be told', 'the foregoing has the ring of a biography'; there is Dick speaking of himself, but in the third person; there is a passage of interior monologue which gives Dick's thoughts in the first person; and there is an extended piece of direct speech from 'a young Rumanian intellectual'. This variety of approaches exemplifies the way in which Dick, throughout the novel, is seen from a range of viewpoints: his own, the narrator's, and those of other characters. The extract also places him in the contexts of both Europe and the USA and relates him to an idea of the American hero, epitomized in this case by General Ulysses S. Grant.

The passage both reveals and casts doubt on the nature and quality of Dick's intellect. The long, complex opening sentence conveys Dick's confidence, at this stage in his life, in his own abilities. His academic achievements – Yale, a Rhodes scholarship to Oxford, a final year at Johns Hopkins University – seem to justify this. But it could also indicate a touch of hubris, of excessive pride. His textbook-burning has a destructive aspect; he is consuming intellectual resources to assuage the urgings of the flesh; it may be necessary in these circumstances, but it anticipates the way in which he will consume those resources and pursue sensuous pleasures when he no longer really has to. Moreover, Dick's low regard for textbooks is ironic in the light of the fact that he will later publish a textbook. It is as if he is devaluing, in advance, the kind of book he will produce. The claim that Dick burnt the books 'with the fine quiet of the scholar which is nearest of all things to heavenly peace' also has an ironic ring; for Dick is destroying one of the means of scholarly study.

The next paragraph shows Dick himself faintly doubting, for the first time in his life, 'the quality of his mental processes' when he feels his thinking is not deeply different from that of his American flatmate Ed Elkins, who has had a good education but seems, in his leisure time, to devote his retentive memory to recalling a list of Yale footballers. List-making is an ambivalent activity in Fitzgerald; as we shall see, he employs it to great effect as a narrative technique in both *Gatsby* and *Tender*, for example in the list of Gatsby's guests and of Nicole Diver's purchases; but in both those cases it displays a promiscuous mingling of categories which challenges the orderly arrangement and categorization usually associated with lists. Elkins's list, however, sticks to one category and, presumably, to a chronological ordering: in doing so it could seem to show a lack of imagination and a repetitive, even slightly obsessive quality. It is implied that Dick's intellect might have similar limitations. The doubt Dick himself experiences at this point is, in the context of the whole novel, a harbinger of his future intellectual decline, implicitly posing the question: how clever and original is he really?

Whatever his doubts about his intellect, Dick seems confident at this stage about his body, hardened by gymnasium exercises at Harvard – 'the flying rings' – and by winter swimming in the Danube; it is as if he employs the artificial resources of America and the natural resources of Europe to keep in peak physical condition, as if he can move with assurance in the elements of air and of water. The adjective 'flying' could echo the 'daring young man on the flying trapeze' of the nineteenth-century popular song who 'flies through the air with the greatest of ease'. But as we shall see in chapter 5 of this book, the failure of his ageing body will later provide a mocking mirror of his youthful physical prowess and the 'rings' will recur with an ironic echo in the 'swinging rings' (*TN* 303) in Book 3, chapter 7 of *Tender*.

In the next paragraph Dick speaks to and of himself in the third person, as if he were dramatizing himself as a character in a novel. Here he repudiates being a 'clever' man, perhaps implying that being 'clever' means achieving easy success. He wants instead to be less 'intact' – a key word in *Tender*. To be 'intact' means to be undamaged or unimpaired; its Latin root, 'intactus', links it with the idea of being untouched ('in' means 'not', 'tactus' is the past participle of 'tangere', to touch). So Dick wants to be damaged and impaired to some extent and 'even to be faintly destroyed'. And 'life' must do this. Dick makes a distinction here between 'life' and specific traumas which can be identified in the discourses of medicine (a disease), popular emotion (a broken heart) or psychology (an inferiority complex). He acknowledges that it would give pleasure and satisfaction to try to repair such a trauma in a way that would improve the damaged part and the whole person and it is significant that he employs an architectural metaphor here: 'to build out some broken side until it was better than the original structure'. The metaphor has an aesthetic element, contributing to the idea of Dick as a kind of artist. It also makes an intertextual allusion to the Bible, to the creation of Eve out of Adam's side in the Book of Genesis (2:20–3), which anticipates the way in which Dick will rebuild Nicole partly from his own resources, leaving him lessened.

In Dick's view, however, to suffer an identifiable trauma could not replace what he wants: the damage or impairment produced by a more complex, less easily nameable experiential process. His desire for this might help to explain why he later behaves in ways that seem self-destructive and could cast doubt on the judgement that Dick is simply a failure: if his aim at this stage of his life is to be 'less intact, even faintly destroyed', he later achieves it, though his destruction may be more than faint. In the following paragraph, Dick mocks his own reflections and judges them to be 'American' because he associates America with phrase-making that does not employ the intellect. The narrator, however, does not endorse this dismissal but confirms the importance of becoming less intact and introduces a further idea: that 'intactness' is bought at the cost of 'incompleteness'. The implication is that losing a measure of intactness is not merely negative but a means towards completion.

In the eighth paragraph, the narrator provides a direct diagnosis of Dick. The image of 'less Achilles' heels than would be required to equip a centipede' is partly jocular, and partly a mythical allusion, an example of an intertextual link between *Tender* and another cultural text, that of ancient Greek myth. Achilles was a Greek hero whose mother, Thetis, dipped him into the River Styx, making him invulnerable except for the heel by which she held him and which stayed dry. The combination of invulnerability and a susceptibility to wounding symbolized in this myth is also evident in Dick Diver and acquires wider significance as the narrator goes on to present Dick as a bearer, not only of individual illusions, but also of national, American ones: 'the illusions of a nation', which are identified as 'the illusions of eternal health and strength, and of the essential goodness of people'. The narrator traces these back to the origins of the USA and to the bond between mother and child, at which point 'illusions' shifts into the stronger term 'lies': the 'lies of generations of frontier mothers' who had to reassure their children they were safe. The implication here is that these illusions, though necessary at a certain stage in the development of a child and of a nation, have an infantile quality. As at the end of *Gatsby*, there is an attempt here to endow the protagonist with national significance.

In the final paragraph of the extract, the narrator comments on what has gone before. He points out that it sounds like a biography but that, unlike the biography of a 'hero' – General Grant, for example – we do not yet know whether the person it describes is to be called to 'an intricate destiny'. It is worth briefly outlining Grant's life here, for it is important in *Tender* and, as we shall see in chapter 6 of this book, will recur significantly in the last sentence of the novel. Originally christened Hiram Ulysses Grant, his adopted name of Ulysses S. Grant (the 'S' did not stand for anything) gave him the same first two initials as his nation. Born in Port Pleasant, Ohio, he graduated from the US Military Academy in 1843 and took part in the Mexican–American war, but resigned from the Army in 1854 and, after some financial failures in St Louis, worked as a clerk in his father's tannery shop at Galena, Illinois – the comparison of Dick to Grant 'lolling in his general store in Galena' refers to this phase of Grant's life. At that stage, Grant might have seemed destined for obscurity. But in the US Civil War, he rapidly distinguished himself as a soldier and strategist, became Commanding General of the US Army, and accepted the surrender of the Confederate leader Robert E. Lee in 1865. Elected President of the USA in 1868, he served two full terms. He played a key role in Reconstruction in the South but his presidency was marred by bribery and corruption scandals. After leaving office, he went on a world tour, where he was well received, but on his return home an unwise investment left him virtually bankrupt. He was, however, able to earn money and make a reputation as a writer by producing his *Memoirs*, which were widely praised; he died with his reputation on the rise again. Even this brief sketch indicates the appropriateness of the adjective 'intricate', which Fitzgerald applies to Grant's destiny. But Grant became an American hero, whose failures and flaws could be seen as adding to his stature because of his ability to transcend them: the question posed at this stage of *Tender* is whether Dick will do the same.

Conclusions

We have analysed the opening passages of *Gatsby* and *Tender* and a further extract from each novel which occurs later in the text but which could, in a more chronologically straightforward story, serve as the opening passage (and in the case of *Tender*, the further extract did become part of the opening passage in the posthumously published text revised by Malcolm Cowley). The two actual opening passages of each novel are notable for their indirectness and elaborateness. In the opening passage of *Gatsby*, the narrator supplies little specific information about himself and offers abstract and general descriptions of Gatsby. In the opening passage of *Tender*, the protagonist, Dick Diver, is not mentioned at all.

Nonetheless the opening passages do quite a lot of work. First, their indirectness and elaborateness establish a narrative strategy, a way of telling a story, for both novels; neither will release information about its characters and themes in a straightforward way but will use indirection, delay and chronological scrambling to sharpen the reader's curiosity. The *Gatsby* opening introduces Nick's narrative voice – a voice sometimes inclined to circumlocution and euphemism, to approaching subjects indirectly – and also establishes Nick as a person in whom others confide, which is important for the subsequent development of a narrative in which some key events are not witnessed directly by the narrator but which he learns about, and retails, after hearing them from others. Moreover, the opening shows Nick as a morally concerned person anxious that people should behave properly and thus raises at the outset ethical questions which recur throughout the novel, though they may sometimes become invisible in the bright play of spectacle and sensation. But some of his diction, his terms of approbation, suggest that he is also a romantic. This combination of moral concern and romanticism relates to another feature of Nick which the opening strongly conveys: his ambivalence in relation to Gatsby, his mixture of admiration and disapproval.

The *Tender* opening also introduces a distinctive narrative voice, this time a third-person one. It is a resourceful voice which can encompass precise description, lyricism, imagery and humour (as in the description of the man bathing). The opening of *Tender* is also important for the way in which it gives a sense of time and geographical location, and sets a scene – the hotel, the beach and the sea – which will be crucial when Dick is introduced: it is the setting in which he will play out key parts of his drama. In portraying two women who are initially defined by their family relationship – mother and daughter – it introduces the theme of families but also adumbrates the way in which families in the novel will be seen as incomplete – in the case of this mother and daughter, the father is absent – or flawed (Dick and Nicole and their two children form a young family in the conventional sense, but this unit is ultimately doomed in *Tender*). By focusing on the difference in the physical appearance of the mother and daughter, it sets up a contrast between youth and age which will also be important in the novel, given the age gap between Dick and Rosemary, and the gulf between Dick's youthful and older self. The extended description of Rosemary has a voyeuristic quality which links with her identity as a film star and it also stresses her innocence, cueing a theme of innocence violated which is also crucial in the novel.

The two subsequent passages we analysed present the earlier life-histories of their protagonists in a comparatively direct way, though they are not wholly straightforward. The passage from *Gatsby* zigzags chronologically and the passage from *Tender* adopts a variety of perspectives on Dick – the narrator's, Dick's own, in his conversations with himself, and a young Rumanian intellectual's. In the account of Gatsby's earlier life, Nick only twice appears in the first person, but there is a sense of a voice shaping and presenting what we hear; we are not given Gatsby's words directly but Nick's paraphrase of them and Nick, like a third-person narrator, varies his distance from what he describes, seeing Gatsby sometimes from the inside and describing how he felt, and offering analyses of him in terms that Gatsby himself might not have employed (for example, 'he was born from his Platonic conception of himself'). The account of a key segment of Dick's earlier life in *Tender* also varies its distance from him; in order to get closer to him, it uses both a section in which Dick is talking or thinking to himself in the third person and a passage of interior monologue in which Dick's thoughts are given in the first person. But both Gatsby and Dick can be seen to embody idealist and romantic aspirations which are also bound up with American national identity and the 'American Dream'.

Methods of Analysis

- We explored how the beginnings of *Gatsby* and *Tender* might appear to a first-time reader with little or no knowledge of its plot or characters.
- We considered how the beginnings of each novel might appear to a reader approaching the novel for a second or subsequent time.
- We examined the kinds of sentences used (e.g. the multiple sentence in the third paragraph of *Gatsby*; the long, complex opening sentence of the *Tender* extract).
- We noted Fitzgerald's fondness for dashes in his narrative prose and focused on an example of this (in the 'Gatz/Gatsby' sentence in extract 3).
- We discussed the diction – the choice of words – and focused on words that seemed significant (e.g. the romantic language Nick employs in *Gatsby*; the lyrical terms used to describe Rosemary's face in *Tender*).
- We identified key examples of imagery (e.g. the technological image of 'the intricate machine' which registers distant earthquakes in *Gatsby*; the simile of 'children after their cold baths' in *Tender*).
- We observed the time signals and scales in the extracts (e.g. the vague time signals in the *Gatsby* opening, the more definite ones at the start of *Tender*).
- We drew attention to significant *intratextual* links – i.e. links between our excerpts and other parts of the novels within which they occur (e.g. the link between the circumlocution and euphemism at the start of *Gatsby* and in Nick's account of finding

Gatsby's body in chapter 5; or, in *Tender*, the link between the 'flying rings' of Book 2, chapter 1 and the 'swinging rings' of Book 3, chapter 7).

- We pointed out important *intertextual* links – that is, links between the passages we considered and other cultural texts (e.g. the phrase from the New Testament in *Gatsby*, the allusions to the Greek myth of Achilles and the partly historical, partly folk-mythical figure of General Grant in *Tender*).

Suggested Work

Using the methods demonstrated in this chapter, examine the following passages, each of which describes a further important beginning: the start of the major relationship in each novel – between Gatsby and Daisy in *Gatsby*, and between Dick and Nicole in *Tender*. Analyse the way in which the kinds of sentences, diction, imagery, time signals, and any intratextual and intertextual references contribute to the portrayal of the beginning of each relationship. Explore how these relationships may be linked with wider cultural, social, national and philosophical contexts.

[a] *Gatsby*. From 'I stayed late that night.' to ' ... what I had almost remembered was uncommunicable forever.' (*GG* 105–7)

[b] *Tender*. From 'They went down two steps to the path ... ' to 'bringing him the essence of a continent. ... ' (*TN* 150–2)

2

Society

Parties.

The society portrayed in *Gatsby* and *Tender* is one in which the bonds of
family and community seem ineffectual or oppressive and in which the
chief social mode in which people meet and try to relate to one another
is the party. In both novels, parties both large and small provide stages on
which to portray the tensions, desires and concealments of a society in
flux. The first extract we shall examine is from Nick's account in chapter 1
of *Gatsby* of Nick's first visit to a small dinner party held by his second
cousin, Daisy, and her husband Tom Buchanan, at their large East Egg
home. A young female golf champion, Jordan Baker, is also present and,
through the medium of the telephone, a fifth guest intrudes.

The Fifth Guest: *The Great Gatsby*, pp. 19–21

The butler came back and murmured something close to Tom's ear,
whereupon Tom frowned, pushed back his chair, and without a word
went inside. As if his absence quickened something within her, Daisy
leaned forward again, her voice glowing and singing.

'I love to see you at my table, Nick. You remind me of a – of a rose, an
absolute rose. Doesn't he?' She turned to Miss Baker for confirmation.
'An absolute rose?'

This was untrue. I am not even faintly like a rose. She was only
extemporizing, but a stirring warmth flowed from her, as if her heart
was trying to come out to you concealed in one of those breathless,

thrilling words. Then suddenly she threw her napkin on the table and excused herself and went into the house.

Miss Baker and I exchanged a short glance consciously devoid of meaning. I was about to speak when she sat up alertly and said 'Sh!' in a warning voice. A subdued impassioned murmur was audible in the room beyond, and Miss Baker leaned forward unashamed, trying to hear. The murmur trembled on the verge of coherence, sank down, mounted excitedly, and then ceased altogether.

'This Mr Gatsby you spoke of is my neighbour – ' I began.

'Don't talk. I want to hear what happens.'

'Is something happening?' I inquired innocently.

'You mean to say you don't know?' said Miss Baker, honestly surprised. 'I thought everybody knew.'

'I don't.'

'Why – ' she said hesitantly. 'Tom's got some woman in New York.'

'Got some woman?' I repeated blankly.

Miss Baker nodded.

'She might have the decency not to telephone him at dinner time. Don't you think?'

Almost before I had grasped her meaning there was the flutter of a dress and the crunch of leather boots, and Tom and Daisy were back at the table.

'It couldn't be helped!' cried Daisy with tense gaiety.

She sat down, glanced searchingly at Miss Baker and then at me, and continued: 'I looked outdoors for a minute, and it's very romantic outdoors. There's a bird on the lawn that I think must be a nightingale come over on the Cunard or White Star Line. He's singing away – ' Her voice sang. 'It's romantic, isn't it, Tom?'

'Very romantic,' he said, and then miserably to me: 'If it's light enough after dinner, I want to take you down to the stables.'

The telephone rang inside, startlingly, and as Daisy shook her head decisively at Tom the subject of the stables, in fact all subjects, vanished into air. Among the broken fragments of the last five minutes at table I remember the candles being lit again, pointlessly, and I was conscious of wanting to look squarely at every one, and yet to avoid all eyes. I couldn't guess what Daisy and Tom were thinking, but I doubt if even Miss Baker, who seemed to have mastered a certain hardy scepticism, was able utterly to put this fifth guest's shrill metallic urgency out of mind. To a certain temperament the situation might have seemed intriguing – my own instinct was to telephone immediately for the police.

This extract brings a specific scene vividly before us through a mixture of description and dialogue. The descriptive sections are in the past tense, the most common tense for narration in a novel, but in contrast to the extracts we discussed in the first chapter, which distanced the narrated events in time and, in the case of the early histories of Gatsby and Dick Diver, summarized them, this passage gives a sense that we are witnessing the event as it happens (even though the account is selective – for example, though we learn that Nick drinks claret at the party, we learn nothing of the food served there). It is only in the final paragraph that the narrative speeds up slightly and is distanced in time a little, with a summary of the last five minutes replacing the description/dialogue mixture, and a reminder to the reader, in the words 'I remember', that Nick is giving a retrospective account.

Dashes are deployed to good effect in this extract. As we observed in the previous chapter, the dashes in Fitzgerald's narrative prose tend to sharpen the reader's attention to meaning. We see an example in the sentence 'To a certain temperament the situation might have seemed intriguing – my own instinct was to telephone immediately for the police.' The dash here highlights the contrast between two possible responses and suggests the urgency of Nick's own reaction; it is almost as if he were about to launch into one of his more elaborate explorations of how 'a certain temperament' might have found the situation 'intriguing' but broke off because of the pressure of his own feelings and declared his personal reaction instead. When dashes occur in Fitzgerald's dialogue, they also sharpen the reader's attention to meaning, often to points at which meaning breaks down or shifts: they can signify a searching for the right word, as when Daisy says to Nick 'You remind me of a – ' or Jordan says 'Why – '; they can indicate an interruption, for instance Jordan's interruption of Nick when he starts to say, 'This Mr Gatsby you spoke of is my neighbour – '; or they can signal a change of direction in discourse, as when Daisy declares of the bird she imagines to be a nightingale 'He's singing away – ' and then, her own voice singing, directly addresses Tom.

The extract contains several finite verbs denoting physical action; most of these are phrasal verbs (that is, they are made up of a verb and a preposition or adverb): 'came back'; 'pushed back'; 'went inside' (twice); 'leaned forward'; 'threw ... on'; 'sat up'; 'shook her head'. Some of the adverbs intensify the sense of energetic activity: 'suddenly'; 'alertly'; 'decisively', 'searchingly', 'startlingly' (this last is applied not to human agency but to the telephone, but the telephone is a kind of presence at the party). At other times, however, the adverbs denote actual or assumed naivety, hesitancy, incomprehension or low spirits: 'innocently', 'hesitantly', 'blankly'; 'miserably'; this combination of bursts of energy with blockages of momentum when understanding or words or optimism fail is a key element of this extract. It also occurs in another extract from the account of the same evening which we shall consider in chapter 4 of this book, and it could be said to feature throughout *Gatsby* and to provide an opposition – energy/blockage – which structures the whole novel. The adverbial phrase 'tense gaiety' is almost an example of an oxymoron, a figure of speech in which two contradictory terms are yoked together, as in 'bitter-sweet' or 'living death'; here it effectively conveys the mixed aspects of Daisy's manner and of the party itself.

Lyrical and romantic diction is also prominent in this extract: 'glowing', 'love'; 'singing', 'rose' (repeated three times, if facetiously); 'stirring'; 'warmth'; 'heart'; 'breathless'; 'thrilling'; 'impassioned'; 'nightingale'; and the term 'romantic' (repeated three times, though in an ironic context; one of the key romantic props, a nightingale, is in fact absent – nightingales are not native to America – and Tom's phrase 'very romantic' hardly seems heartfelt). This kind of diction is concerned with sensation and feeling, but there is another strand of vocabulary in the passage which could be called cognitive, concerned with knowing and understanding: 'meaning' occurs twice, first when Jordan Baker and Nick exchange a short glance 'consciously devoid of meaning', and then when Tom and Daisy return almost before Nick has grasped Jordan's meaning (after she has told him that Tom has 'got some woman in New York'). The adverb 'blankly', applied to Nick's echo of Jordan's words 'got some woman', also conveys incomprehension, and the idea of meaning which cannot quite be grasped is exemplified by the murmur which Jordan tries, unsuccessfully, to hear but which never becomes coherent.

Imagery is used to convey changes in Daisy's emotional state: when Tom goes out to take the first phone call, it is 'as if his absence' quickens something within her, where 'quickens' has the sense of both 'stimulates' and 'restores life to'. When she compares Nick to a rose, it is 'as if her heart was trying to come out to you concealed in one of those breathless, thrilling words'. Fitzgerald also makes significant use in this section of the device of metonymy, in which a part belonging to a thing or associated with it stands for that thing. After the first exit of Tom and Daisy, their return is evoked by 'the flutter of a dress [Daisy] and the crunch of leather boots [Tom]', sounds which reinforce a contrast between Daisy's lightness and Tom's hardness. The telephone which rings twice during the evening is a metonymy for Tom's mistress and his affair with her. It also provides an example of that form of imagery called personification, in which inanimate objects are given human attributes: after it rings for the second time, Nick refers to it as the 'fifth guest' at the dinner party.

When Nick sums up the last five minutes at the table, after Daisy has indicated to Tom that he should not answer the second phone call, he uses the image of 'broken fragments' to describe how the cohesion of the evening has been shattered; this links up with Tom's own remark earlier in this scene, 'Civilization's going to pieces' (*GG* 18), a break-up which he attributes to the rise of the coloured races but for which, in the context of this evening, he is responsible. The phrase 'broken fragments' could also be heard as an intertextual echo of the lines 'A heap of broken images' (22) and 'These fragments I have shored against my ruins' (430) in T. S. Eliot's poem *The Waste Land* (1922).

The dinner party at the Buchanans puts Nick in a situation which recurs in *Gatsby*, in which he is the observer and participant in a drama he only partly understands. In this case, however, he understands enough to be disturbed by it. He claims that his own instinct is to telephone immediately for the police; the sense that a person like Tom can no longer control himself or be controlled by the social world he inhabits, so that an external agency is necessary, could be seen as symptomatic of a wider social breakdown.

The next extract, from *Tender*, also takes up the topic of the dinner party as a way of meeting which goes wrong. This extract is from the account, in Part 1, chapter 7, of the dinner party hosted by Dick and Nicole Diver at their Riviera home, the Villa Diana; this aims to bring together Abe North and Tommy Barban, who are already part of the Divers' circle, with a range of new associates: Rosemary and Mrs Speers, Earl Brady, Violet and Albert McKisco, Royal Dumphrey, Luis Campion and Mrs Abrams. When the extract starts, they are dining in the open air and have already been sitting at the table for over half an hour.

The Vanishing Hosts: *Tender is the Night*, pp. 43–6

Rosemary, as dewy with belief as a child from one of Mrs Burnett's vicious tracts, had a conviction of homecoming, of a return from the derisive and salacious improvisations of the frontier. There were fireflies riding on the dark air and a dog baying on some low and far-away ledge of the cliff. The table seemed to have risen a little toward the sky like a mechanical dancing platform, giving the people around it a sense of being alone with each other in the dark universe, nourished by its only food, warmed by its only lights. And, as if a curious hushed laugh from Mrs McKisco were a signal that such a detachment from the world had been attained, the two Divers began suddenly to warm and glow and expand, as if to make up to their guests, already so subtly assured of their importance, so flattered with politeness, for anything they might still miss from that country well left behind. For just a moment they seemed to speak to everyone at the table, singly and together, assuring them of their friendliness, their affection. And for a moment the faces turned up toward them were like the faces of poor children at a Christmas tree. Then abruptly the table broke up – the moment when the guests had been daringly lifted above conviviality into the rarer atmosphere of sentiment was over before it could be irreverently breathed, before they had half realized it was there.

But the diffused magic of the hot sweet South had withdrawn into them – the soft-pawed night and the ghostly wash of the Mediterranean far below – the magic left these things and melted into the two Divers and became part of them. Rosemary watched Nicole pressing upon her mother a yellow evening bag she had admired, saying, 'I think things ought to belong to the people that like them' – and then sweeping into it all the yellow articles she could find, a pencil, a lipstick, a little note book, 'because they all go together'.

Nicole disappeared and presently Rosemary noticed that Dick was no longer there; the guests distributed themselves in the garden or drifted in toward the terrace.

'Do you want,' Violet McKisco asked Rosemary, 'to go to the bathroom?'

Not at that precise moment.

'I want,' insisted Mrs McKisco, 'to go to the bathroom.' As a frank outspoken woman she walked toward the house, dragging her secret after her, while Rosemary looked after with reprobation. Earl Brady proposed that they walk down to the sea wall but she felt that this was her time to have a share of Dick Diver when he reappeared, so she stalled, listening to McKisco quarrel with Barban.

'Why do you want to fight the Soviets?' McKisco said. 'The greatest experiment ever made by humanity? And the Riff? It seems to me it would be more heroic to fight on the just side.'

'How do you find out which it is?' asked Barban dryly.

'Why – usually everybody intelligent knows.'

'Are you a Communist?'

'I'm a Socialist,' said McKisco, 'I sympathize with Russia.'

'Well, I'm a soldier,' Barban answered pleasantly. 'My business is to kill people. I fought against the Riff because I am a European, and I have fought the Communists because they want to take my property from me.'

'Of all the narrow-minded excuses,' McKisco looked around to establish a derisive liaison with some one else, but without success. He had no idea what he was up against in Barban, neither of the simplicity of the other man's bag of ideas nor of the complexity of his training. McKisco knew what ideas were, and as his mind grew he was able to recognize and sort an increasing number of them – but faced by a man whom he considered 'dumb', one in whom he found no ideas he could recognize as such, and yet to whom he could not feel personally superior, he jumped at the conclusion that Barban was the end product of an archaic world, and as such, worthless. McKisco's contacts with the princely classes in America had impressed upon him their uncertain and fumbling snobbery, their delight in ignorance and their deliberate rudeness, all lifted from the English with no regard paid to factors that make English philistinism and rudeness purposeful, and applied in a land where a little knowledge and civility buy more than they do anywhere else – an attitude which reached its apogee in the 'Harvard manner' of about 1900. He thought that this Barban was of that type, and being drunk rashly forgot that he was in awe of him – this led up to the trouble in which he presently found himself.

Feeling vaguely ashamed for McKisco, Rosemary waited, placid but inwardly on fire, for Dick Diver's return. From her chair at the deserted table with Barban, McKisco, and Abe she looked up along the path edged with shadowy myrtle and fern to the stone terrace, and falling in love with her mother's profile against a lighted door, was about to go there when Mrs McKisco came hurrying down from the house.

She exuded excitement. In the very silence with which she pulled out a chair and sat down, her eyes staring, her mouth working a little, they all recognized a person crop-full of news, and her husband's 'What's the matter, Vi?' came naturally, as all eyes turned toward her.

'My dear – ' she said at large, and then addressed Rosemary, 'my dear – it's nothing. I really can't say a word.'

'You're among friends,' said Abe.

'Well, upstairs I came upon a scene, my dears – '

Shaking her head cryptically, she broke off just in time, for Tommy arose and addressed her politely but sharply:

'It's inadvisable to comment on what goes on in this house.'

This extract evokes a movement from apparent harmony to disharmony and finishes on the edge of a revelation which seems as though it could radically reconfigure all that has gone before. The narrative voice here is that of a third-person storyteller who mixes his own observations and analyses with a portrayal of Rosemary's point of view (as well as making an excursion into Albert McKisco's point of view and noting its limitations). The extract mixes summarizing narrative description with fragments of dialogue. Summarizing description, for example, is the exclusive mode of the first paragraph, which contains no dialogue at all. We are not told what the Divers said as they 'began suddenly to warm and glow and expand'; the focus is on their effect on Rosemary and the other guests.

The diction of the extract includes a range of terms which convey the peculiar quality of the evening, its mixture of congenial and inimical elements. The adjective 'magic' occurs twice, first applied to the natural surroundings (night, sea), then transferred to the Divers; this transfer is denoted by the phrasal verb 'melted into', suggesting an imperceptible (indeed magical) metamorphosis. There are nouns with positive associations: 'homecoming'; 'lights', 'food', 'friendliness', 'affection', 'conviviality', 'sentiment' (this seems primarily used in its older sense of 'refined and elevated feeling', though its dominant modern meaning of 'exaggerated and self-indulgent feelings' is still present in the background, particularly perhaps in relation to Rosemary's perception of the occasion). There are also positive verbs and adjectives: 'to warm', 'glow', 'expand'; 'nourished', 'warmed', 'hot' and 'sweet'. But negative terms are apparent as well: 'vicious', 'derisive' (which occurs twice), 'salacious'; 'worthless', 'uncertain', 'fumbling', 'dark'. Present participles help to give a sense of ongoing action: 'riding', 'baying', 'giving', 'assuring', 'pressing', 'saying', 'sweeping', 'dragging', '[f]eeling', 'falling', 'hurrying', 'staring', 'working', '[s]haking'.

The imagery is varied. Rosemary is described as being 'as dewy with belief as a child from one of Mrs Burnett's vicious tracts': 'dewy' takes up the image that 'the dew was still on her' from the first extract we analysed, and here once again it suggests innocence, but also, now, naivety and credulity, especially when followed by the phrase 'with belief'. The comparison of Rosemary to a child also links up with the initial description of Rosemary as 'on the last edge of childhood'. But here Rosemary is not seen in terms of a general idea of childhood, but, in an explicit intertextual reference, likened to the specific kind of fictional child that features in the work of Frances Hodgson Burnett (1849–1924), a writer of romantic stories, many of which were for children, such as *Little Lord Fauntleroy* (1886) and *The Secret Garden* (1911). The condemnatory adjective 'vicious', meaning 'immoral' in this context, constitutes a limiting judgement, not only on Rosemary as an individual, but also on the cultural construction of children by a certain kind of popular sentimental fiction and links up with the novel's critique of the construction of children and of the parent–child relationship in popular film, such as the movie in which Rosemary starred, *Daddy's Girl*.

To convey Rosemary's sense that the table has been uplifted, Fitzgerald employs an image from modern technology and the 1920s leisure industry, comparing the supposedly raised table to 'a mechanical dancing platform' – a further example of his romantic modernism, in which a technological comparison is applied to a romantic experience. The faces turned up to the Divers seem for a moment 'like the faces of poor children at a Christmas tree', implying a kind of neediness in the guests, an emotional rather than a material impoverishment, which the Divers seem to be about to assuage with gifts. The night is described as 'soft-pawed', as if it were an animal, apparently benign at this point but perhaps capable of unsheathing its claws. When Rosemary waits for Dick to return after he disappears, she is 'inwardly on fire', suggesting the intensity of her feelings for Dick. Each of these images raises questions about the quality of Rosemary's perception and experience and about the real nature of the evening.

The extract starts at a point when the party, which has been in progress for some time, enters a quasi-magical phase. This is characterized, for

Rosemary, by 'a conviction of homecoming from the derisive and salacious improvisations of the frontier'. The 'frontier' here is perhaps the last American frontier represented by Hollywood, and there is a sense that Rosemary is returning to a supposedly more civilized version of American life, embodied in Europe by the expatriate Divers. The people gathered at the table seem to become detached from the world and the Divers start to work together to make sure their guests are not missing the world they have moved above. As mentioned earlier, we are not told what the Divers said but the narrator sums up its effect: 'they seemed to speak to every one at the table, singly and together, assuring them of their friendliness, their affection'. The Divers' words at this point seem to make an impression on individuals similar to that of Gatsby's smile: it 'concentrated on *you* with an irresistible prejudice in your favour' (*GG* 49). But just as Gatsby's smile vanishes quickly, so does the instant when the Divers seem to speak individually and collectively to all their guests. Its transience is stressed by the repetition, in the last three sentences of the paragraph, of the word 'moment': 'For just a moment'; 'And for a moment'; 'the moment … was over'. In that 'moment', it seems to Rosemary – and the narrator's description partly endorses her perception – that the dinner party has achieved a heightened, magical reality, has become a utopian space, and that the Divers make a crucial contribution to this. But even then, the image of the guests' momentary attitude towards the Divers as 'like the faces of poor children at a Christmas tree' suggests to the reader (if not to Rosemary) a relationship between the Divers and the other people at the table which is not reciprocal but hierarchical, akin to that between the dispensers and recipients of charity. It is a relationship in which the Divers have power. At the end of the paragraph, the mood of harmony breaks up 'abruptly' and the evening starts to fragment.

In the next phase of the evening, a certain magic lingers – 'the diffused magic of the hot, sweet South … melted into the two Divers' – but it does not last long. Although they are called 'the two Divers', Dick and Nicole are no longer working together; Nicole has struck out on her own, putting pressure on Rosemary's mother to accept the yellow gifts. Compared to Dick and Nicole's combined effect on the guests a short time before and the harmony it momentarily created, Nicole's attempt to construct a kind of connection with Mrs Speers, by grouping objects according to a colour and giving them as a gift, is clumsy; Fitzgerald makes use here of one of his key devices, the list, although this one is short ('a pencil, a lipstick, a little note book'), a kind of rehearsal for the much longer list that will come later, when Nicole goes on her shopping spree. We have a snatch of dialogue from Nicole, but we do not hear the response of Rosemary's mother. Nicole's insistence has an uncomfortable aspect, however, as she plays the role of a rich woman dispensing largesse. It exemplifies and reinforces the sense of an unequal relationship between the givers and receivers of charity which the earlier 'Christmas tree' image conveyed, and it suggests that such inequality is, at least in part, economic. In relation to the broader themes of the novel, it echoes and extends the uneasiness which arises from Nicole's economic power over Dick.

Immediately after this, at the start of the third paragraph, a further phase of the evening is triggered when we are simply told that 'Nicole disappeared', without explanation, as if, given the magical quality of the earlier part of the evening, she were a conjuror who had vanished. Then Rosemary notices that Dick is also absent, again without explanation. Given the centrality of Dick and Nicole to the harmony and atmosphere of the dinner party in the first paragraph, this sudden joint disappearance is strange, the first of the two enigmas the evening will pose. In contrast to this mystery, Violet McKisco is, for the time, bluntly outspoken in her announcement that she wants to go to the bathroom.

The aftermath of the Divers' departure suggests how much the party guests rely on the guiding presence of the couple for cohesion; in their absence, the party fragments as the guests separate, and, after Violet McKisco departs for the bathroom, a quarrel breaks out between her husband and Tommy Barban. This is evoked in a question-and-answer dialogue between the two men which illustrates political tensions in the wider world. The narrator then follows up the dialogue with an extended account of McKisco's inability to grasp the kind of person Barban is, because he sees him in American terms. This account ends with the ominous indication that this inability will lead McKisco into trouble. At this point, the trouble is not specified, but the reader later discovers that it is a duel between Barban and McKisco.

Rosemary is about to go to her mother when Violet McKisco returns. Another stretch of dialogue ensues, in which Violet tantalizingly evokes the 'scene' in the bathroom but breaks off three times ('My dear – '; 'my dear – '; 'My dears – '). We see Fitzgerald making use of the dash again and, on the three occasions he does so here, it indicates an aposiopesis – a rhetorical term for a sentence which breaks off suddenly and is left unfinished (in contrast, the broken-off sentences in the first passage we discussed in this chapter were either completed once the speaker had found a suitable word or were left incomplete because of an interruption by another speaker). An aposiopesis indicates that a speaker has come to a point where words fail because of strong emotion or incomprehension or a mixture of both. Violet McKisco has previously been portrayed as very outspoken, so the failure of words at this point suggests the deep effect of what she has seen. For Rosemary, and for the first-time reader of the novel who does not know the plot, Violet's aposiopeses and hints, and the strategic silence of the third-person narrator at this point, create the second enigma of the evening. The two enigmas (why did Nicole and Dick disappear? what did Violet see in the bathroom?) will not be resolved until the end of Part 1 of *Tender*, when Rosemary witnesses a similar scene in another bathroom and knows, in retrospect, what Violet McKisco saw in the bathroom at the Villa Diana. Already, however, the momentary magical harmony which the Divers created has given way to tension, friction, unease and puzzlement.

Both the extracts we have considered so far in this chapter evoke small dinner parties fairly directly. But it is the presentation of large parties for which *Gatsby* is famous, and we shall now look at one of the ways Fitzgerald portrays these – by the indirect device of the famous list which shows the diversity of Gatsby's guests and offers a cross-section through metropolitan society in modern America.

Gatsby's Guests: *The Great Gatsby*, pp. 60–2

Once I wrote down on the empty spaces of a time-table the names of those who came to Gatsby's house that summer. It is an old time-table now, disintegrating at its folds, and headed 'This schedule in effect July 5th, 1922'. But I can still read the grey names, and they will give you a better impression than my generalities of those who accepted Gatsby's hospitality and paid him the subtle tribute of knowing nothing whatever about him.

From East Egg, then, came the Chester Beckers and the Leeches, and a man named Bunsen, whom I knew at Yale, and Doctor Webster Civet, who was drowned last summer up in Maine. And the Hornbeams and the Willie Voltaires, and a whole clan named Blackbuck, who always gathered in a corner and flipped up their noses like goats at whosoever came near. And the Ismays and the Chrysties (or rather Hubert Auerbach and Mr Chrystie's wife), and Edgar Beaver, whose hair, they say, turned cotton-white one winter afternoon for no good reason at all.

Clarence Endive was from East Egg, as I remember. He came only once, in white knickerbockers, and had a fight with a bum named Etty in the garden. From farther out on the Island came the Cheadles and the O. R. P. Schraeders, and the Stonewall Jackson Abrams of Georgia, and the Fishguards and the Ripley Snells. Snell was there three days before he went to the penitentiary, so drunk out on the gravel drive that Mrs Ulysses Swett's automobile ran over his right hand. The Dancies came, too, and S. B. Whitebait, who was well over sixty, and Maurice A. Flink, and the Hammerheads, and Beluga the tobacco importer, and Beluga's girls.

From West Egg came the Poles and the Mulreadys and Cecil Roebuck and Cecil Schoen and Gulick the State senator and Newton Orchid, who controlled Films Par Excellence, and Eckhaust and Clyde Cohen and Don S. Schwartz (the son) and Arthur McCarty, all connected with the movies in one way or another. And the Catlips and the Bembergs and G. Earl Muldoon, brother to that Muldoon who afterward strangled his wife. Da Fontano the promoter came there, and Ed Legros and James B. ('Rot-Gut') Ferret and the De Jongs and Ernest Lilly – they came to gamble, and when Ferret wandered into the garden it meant he was cleaned out and Associated Traction would have to fluctuate profitably next day.

A man named Klipspringer was there so often that he became known as 'the boarder' – I doubt if he had any other home. Of theatrical people there were Gus Waize and Horace O'Donavan and Lester Myer and George Duckweed and Francis Bull. Also from New York were the Chromes and the Backhyssons and the Dennickers and Russel Betty and the Corrigans and the Kellehers and the Dewars and the Scullys and S. W. Belcher and the Smirkes and the young Quinns, divorced now, and Henry L. Palmetto, who killed himself by jumping in front of a subway train in Times Square.

Benny McClenahan arrived always with four girls. They were never quite the same ones in physical person, but they were so identical one with another that it inevitably seemed they had been there before. I have forgotten their names – Jaqueline [*sic*], I think, or else Consuela, or Gloria or Judy or June, and their last names were either the melodious names of flowers and months or the sterner ones of the great American capitalists whose cousins, if pressed, they would confess themselves to be.

In addition to all these I can remember that Faustina O'Brien came there at least once and the Baedeker girls and young Brewer, who had his nose shot off in the war, and Mr Albrucksburger and Miss Haag, his fiancée, and Ardita Fitz-Peters and Mr P. Jewett, once head of the American Legion, and Miss Claudia Hip, with a man reputed to be her chauffeur, and a prince of something, whom we called Duke, and whose name, if I ever knew it, I have forgotten.

All these people came to Gatsby's house in the summer.

This passage adapts one of the most ancient of literary devices, the roll-call of names, used, for example, in the catalogue of the captains and ships in Homer's ancient Greek epic poem, *The Iliad* (Book 2, lines 494–877), and employs it to portray a vivid, mobile society in which established class and other barriers have become blurred to some extent. Although Nick is supposed to be writing his story one to two years after the events he describes, three of the terms with which he introduces the list suggest a much older document concerning events long ago: the time-table is 'old' and 'disintegrating', as if it were a crumbling parchment, and the names are 'grey', as if aged. It is not clear what the time-table was for – perhaps trains, since Nick will later, sitting in his office on the day of Gatsby's death, take out his 'time-table' (the only other occurrence of the word in *Gatsby*) and draw a circle around the three-fifty train which he intends to catch back to West Egg later that afternoon (*GG* 148). In this respect, the mention of a 'time-table' at this point anticipates Gatsby's death, which Nick will not be in time to try to prevent, and also relates to the overall concern in the novel with time. It is worth noting as well that the heading of the time-table calls it a 'schedule' and this anticipates the boyhood 'SCHEDULE' of Jimmy Gatz, which his father shows to Nick after his son's death (*GG* 164). These intratextual repetitions of words in different parts of the narrative help to bind it together and create internal echoes.

Continuing the concern with time, a definite date is given – 'July 5th, 1922' – which is significant because it is the day after 4 July, American Independence Day. 5 July is not, however, the date of a particular Gatsby party which the listed guests attended; it is the date on which the schedule, the time-table, comes into effect. The list, as Nick indicates here and at the end of the passage, is a list of those who came to Gatsby's house in the summer of 1922 and who may have visited several parties. Nick also indicates that these guests did not know Gatsby personally; in a sense, it is a tribute to Gatsby's success as a stage-manager of huge and spectacular parties that it attracted those who had no personal acquaintance with, or knowledge of, the host.

There are 42 definitely named individuals on the guest list (if we count as individuals Hubert Auerbach and Mr Chrystie's wife, who are initially referred to as 'the Chrysties') and 28 named couples, families, groups or clans. There are also some individuals and groups without names or whose names are uncertain: the man reputed to be Miss Claudia Hip's chauffeur; the 'prince of something, whom we called Duke' and whose name Nick has forgotten, if he ever knew it; Beluga's girls; and the four girls, 'never quite the same ones in physical person' but virtually 'identical one with another' with whom Benny McClenahan always arrives (*GG* 62). The names suggest how the USA in 1922 is made up of people from families with a variety of national origins. Nine sound German: Albrucksburger, Auerbach, Becker, Baedeker, Bunsen, Myer, Schoen, Schraeder, Waize. Two could be Dutch or German: Gulick and Schwartz. Others are more definitely Dutch: Backhysson (as a version of Backhuysen), De Jong (one of the most common Dutch surnames), Snell. Seven are Irish: Corrigan, Kelleher, McCarty, Muldoon, Mulready, O'Donavan, Quinn, Scully. There are also English names (Ismay, Leech, Pole, Smirke); French names (Legros, Voltaire); and an Italian one (Da Fontana).

As well as these indications of national origins, some of the guests are identified by where they currently live. Edgar Beaver, Bunsen, Civet, Clarence Endive and Willie Voltaire, and the Blackbucks, Chester Beckers, Chrysties, Hornbeams, Ismays and Leeches all come from East Egg. As East Egg is the more established community, the home of old – or at least older – money, their presence indicates the power of Gatsby's parties to attract people from such a place, even though they have not, as yet, attracted Tom Buchanan and Daisy. Clyde Cohen, Eckhaust, Gulick, Arthur McCarty, Newton Orchid, Cecil Roebuck, Cecil Schoen, Don S. Schwartz and the Poles and Mulreadys come from West Egg. The Abrams, Cheadles, Fishguards, Schraeders and

Snells come from 'farther out on the island'. S. W. Belcher, Russel Betty and Henry L. Palmetto and the Backhyssons, Chromes, Corrigans, Dewars, Dennickers, Kellehers, Quinns, Scullys and Smirkes come from New York. The different places from which Gatsby's guests come give a sense of the disparate social worlds which meet at his parties.

The occupations of 15 of the named individuals are also provided: significantly, ten of these work in the entertainment industry: five in the traditional mode of theatre – Guz Waize, Horace O'Donavan, Lester Myer, George Duckweed and Francis Bull – and five in the up-and-coming twentieth-century mode of movies: Newton Orchid, the controller of Films Par Excellence (a film company which also features in Fitzgerald's second novel, *The Beautiful and Damned* (1922)) and, in unspecified capacities, Eckhaust, Clyde Cohen, Don S. Schwartz and Arthur McCarty. This reflects the importance of the theatre and movies in American commerce and culture at this time and the way in which Gatsby's parties are open to these worlds (in a way that Tom Buchanan's house might not be). In the account of the later Gatsby party which Daisy and Tom attend, theatre is seen as the progenitor of West Egg itself – 'this unprecedented "place" that Broadway had begotten upon a Long Island fishing village' (*GG* 103). The theatre and movie guests at Gatsby's parties, and the sense that Broadway has fathered West Egg, link up with the idea that Gatsby himself is a theatrical or movie figure, a kind of producer, director and performer who creates spectacular entertainments in the form of parties on the 'studio lot' of his house and gardens, where he himself and his guests are both cast and audience; he is, in the Owl-Eyed Man's words, 'a regular Belasco', referring to the Broadway producer David Belasco (*GG* 47).

Other occupations represented in Gatsby's guest list include that of doctor (Civet), tobacco importer (Beluga), state senator (Gulick), promoter (Da Fontana) and former head of the American Legion (Mr P. Jewett), the mutual-aid organization for US armed forces war veterans founded in 1919 after the First World War – it is this organization which Wolfshiem, soon after taking up Gatsby when he is a penniless ex-soldier, makes Gatsby join, presumably to provide a respectable front. There are also party guests whose occupations are less clear or nonexistent. Snell 'went to the penitentiary', suggesting that he is a criminal; Ferret seems to be a gambler and share speculator and possibly a bootlegger, if his nickname, 'Rot-Gut', is taken to be the effect of the illicit alcohol he provides; Etty is a bum and Klipspringer, the 'boarder' at Gatsby's, virtually lives in the house, with no visible means of support. The range of occupations of the guests contributes to the sense of the diverse worlds which mix at Gatsby's parties.

The list can be very funny, playing on words and common associations and highlighting the comic incongruities which arise in such a mixed and mobile society. For instance, 'Bunsen' almost irresistibly invites the noun 'burner', while 'Edgar Beaver' sounds like a garbling of the phrase 'eager beaver'. Some of the surnames pun on grosser corporeal processes: Mrs Ulysses Swett calls to mind the unladylike image of Shakespeare's Falstaff, who 'sweats to death, / And lards the lean earth as he walks along' (*Henry IV 1*; 2:2:79–80); Belcher and the Smirkes, in a kind of compressed anecdote, suggest the noisy emission of wind from the stomach through the mouth and the smug or silly smiles it may produce in those who hear it; the surname Eckhaust, as well as connoting fatigue, implies a scatological analogy between the expulsion of waste gases from a machine such as an automobile, and the expulsion of gas from the human body in breaking wind. Here Fitzgerald draws, as he did in the revues he wrote at Princeton, on popular American traditions of burlesque and vaudeville which link back, through the ages, with the medieval carnivals in which the hierarchy between higher and lower bodily functions was inverted and the latter were subversively elevated.

Incongruities also arise from intertextual references to high-cultural figures. Mrs Ulysses Swett's husband bears the forename which the ancient Romans gave to the Greek epic hero Odysseus and which in American history calls to mind the folk-hero discussed in chapter 1, General Ulysses S. Grant; Willie Voltaire's surname is also the pen-name of the great French Enlightenment writer and *philosophe*; Etty and Mulready were the surnames of two nineteenth-century British painters who were highly respected in their day; Faustina was the third wife of the ancient Roman emperor Constantius II and, more immediately, 'Faustine' was the title of a notorious poem by the later nineteenth-century English poet Algernon Charles Swinburne, whose work the young Fitzgerald admired.

It is significant that several of the guests are associated with violence, injury or death in the recent past, present or near future: young Brewer had his nose shot off in the war; Endive and Etty fight in Gatsby's garden; Mrs Ulysses Swett's automobile runs over Ripley Snell's hand; Doctor Civet will drown in Maine; G. Earl Muldoon's brother will strangle his wife; Henry L. Palmetto will kill himself by jumping in front of a subway train in Times Square. These elements link up with the other violent incidents and deaths which the novel evokes: Tom's breaking of Myrtle's nose (*GG* 39); the 'piles of dead' in the Argonne Forest battle in the First World War in which Gatsby fought (*GG* 64–5); the murder of Rosy Rosenthal which Wolfshiem recalls (*GG* 68–9); Myrtle's mutilated body after Gatsby's car has struck it (*GG* 131); Wilson's shooting of Gatsby and then himself.

Many of the names in the guest list are drawn from the nomenclature of the natural world – from the plant, tree, fish, invertebrate and mammalian kingdoms. Some of the creatures and plants invoked, and their supposed characteristics, are widely familiar; bull, ferret, leech, orchid. Others may be less well known. Duckweed is a tiny aquatic flowering plant that floats in large quantities on still water. An endive is an edible Mediterranean plant whose bitter leaves can be blanched and used in salads – in North America, it is called 'chicory' and 'endive' refers to the crown of the chicory. A hornbeam is a deciduous tree of hard, pale wood (its name, from Middle English, means 'hard wood'). A beluga is a small white-toothed whale of Arctic coastal waters, related to the narwhal, or a very large sturgeon occurring in the inland seas and rivers of central Eurasia, which is a source of caviar. A hammerhead is a shark with flattened blade-like extensions on either side of the head (it can also be an alternative term for a hamerkop, a brown African marshbird). Whitebait is a term for the small silvery-white young of herrings, sprats and similar marine fish when used as food. A blackbuck is a small Indian gazelle. A civet is a slender cat with a barred and spotted coat, native to Asia and Africa; the word is also used for the strong musky perfume extracted from its scent glands. A klipspringer is a small rock-dwelling antelope with a yellowish-grey coat, native to southern Africa. A roebuck is a male roe deer.

To some extent, this use of names drawn from the natural world recalls the literary genres of the bestiary, in which animals are used allegorically to represent human characteristics, and of satire, in which names drawn from natural history indicate human traits; for example, in Ben Jonson's play *Volpone* (1607), an attack on the attitudes of the rising merchant class, the name of the title character means 'fox' and other characters include Mosca (fly), Corbaccio (crow) and Corvino (raven). We feel that the names of Gatsby's guests indicate something about the people who bear them – for example, the Leeches call to mind the metaphorical use of the term 'leech' to refer to a person who extorts profit from or lives off others. We have little chance to verify this, however, as we encounter all but three of them only in this list: the three who reappear are, most prominently, Klipspringer, 'the boarder', whom Gatsby orders to play the piano when he is showing Daisy round his house for the first time (and whose forename is then revealed as Ewing) (*GG* 91–3) and who rings up, after Gatsby's death, to ask for his tennis shoes to be sent on (to Nick's disgust) (*GG* 160–1); and Dr Civet and Miss Baedeker, presumably one of 'the Baedeker girls', who reappear at the Gatsby party which Tom and Daisy attend (*GG* 102, 103).

Apart from Nick himself, none of the guests named here or elsewhere in the text comes to Gatsby's funeral, except the Owl-Eyed Man, whose proper name we never know, though his nickname links him with Minerva, the ancient Greek goddess of wisdom, the arts and just war, whose symbol is an owl. But the natural-history names also contribute to the sense of the presence of nature pulsing through the urban and suburban settings of the novel. Along with the invocations at significant moments of the sun, moon and sea, and the pastoral intimations which Nick experiences even in the heart of New York, they serve to remind the reader of the natural forces which underlie and feed into the world of high artifice that the characters inhabit. *Gatsby* does not, however, imply a simple opposition between nature and artifice. The novel does suggest that natural forces are ultimately stronger than artificial constructions and may threaten and challenge them; but it also indicates how such forces can be complicit with those constructions and serve to mollify them, for good and bad. This mollifying complicity is suggested by Nick's remark that the surnames of Benny McClenahan's girls, which he has forgotten or never knew, 'were either the melodious names of flowers and months or the sterner ones of the great American capitalists'. There is a sense here that floral, calendric and financial signifiers are interchangeable, apart from the tunefulness of the first and second categories, which serve only to soften the sternness of the third; and in this they link up with

Daisy Buchanan, who bears the forename of a flower and the surname of a family with a fortune.

The extract we have been analysing gives a remarkable impression of a whole segment of American society at a particular time. By its accumulation of names suggesting different nationalities and ethnic provenances, by its details about people's jobs and lives, by its comic incongruities, it conveys a sense of the multiplicity and variety of life but also of the way in which people may be drawn together in the pursuit of happiness. This pursuit may seem to become trivial, to exclude more serious concerns; and the references to injury, violence and death exemplify the darker world which surrounds and sometimes invades the bright gaiety of Gatsby's parties; but it could also be seen, within its limits, as an anticipation of a world in which people could meet and mingle freely in the quest for pleasure and fulfilment. Gatsby's parties hover between hell and utopia; on the one hand they may seem pits in which people are endlessly consumed by unassuageable desires; on the other they can appear as elevated plateaux on which to explore the performance and reinvention of human identities and relationships with unprecedented freedom. Either way, the sheer scale of Gatsby's parties is overwhelming, compared to the small dinner parties at the Buchanan house or the Villa Diana. With our next passage, from *Tender*, we return to a small party, but it differs from the previous parties we have discussed in two respects: it is mobile rather than confined to one place (even the capacious space of Gatsby's house and gardens); and it is set in a metropolis rather than in the prosperous suburbs (East Egg or West Egg) or a seaside village (the Villa Diana).

Quick Odyssey: *Tender is the Night*, pp. 88–9

> The party that night moved with the speed of a slapstick comedy. They were twelve, they were sixteen, they were quartets in separate motors bound on a quick Odyssey over Paris. Everything had been foreseen. People joined them as if by magic, accompanied them as specialists, almost guides, through a phase of the evening, dropped out and were succeeded by other people, so that it appeared as if the freshness of each one had been husbanded for them all day. Rosemary appreciated how different it was from any party in Hollywood, no matter how splendid in

scale. There was, among many diversions, the car of the Shah of Persia. Where Dick had commandeered this vehicle, what bribery was employed, these were facts of irrelevance. Rosemary accepted it as merely a new facet of the fabulous, which for two years had filled her life. The car had been built on a special chassis in America. Its wheels were of silver, so was the radiator. The inside of the body was inlaid with innumerable brilliants which would be replaced with true gems by the court jeweller when the car arrived in Teheran the following week. There was only one real seat in back, because the Shah must ride alone, so they took turns riding in it and sitting on the marten fur that covered the floor.

But always there was Dick. Rosemary assured the image of her mother, ever carried with her, that never, never had she known any one so nice, so thoroughly nice as Dick was that night. She compared him with the two Englishmen, whom Abe addressed conscientiously as 'Major Hengist and Mr Horsa', and with the heir to the Scandinavian throne and the novelist just back from Russia, and with Abe, who was desperate and witty, and with Collis Clay, who joined them somewhere and stayed along – and felt there was no comparison. The enthusiasm, the selflessness behind the whole performance ravished her, the technic of moving many varied types, each as immobile, as dependent on supplies of attention as an infantry battalion is dependent on rations, appeared so effortless that he still had pieces of his own most personal self for everyone.

– Afterward she remembered the times when she had felt the happiest. The first time was when she and Dick danced together and she felt her beauty sparkling bright against his tall, strong form as they floated, hovering like people in an amusing dream – he turned her here and there with such a delicacy of suggestion that she was like a bright bouquet, a piece of precious cloth being displayed before fifty eyes. There was a moment when they were not dancing at all, simply clinging together. Some time in the early morning they were alone, and her damp powdery young body came up close to him in a crush of tired cloth, and stayed there, crushed against a background of other people's hats and wraps ....

The time she laughed most was later, when six of them, the best of them, noblest relics of the evening, stood in the dusky front lobby of the Ritz telling the night concierge that General Pershing was outside and wanted caviare and champagne. 'He brooks no delay. Every man, every gun is at his service.' Frantic waiters emerged from nowhere, a table was set in the lobby, and Abe came in representing General Pershing while they stood up and mumbled remembered fragments of war songs at him. In the waiters' injured reaction to this anti-climax they found themselves neglected, so they built a waiter trap – a huge and fantastic device constructed of all the furniture in the lobby and functioning like one of the bizarre machines of a Goldberg cartoon. Abe shook his head doubtfully at it.

This extract portrays a party different from the comparatively static small dinner parties at the Buchanans and Divers or the huge assemblies in the gardens of Gatsby's house. It shares a magical quality with Gatsby's extravaganzas and the brief moment of harmony at the Villa Diana, but it is a mobile party which moves across a big city. It has its own kind of high-life flourishes, involving the Shah of Persia's borrowed car and an attempt to impersonate General Pershing at the Ritz; but it also partakes of the humbler pleasures of motion and improvisation. For all its improvisatory air, however, it is highly organized by Dick, who emerges as a kind of artist expending considerable energy on trying to create a form of sociability that can bind together, if only temporarily, the rootless expatriates, the urban wanderers of the night.

The extract is told in the third person but mainly from Rosemary's point of view. Sometimes her thoughts are summarized in words she might use herself – for example, 'Rosemary appreciated how different it was from any party in Hollywood' – while at other times the vocabulary and imagery seem more likely to be those of the third-person narrator, for instance the simile of the 'infantry battalion dependent on rations', which we will discuss below. On one occasion, Rosemary's thoughts are given in indirect discourse: 'Rosemary assured the image of her mother that ... never, never had she known any one so nice, so thoroughly nice, as Dick was that night'. There is also a moment when the point of view – or perhaps more precisely, point of sensation – seems to shift implicitly to Dick's, in the part of the last sentence of the third paragraph which runs 'her damp powdery young body came up close to him in a crush of tired cloth'. It may be that Rosemary is experiencing her own body as damp and powdery, but when these adjectives are coupled with 'young', this seems more likely to be Dick's experience more than Rosemary's. The words reinforce what we already know – that Rosemary is attracted to Dick – but they also imply Dick's erotic experience of her, and the way in which this is bound up with her youth.

The account is in summary form and it sometimes encapsulates recurrent experiences of the evening in one description which aims to give their essential elements – for example, the way in which new people keep joining the party. It purports to be selective, so that the commandeering of the Shah of Persia's car is only one, albeit spectacular incident on a night of 'many diversions'. This suggests a profusion of activity and incident beyond what is actually described. But Rosemary's constant awareness of Dick gives the whole evening continuity for her and also provides a running thread for the reader. The time signals vary between immediacy and recollection: although most of the passage is written in the past tense and in summary form, it nonetheless gives a sense of Rosemary's immediate involvement in the events of 'that night', but there are also phrases, strategically placed at the start of the third and fourth paragraphs, which suggest that Rosemary is experiencing the night in retrospect rather than on the spot: 'Afterwards she remembered the times …'; 'The time she laughed most'. This fluctuation between involvement and slight distancing provides the reader with a double viewpoint which sets the events evoked in both an immediate and longer perspective and enables reflection on them, bringing the past under the scrutiny of the present.

The sentences in the extract move between fairly short and direct sentences which convey the pace and nature of the party and sum up Rosemary's feelings, and more elaborate ones which suggest the rich intensity of its key events. For example, the extract starts with a simple sentence, followed by one which begins by employing parallelism, repeating the formula 'they were' three times, followed by an indication of number: 'They were twelve, they were sixteen, they were quartets.' By summing up the changes of number in the party with no mention of intervening incidents, the sentence reinforces the sense of fast movement. A short, four-word sentence follows, but with a passive verb: 'Everything had been foreseen.' The absence of a subject for the verb here might prompt the question: foreseen by whom? By Dick? Or by some kind of benevolent precognitive spirit guiding the evening? A much longer sentence (45 words) follows which describes a repeated experience of the evening: the appearance of new people who stay with them for a time then drop out to be replaced by others. The length of the sentence conveys a sense of flow – this is something that keeps on happening – while allowing space for comparisons which convey the quality of the experience.

The diction of the extract includes words which convey pace ('speed', 'quick'), a sense of the extraordinary ('fabulous') and an impression of glitter and gleam which encompasses both the Shah of Persia's car ('silver', 'brilliants', 'gems') and Rosemary ('sparkling bright'). There is also a repertoire of terms which Rosemary applies to Dick in her imaginary conversation with her mother. She calls him 'nice', a word which covers his physical attractiveness, his capacity to give pleasure and his good manners (it may also include a suggestion of the grace which comes with wealth – in *Gatsby*, Daisy is described as 'the first "nice" girl [Gatsby] had ever known' (*GG* 141). Rosemary inwardly approves of the 'enthusiasm' and 'selflessness' of Dick's whole 'performance' during the evening which 'appeared so effortless that he still had pieces of his own most personal self for everyone'. The use of the terms 'performance' and 'appeared' here implicitly raises the question – though not one Rosemary puts to herself – of whether there is a contradiction between the 'performance' Dick mounts and his actual feelings. It is also worth noting that the precise verb Fitzgerald uses for her feelings about Dick's 'performance' is 'ravished', which means 'enraptured' but can also signify forcible seizure and rape. These darker meanings have particular relevance to Rosemary; Dick's attitude to this young, attractive and inexperienced woman has a predatory element which can be linked with Devereux Warren's predatory attitude to the young daughter he rapes. But these darker meanings might also apply more widely to the way in which Dick organizes people; there could be a subtly coercive element in it, as he makes them do what he wants them to do, even if this involves directing and gratifying their own desires. This links as well with his organization of Rosemary.

A range of similes is used to convey the quality of the evening. Comparisons are drawn from cinema, magic, husbandry, soldiering, dream, flowers, cloth and elaborate machinery. The party's speed of movement is compared to that of 'a slapstick comedy', presumably a movie comedy. People join the party 'as if by magic', suggesting the quasi-supernatural, slightly unreal nature of the way in which people appear ('magic' also featured in the account of the Divers' dinner party discussed earlier in this chapter). But there is also a sense that this magical effect is the result of planning or at least of resourceful improvisation; it is as if, when each new person joins the party, 'the freshness of each one had been husbanded for them all day'. 'To husband' means to use resources economically and implies that someone is doing the 'husbanding'; this person is Dick but the verb also reminds us of his status as a 'husband' – Nicole's, not Rosemary's. The idea that Dick is planning and managing the party is strengthened when the types of people with whom Dick has to deal during the evening are characterized in a military simile as being 'as dependent on supplies of attention as an infantry battalion is dependent on rations', an image which emphasizes the efficiency and discipline which the organization of the party requires but also invokes the First World War, in which many efficient and disciplined infantry battalions went to their deaths. When Dick and Rosemary dance, they hover 'like people in an amusing dream' which enhances the sense of unreality. Rosemary herself, when Dick turns her in the dance, is 'like a bright bouquet' and 'a piece of precious cloth being displayed before fifty eyes': this reinforces the sense of Rosemary as an object combining nature and artifice (like a bouquet or piece of cloth) who is put on show for the eyes of others (primarily men); it links up with her identity as a film actress. The way in which artifice can be enmeshing is suggested by the 'waiter trap' constructed in the lobby of the Ritz which is likened to 'one of the bizarre machines' of a cartoon by Rube Goldberg (1883–1970), who drew complex contraptions which performed simple tasks.

The metaphor of Dick having 'pieces of his own most personal self for everyone' has both cannibalistic and religious implications. It suggests that his guests are devouring him intimately and in that respect recalls the military simile discussed in the previous paragraph; he provides the 'rations' on which soldiers are dependent. The metaphor could also allude to the image, which goes back to medieval times, of Christ as a pelican, digging into his own body in order to provide sustenance for others; Dick offers pieces of himself in a kind of quasi-spiritual Eucharist, the ceremony in which worshippers partake of the body and blood of Christ. (Gatsby does something similar in his role as 'host', a term which can mean 'the bread consecrated in the Eucharist'.) The idea of Dick as a self-sacrificing Christ-figure would link up with the other religious references in *Tender* – the metaphor of the beach as a 'bright tan prayer rug' (*TN* 11) at the beginning, Dick blessing the beach 'with a papal cross' (*TN* 337) near the end – and with Fitzgerald's own description of

Dick, in his notes for the novel, as 'a spoiled priest' (qtd *SG* 393). As well as this possible Christian allusion, there is an explicit Classical allusion in the metaphor of an 'Odyssey' which is used to describe the passage of the party across Paris. This is an intertextual reference to Homer's ancient Greek epic *The Odyssey* which describes the long journey home from Troy to Ithaca of the warrior Odysseus (whose ancient Roman name, Ulysses, also invokes, as our discussion of Gatsby's guest list mentioned, Ulysses S. Grant, an American hero who, as we have seen, figures at key points in *Tender*). But in this extract, the unexpected adjective 'quick' which precedes 'Odyssey' gives the latter a pace appropriate to modern life and perhaps also alludes to the archaic meaning of 'quick' as 'living'. On one level, the invocation of the Odyssey might imply an ironic disjunction between the ancient, heroic epic world and the frenzied modern pursuit of pleasure and sensation which the mobile party exemplifies; on another level, it could seem to endow the party with a mythical dimension, to elevate it to a greater significance than a merely hedonistic and frivolous one. The intertextual allusion might also imply, more broadly, that Dick's peregrinations across Europe which occupy most of the novel constitute a longer-term modern Odyssey in which, like the original Odysseus, he is detained by alluring women (Nicole, Rosemary) before he can finally return to America – although, in contrast to Odysseus, no faithful wife awaits him there.

In the more immediate context of the extract, the allusion to Odysseus, a soldier returning from the wars, also links up with the figure invoked in the hoax at the Ritz: General Pershing, the commander of the American expeditionary forces in the First World War. Like the image of infantry battalions earlier in the passage, the hoax recalls that war and the visit to the battlefield in chapter 13 of the novel, and implies a contrast between the pursuit of pleasure by Dick's party and the loss and sacrifice of combat. The hoax also suggests the selfish aspect of the behaviour of Dick's party by demonstrating a lack of consideration for the extra work and disturbance it causes, especially to the hotel waiters.

Conclusions

Our analysis has shown the skill with which Fitzgerald evokes a variety of parties – the small dinner parties at the Buchanans and Divers, the quick Odyssey in Paris, and Gatsby's vast congregations. In the descriptions of the small dinner parties at the Buchanans and the Divers and of the mobile party in Paris he focuses on the point of view of one of the guests – the narrator, Nick Carraway, in the case of *Gatsby* and Rosemary Hoyt, in the case of *Tender*. He mixes narrative with dialogue, relying more on dialogue in the extract from *Gatsby* and more on summarizing narrative with occasional snatches of dialogue in the extracts from *Tender*. The narrative prose sometimes employs elaborate sentences and sometimes shorter, more direct ones. Dashes are deployed to good effect in both the dialogue and narrative prose.

A range of imagery is used to vivify the scenes and enhance their significance: for example, in the account of the dinner party at the Buchanans, the phone is personified as a 'fifth guest'; in the magical moment at the Villa Diana, the table seems to rise 'like a mechanical dancing platform'; the mobile party in Paris is seen as 'a quick Odyssey'. In his account of the guests who come to Gatsby's party, Fitzgerald uses a different technique, that of the list; it is a technique he employs elsewhere in his fiction, and we shall examine a further example in chapter 3 of this book, but this list is uniquely copious, generating names and further details which give a sense of the multitudinous variety of Gatsby's parties and of the social (and natural) worlds which lie beyond them.

All the parties portrayed in both novels are attempts at human sociability in a society in which the bonds of family and traditional community have been weakened. The parties are flawed by a variety of tensions which exemplify those of the wider society at this time and still resonate with us today: flagrant marital infidelity, potentially violent political conflict, concealed sexual abuse, psychological trauma, organized crime, excessive drinking, financial extravagance, a frenetic and frivolous pursuit of pleasure and sensation. The party which comes closest to a traditional family gathering is the one Nick attends at Tom and Daisy's. The Buchanans are a married couple with a young daughter and Nick Carraway is related to Daisy; but the focus is not on the family and the marriage of Tom and Daisy is riven by Tom's infidelity, which, by means of the telephone, interrupts and invades the party. The Divers' party also takes place at the family home and for a moment does seem to achieve a quasi-magical harmony; but this is fleeting, and underlying tensions emerge which reflect the political divisions in the wider world – in the argument between McKisco and Barban – and hint that the house has an unmentionable secret which will be revealed later in the novel as Nicole's madness and its cause, an act of incest with her father: a violation that invades the core of family relationships. The parties at Gatsby's are spectacular in their scale and the range of people they attract, as Nick's guest list shows. But they are also occasions for excess; they are shadowed by violence and premature death; they are, as we later learn, financed by the proceeds of organized crime. The mobile party across Paris in *Tender* is colourful and inventive; but there is also a sense of an ultimately futile pursuit of sensation.

For all their flaws, however, Gatsby's huge parties and the Divers' smaller parties have an aesthetic, utopian dimension, creating spaces in which people can, for a brief space, live more intensely and freely. Both Gatsby and Dick are, in a sense, artists of the event, presidents of their mini-republics. In their aesthetic, utopian dimension, the parties can be related to the artistic and political projects of the earlier twentieth century which tried to create new forms which would organize chaos and amplify newly liberated energies.

Methods of Analysis

- We examined the kinds of sentences used in the extracts, looking at their length and structure and, where appropriate, suggesting how these contributed to their meaning (e.g. the sentence in *Gatsby* in which Nick shifts, via a dash, between two possible responses to the fraught situation in the Buchanan household (finding it intriguing, sending for the police); the parallelism in the sentence from *Tender* which conveys the quick changes of number in the Paris party).

- We considered Fitzgerald's use of dashes in his narrative prose and in his dialogue and the ways in which they can highlight a shift in meaning and indicate interruption or aposiopesis, a sudden breaking-off of a sentence (e.g. Jordan's interruption of Nick as he is about to talk about Gatsby; Violet McKisco's truncation of her account of the scene in the Divers' bathroom in *Tender*).

- We discussed the diction – the choice of words – and focused on words that seemed significant (e.g. the lyrical, romantic and cognitive diction in *Gatsby*; the use of the term 'magic' in *Tender*).

- We explored examples of imagery – of simile, metaphor, metonymy and personification – and considered what these might convey (e.g. in *Gatsby*, the telephone as 'the fifth guest'; in *Tender*, the simile of the Divers' dining table as 'a mechanical dancing platform').
- We identified the time signals and scales in the extracts (e.g. the dating of Gatsby's guest list and the adjectives which might make it seem much older; the fluctuation between immediacy and recollection in the account of the mobile party).
- We analysed Gatsby's guest list and the significance of the names and extra details it contains (e.g. the many natural-history names, the association of some guests with violence and death).
- We drew attention to significant *intratextual* links (e.g. the energy/ blockage motif in the Buchanans' dinner party which recurs throughout Gatsby; the way the list of the yellow objects Nicole presses on Rosemary's mother in *Tender* anticipates the much longer list of Nicole's purchases on her shopping spree).
- We pointed out important *intertextual* links – (e.g. the phrase 'broken fragments' in *Gatsby* and the 'fragments shored against my ruins' in Eliot's *Waste Land*; the 'quick Odyssey' of the mobile Paris party in *Tender* and Homer's *Odyssey*).
- We traced ways in which the parties might relate to the wider tensions and possibilities of the societies in which they occur (e.g. Gatsby's parties as gatherings shadowed by violence and death; the mobile Paris party as a form of creative improvisation).

Suggested Work

Examine the two following passages, each of which evokes a further significant party in each novel – the party at Myrtle's apartment in *Gatsby* and at Voisins in *Tender*. Analyse the style of these passages, try to sum up the key qualities of each of the gatherings and explore their possible relationships to the wider society of the time (e.g. Myrtle's party has an illicit dimension both because she is the mistress of a married man and because much alcohol is being consumed in the era of Prohibition; while the account of the party at Voisins is preoccupied with the behaviour and identity of Americans in Europe in the 1920s).

[a] *Gatsby*. From 'The apartment was on the top floor ... ' to "" ...
    If Chester could only get you in that pose I think he could make
    something of it"' (*GG* 31–3)

[b] *Tender*. From 'They were at Voisins waiting for Nicole ... ' to ' ...
    ask for Mr. Crowder' (*TN* 61–4)

Analysing The Great Gatsby and Tender...

New York. At the newsstand she ...
moving-picture magazine, and ...
and a small flask of perfu...
four taxicabs drive ...
with the grey uph...
into the ...

60

N.

In a review of *Tender* in the *New Yorker* ... 1934), the American writer and media intellectual Clifton ...uman remarked that, in Fitzgerald's case, 'money is the root of all novels' (*FR* 301). There can be no doubt of the importance of money in Fitzgerald's fiction; but one of his strengths is that he does not assume that money is a simple matter; rather, he attempts to grasp money in its full complexity, not only as a means of exchange but also as an element that enters, materially and symbolically, into the surfaces and depths of identity, behaviour and relationship. This chapter considers the role of money in *Gatsby* and *Tender*, examining the vivid examples of modern consumerism both novels provide and the ways in which money moulds Gatsby's courtship of Daisy and Nicole's marriage to Dick. The first extract we shall explore is Myrtle's display of her buying power in chapter 2 of *Gatsby*.

Buying Power: *The Great Gatsby*, pp. 29–30

So Tom Buchanan and his girl and I went up together to New York – or not quite together, for Mrs Wilson sat discreetly in another car. Tom deferred that much to the sensibilities of those East Eggers who might be on the train.

She had changed her dress to a brown figured muslin, which stretched tight over her rather wide hips as Tom helped her to the platform in

ought a copy of *Town Tattle* and a
in the station drug-store some cold cream
e. Upstairs, in the solemn echoing drive she let
way before she selected a new one, lavender-coloured
stery, and in this we slid out from the mass of the station
owing sunshine. But immediately she turned sharply from the
ow and, leaning forward, tapped on the front glass.

'I want to get one of those dogs,' she said earnestly. 'I want to get one
for the apartment. They're nice to have – a dog.'

We backed up to a grey old man who bore an absurd resemblance to
John D. Rockefeller. In a basket swung from his neck cowered a dozen
very recent puppies of an indeterminate breed.

'What kind are they?' asked Mrs Wilson eagerly, as he came to the
taxi-window.

'All kinds. What kind do you want, lady?'

'I'd like to get one of those police dogs; I don't suppose you got that
kind?'

The man peered doubtfully into the basket, plunged in his hand and
drew one up, wriggling, by the back of the neck.

'That's no police dog,' said Tom.

'No, it's not exactly a police dog,' said the man with disappointment
in his voice. 'It's more of an Airedale.' He passed his hand over the brown
washrag of a back. 'Look at that coat. Some coat. That's a dog that'll never
bother you with catching cold.'

'I think it's cute,' said Mrs Wilson enthusiastically. 'How much is it?'

'That dog?' He looked at it admiringly. 'That dog will cost you ten
dollars.'

The Airedale – undoubtedly there was an Airedale concerned in it
somewhere, though its feet were startlingly white – changed hands and
settled down into Mrs Wilson's lap, where she fondled the weather-proof
coat with rapture.

'Is it a boy or a girl?' she asked delicately.

'That dog? That dog's a boy.'

'It's a bitch,' said Tom decisively. 'Here's your money. Go and buy ten
more dogs with it.'

Although this extract forms part of Nick Carraway's first-person narrative, he himself does not speak or act in it, except to observe and
accompany Tom and Myrtle. He only once uses the pronoun 'I', in the
first sentence, and then he is describing a joint action, as he is when he

employs the first-person plural 'we' in the second paragraph. Otherwise, the account could be that of a third-person narrator. The start of the extract emphasizes the illicit nature of Tom and Myrtle's relationship and, once again, Fitzgerald employs the dash to good effect. Two terms are used to denote Myrtle, before and after the dash: she is first called 'his girl', the pronoun 'his' showing Tom's possession of her and the term 'girl' functioning as a euphemism for 'mistress' (as well as suggesting, ironically, a youthfulness that Myrtle has passed beyond); she is then called 'Mrs Wilson', a formal title indicating that she is legally possessed by someone else, Mr Wilson, not Mr Buchanan. The use of these terms within the same sentence also highlights the division between Myrtle's two identities – Tom's girl, Wilson's wife – which will ultimately prove fatal to her. The illicit nature of the relationship is further stressed by the way in which the adverb 'together' is amended, after the dash, to 'not quite together' and by the statement that Myrtle 'sat discreetly' in another carriage, indicating the need to conceal her relationship with Tom, at least from the eyes of the other inhabitants of East Egg. This physical separation also indicates the social division between them (even if Tom and Myrtle were not married to other people, Myrtle would not be socially acceptable to the East Eggers). Although Myrtle is the subject of the verb 'sat', the second and last sentence of the paragraph suggests that she is acting under Tom's orders rather than on her own initiative.

In the next paragraph, however, Myrtle comes into her own. Apart from 'stretched', 'helped' and 'slid', Myrtle is the subject of all the finite verbs in the paragraph: 'she had changed', 'she bought' (an especially important verb here), 'she let', 'she selected', 'she turned', she 'tapped'. This highlights her role as an active agent. In the first sentence, the pluperfect tense ('she *had* changed'; my emphasis) shows that, even before leaving the garage, she had already started to assert herself, to change her identity by changing her clothes, from the 'spotted dress of dark blue crêpe-de-chine' she was wearing when Nick first saw her (*GG* 28) to 'a brown figured muslin' ('figured' here means 'patterned'). The first sentence also reinforces the impression of powerful physicality which Nick had initially registered at the garage. When the sentence goes on to describe Tom helping her down from the train, it indicates that, though he may still control her, he is publicly acknowledging that they have some kind of relationship and assisting her as a gentleman should.

The transitional space of the train has given way to the metropolis, in which selves and relationships can be paraded and redefined.

In the next three sentences Myrtle emerges as her New York self, constructing and performing her desired city identity. At the station, she becomes an enthusiastic consumer, buying magazines which will inform her of metropolitan and movie gossip (*Town Tattle* and a film magazine) and cosmetics (cold cream and perfume). She then further exercises her power as a consumer by carefully choosing the kind of taxicab she wants and by ordering the driver to stop almost as soon as he has started because (as we learn in the next paragraph) she has seen something else she wants to buy, although this a different sort of commodity since it is alive: a dog.

The second paragraph of the extract features little imagery. All the adjectives and nouns are directly descriptive, almost as if they were items in a list, and this establishes a kind of equivalence between them: the brown patterned muslin dress, the wide hips, the magazines, the cosmetics, the station drive, the four rejected taxicabs, the new lavender one, the glowing sunshine. We are in a world which largely consists of manufactured objects, commodities for sale or hire. Even the natural phenomena mentioned – Myrtle's body and the sunshine – get caught up in this commodification: Myrtle's body is, in a sense, a commodity which Tom has bought; the glowing sunshine is experienced from the hired taxicab and mirrors the reflected glow of the sunshine on the windows of Tom's house when Nick visits it in the first chapter of *Gatsby*, a glow which is aesthetically appealing but also symbolizes money.

The rest of the extract consists largely of dialogue, with some commentary by Nick. At four points adverbs are inserted to indicate the way in which Myrtle speaks. Her desire for a dog is expressed 'earnestly', her question about the kind of dogs for sale is asked 'eagerly' and her comment on its cuteness is made 'enthusiastically'. All these adverbs suggest the intensity of her involvement in her canine purchase and are an index of both her vitality and her naïvety. Her question about the dog's gender, however, is put 'delicately' and this adverb suggests her aspirations to the kind of gentility which she perhaps thinks is appropriate to the kind of person she wants to become – a gentility which Nick probably offers as evidence of her vulgarity and pretentiousness. Tom, the genuinely upper-class figure, cuts through her gentility with his abrasive definition of the dog as 'a bitch', a noun which calls to mind the use of 'bitch' as an insulting term for a woman and the epitaph which the Owl-Eyed Man will later pronounce on Gatsby: 'The poor son-of-a-bitch' (*GG* 166).

The dog salesman is a partly comic image of entrepreneurism – he resembles the Standard Oil billionaire John D. Rockefeller, tries to mislead his customers about the provenance of the product he is selling, and, Tom abrasively implies, profits from a large markup. The exploitation of the dog as an object of exchange and fashionable display weaves into a strand running through *Gatsby* which registers the depredation of the natural world and which could be interpreted today in an ecocritical perspective. Nick's observations and the dialogue between Myrtle, Tom and the dog-seller also raise the question of 'breeding'. The puppies are 'of an indeterminate breed' and attempts to define it break down; neither of the two categories which are proposed – a 'police dog' and an 'Airedale' – quite fits the bill.

On one level, there is a kind of snobbish joke here at the expense of Myrtle's naïve notion that it would be possible to purchase a pedigree dog from a street seller. In a sense, this error echoes the one she made in her choice of her husband, according to the reason she gives, at the party in her apartment later that day, for marrying George Wilson: 'I married him because I thought he was a gentleman … I thought he knew something about breeding, but he wasn't fit to lick my shoe' (*GG* 37) ('breeding' also refers to George's presumed impotence, his inability to perform the act that might lead to 'breeding' in the sense of procreation). But the indeterminacy of the dog's breed relates to a more general theme that runs through *Gatsby*, an uneasiness about a society in which interbreeding has made it more difficult to identify and place, not only animals, but also people. A similar uneasiness, sometimes of an anti-Semitic kind, is evident in some of the names on Gatsby's guest list, such as or 'the Stonewall Jackson Abrams' or 'Mrs Ulysses Swett' (*GG* 61). This uneasiness is an element of the character of Nick, who knows himself to be a Carraway and who comes from a city in which his family and those of similar social rank have supposedly clear identities; but it also represents a wider anxiety which the mobility and mixing of modern society can produce.

Myrtle revels in the purchasing power she enjoys as a result of being Tom's mistress, and she tries to create herself as the sort of person she would like to be by her purchases. The passage conveys the ambiguous promise of consumer culture, suggesting the pleasure and sense of empowerment which shopping can give while also indicating how consumer choices – and, to an extent, identities – are determined by the goods that are available and the kinds of lifestyle that are promoted as fashionable. Myrtle's shopping spree pales, however, before that of the truly rich Nicole in *Tender*, as the next extract shows. It starts just after Rosemary has overheard Nicole and Dick fixing a time to make love later that day.

Shopping Spree: *Tender is the Night*, pp. 64–5

Rosemary stood breathless as the voices moved away. She was at first even astonished – she had seen them in their relation to each other as people without personal exigencies – as something cooler. Now a strong current of emotion flowed through her, profound and unidentified. She did not know whether she was attracted or repelled, but only that she was deeply moved. It made her feel very alone as she went back into the restaurant, but it was touching to look in upon, and the passionate gratitude of Nicole's 'Oh, *do* I!' echoed in her mind. The particular mood of the passage she had witnessed lay ahead of her; but however far she was from it her stomach told her it was all right – she had none of the aversion she had felt in the playing of certain love scenes in pictures.

Being far away from it she nevertheless irrevocably participated in it now, and shopping with Nicole she was much more conscious of the assignation than Nicole herself. She looked at Nicole in a new way, estimating her attractions. Certainly she was the most attractive woman Rosemary had ever met – with her hardness, her devotions and loyalties, and a certain elusiveness, which Rosemary, thinking now through her mother's middle-class mind, associated with her attitude about money. Rosemary spent money she had earned – she was here in Europe due to the fact that she had gone in the pool six times that January day with her temperature roving from 99° in the early morning to 103°, when her mother stopped it.

With Nicole's help Rosemary bought two dresses and two hats and four pairs of shoes with her money. Nicole bought from a great list that ran two pages, and bought the things in the windows besides. Everything she liked that she couldn't possibly use herself, she bought as a present for a friend. She bought colored beads, folding beach cushions, artificial flowers, honey, a guest bed, bags, scarfs, love birds, miniatures for a doll's house and three yards of some new cloth the color of prawns. She bought a dozen bathing suits, a rubber alligator, a travelling chess set of gold and ivory, big linen handkerchiefs for Abe, two chamois leather jackets of kingfisher blue and burning bush from Hermès – bought all these things not a bit like a high-class courtesan buying underwear and jewels, which were after all professional equipment and insurance – but with an entirely different point of view. Nicole was the product of much ingenuity and toil. For her sake trains began their run at Chicago and traversed the round belly of the continent to California; chicle factories fumed and link belts grew link by link in factories; men mixed toothpaste in vats and drew mouthwash out of copper hogsheads; girls canned tomatoes quickly in August or worked rudely at the Five-and-Tens on Christmas Day; half-breed Indians toiled on Brazilian coffee plantations and dreamers were muscled out of patent rights in new tractors – these were some of the people who gave a tithe to Nicole, and as the whole system swayed and thundered onward it lent a feverish bloom to such processes of hers as wholesale buying, like the flush of a fireman's face holding his post before a spreading blaze. She illustrated very simple principles, containing in herself her own doom, but illustrated them so accurately that there was grace in the procedure, and presently Rosemary would try to imitate it.

The opening sentence of this extract emphasizes Rosemary's physical response – she is breathless – to the overheard conversation between Dick and Nicole. The next sentence indicates her astonishment, and then aims to analyse it, marking the moment as one in which her perception of Dick and Nicole has been strikingly altered. But the analysis is not taken too far: the third sentence uses the familiar metaphor of 'a strong current of emotion', and intensifies it by the adjectives at the end of the sentence, 'profound' and 'unidentified'. At this point, the third-person narrator does not try to be all-knowing, but adopts a position of limited omniscience, staying within Rosemary's viewpoint and her inability to determine whether she is 'attracted or repelled'. The narrator then draws back to a more distanced, voice-of-experience stance: the 'particular mood of the passage she had witnessed lay ahead of her'; in other words, she has not yet experienced for herself the intensity of emotion and desire evident in the overheard exchange – 'the passage' – between Dick and Nicole. The following clause, 'her stomach told her it was all right', plays a variation on what could seem a cliché – 'her heart told her it was all right' – and suggests a more visceral 'gut' response than the cardiac image. In analysing Rosemary's response, Fitzgerald also brings in her professional experience of playing love scenes as an actress, some of which aroused her aversion, presumably by their emotional inauthenticity.

The sense of emotional and erotic intensity and promise which the overheard conversation conveys to Rosemary enters into her perception of Nicole on their shopping spree. But money is also part of that perception: Rosemary links Nicole's 'elusiveness' to 'her attitude about money'; Rosemary's own view of Nicole's attitude is conditioned by her mother's view, which is class-determined. For Rosemary there is a clear link between earning money and spending it and an implicit idea that one should not exceed one's income: and if Rosemary's way of earning money as a movie actress is in one sense glamorous, it also involves punishing one's body and risking longer-term damage to one's health, for example by going into a swimming pool with a fever. The nature of Nicole's 'attitude about money' is not stated explicitly; rather it is exemplified in the ensuing description as an attitude of conspicuous consumption in which money is spent without thrift or thought for its source in human labour.

In the first five sentences of the next paragraph, the verb 'bought' occurs seven times, emphasizing the act of purchasing. Rosemary is the subject of the verb only once in the first sentence; the next six times, the subject is Nicole, driving home the identity of the person who does most of the buying (this is similar to the way in which Myrtle is the active consumer in the extract from chapter 2 of *Gatsby* we explored previously in this chapter). Nicole buys from 'a great list' and listing is the means by which the narrator itemizes some of the purchases made on this shopping spree and differentiates between Rosemary and Nicole. The list of Rosemary's purchases is short, consisting of three kinds of items, all with a practical as well as ornamental use (two dresses, two hats, four pairs of shoes); they are specified by noun and quantity but no further description (for example, of colour, style, material) is supplied. In contrast, the list of Nicole's purchases, spread over two sentences, is long; there are 15 items in all and 12 of them are embellished with adjectives or adjectival phrases: for instance, there are 'two chamois leather' jackets 'of kingfisher blue and burning bush from Hermès', a costly and fashionable clothing shop (which still trades today). Some of the items could be (partly) functional, others are for purposes such as decoration, play or leisure activity. They are bought for friends as well as herself. The juxtaposition of different artefacts in the account of Nicole's purchases creates a sense of abundance, of a consumer cornucopia, but also of profligacy.

The rest of the passage strikingly broadens out and shows a different sort of economic and political awareness, more like that of Fitzgerald's friend and fellow-writer John Dos Passos, or even, at moments, of John Steinbeck. Unusually in Fitzgerald, it summons up poor and exploited working people and juxtaposes them with the rich. A very long, 122-word sentence details some of the sources of Nicole's wealth (this contrasts with *Gatsby*, which says nothing of the sources of the vast wealth of Tom Buchanan, who, like Nicole, is from a Chicago 'old-money' family, and which is fairly vague about the sources of Gatsby's riches). The metaphor which occurs early in the sentence, the 'round belly of the continent', suggests both pregnancy and plumpness and stands for a plenty which may swell into excess but casts a large and ironic shadow over the toiling workers who are later invoked. The first half of the sentence, the 74 words up to the dash, stretches out across the USA, from Chicago to California, and into South America, to Brazil. It encompasses a range of products: chicle (the milky latex of the sapodilla tree, used to make chewing gum); toothpaste; mouthwash; coffee (for those who might be inclined to pursue the oral symbolism of the novel, it is worth noting that all these products are taken into the mouth, but three of them – chewing gum, toothpaste and mouthwash – are usually spat or rinsed out eventually rather than swallowed).

The sentence takes in examples of the means of production, distribution and exchange: factories, link belts, vats, copper hogsheads, coffee plantations; freight trains; Five-and-Ten stores. It contains nine active verbs – 'began', 'traversed', 'fumed', 'grew', 'mixed', 'drew', 'canned', 'worked', 'toiled'. Two of the subjects of these verbs are mechanical (trains, link belts), one combines the human and mechanical ('chicle factories') and three are human – 'men', 'girls', 'Indians': this suggests how human beings and machines are equivalent in this 'system' in the sense that both are functional components of it. Moreover, the human beings perform repetitive and demanding tasks; they act on the material world but within limits prescribed by the demands of the system. The adverbs especially emphasize female labour: the girls can tomatoes 'quickly' or work in the Five-and-Tens 'rudely'. In contrast with the human and mechanical agents, the 'dreamers' have only a passive verb, reinforcing the sense of their unsuitability for action which the sentence goes on to emphasize; they are 'muscled out of their patent rights', deprived by corporate heft of the rewards of their inventiveness (the term 'muscled' could suggest an analogy between the might of business corporations and the powerful body of Tom Buchanan in *Gatsby*).

After the accumulation of examples in the sentence, there is a dash – that characteristically Fitzgeraldian way of highlighting a shift of focus – and the narrator then makes a general statement, rich in imagery. The workers give Nicole a 'tithe' – originally, under the feudal system, a tenth of income or produce formerly taken as a tax to support the Church and clergy: here it supports the Church of conspicuous consumption. The system is seen as swaying and thundering onwards, like a large and unstable train, heading for a crash: and in doing so it gives 'a feverish bloom' (rather like the 'hectic red' of autumn leaves in Shelley's 'Ode to the West Wind') to her wholesale buying which is then compared to 'the flush of a fireman's face holding his post before a spreading blaze'. In a novel set in the later 1920s and completed and published in the mid-1930s, this spreading blaze would look like the impending economic crash of 1929 and could also represent what might have seemed, in the 1930s, the widening forces of revolution. Nicole is offered as an illustration of the principles which will bring about the destruction of herself and her class. A more politically intransigent writer than Fitzgerald might have stopped there; but the narrator acknowledges the 'grace' – a word with both aesthetic and religious connotations – with which she illustrates her supposedly self-destructive principles and the desire it arouses in Rosemary to mimic that grace.

The next passage shows how money may enter into an intimate relationship, that between Gatsby and Daisy.

Courtship and Money: *The Great Gatsby*, pp. 141–2

It was this night that he told me the strange story of his youth with Dan Cody – told it to me because 'Jay Gatsby' had broken up like glass against Tom's hard malice, and the long secret extravaganza was played out. I think that he would have acknowledged anything now, without reserve, but he wanted to talk about Daisy.

She was the first 'nice' girl he had ever known. In various unrevealed capacities he had come in contact with such people, but always with indiscernible barbed wire between. He found her excitingly desirable. He went to her house, at first with other officers from Camp Taylor, then alone. It amazed him – he had never been in such a beautiful house before. But what gave it an air of breathless intensity, was that Daisy lived there – it was as casual a thing to her as his tent out at camp was to him. There was a ripe mystery about it, a hint of bedrooms upstairs more beautiful and cool than other bedrooms, of gay and radiant activities taking place through its corridors, and of romances that were not musty and laid away in lavender but fresh and breathing and redolent of this year's shining motor-cars and of dances whose flowers were scarcely withered. It excited him, too, that many men had already loved Daisy – it increased her value in his eyes. He felt their presence all about the house, pervading the air with the shades and echoes of still vibrant emotions.

But he knew that he was in Daisy's house by a colossal error. However glorious might be his future as Jay Gatsby, he was at present a penniless young man without a past, and at any moment the invisible cloak of his uniform might slip from his shoulders. So he made the most of his time. He took what he could get, ravenously and unscrupulously – eventually he took Daisy one still October night, took her because he had no real right to touch her hand.

He might have despised himself, for he had certainly taken her under false pretences. I don't mean that he had traded on his phantom millions, but he had deliberately given Daisy a sense of security; he let her believe that he was a person from much the same strata as herself – that he was fully able to take care of her. As a matter of fact, he had no such facilities – he had no comfortable family standing behind him, and he was liable at the whim of an impersonal government to be blown anywhere about the world.

But he didn't despise himself and it didn't turn out as he had imagined. He had intended, probably, to take what he could and go – but now he found that he had committed himself to the following of a grail. He knew that Daisy was extraordinary, but he didn't realize just how extraordinary a 'nice' girl could be. She vanished into her rich house, into her rich, full life, leaving Gatsby – nothing. He felt married to her, that was all.

When they met again, two days later, it was Gatsby who was breathless, who was, somehow, betrayed. Her porch was bright with the bought luxury of star-shine; the wicker of the settee squeaked fashionably as she turned toward him and he kissed her curious and lovely mouth. She had caught a cold, and it made her voice huskier and more charming than ever, and Gatsby was overwhelmingly aware of the youth and mystery that wealth imprisons and preserves, of the freshness of many clothes, and of Daisy, gleaming like silver, safe and proud above the hot struggles of the poor.

This is a later segment of the story that Gatsby tells Nick on the night after Myrtle's death. Near the start of chapter 4, Nick has already recounted the first part of the story which Gatsby related that night – the account of his boyhood, his meeting with Dan Cody and the subsequent transformation of his life; we analysed this account in chapter 1 of this book. Now we have the story of his early relationship with Daisy. It is not told in Gatsby's own words but summarized, interpreted and retailed by Nick, who acts as a kind of reader and rewriter of Gatsby's oral narrative. Nick registers the extent of Gatsby's defeat by Tom in the simile of 'Jay Gatsby' 'breaking up like glass against Tom's hard malice'. But this shattering also seems to have released something in Gatsby – his capacity to talk about himself, to tell the story of his self-invention.

The image of 'Tom's hard malice', one of the barriers to Gatsby's achievement of what he wants, links up with the image in the next paragraph of 'indiscernible barbed wire' – wire that cannot be seen but that acts as a barrier and has the power to injure. Gatsby finds Daisy 'excitingly desirable', terms which suggest erotic arousal, and we might expect a description to follow of Daisy herself as she then appeared to Gatsby – her face and figure, for example. But instead the focus shifts to Daisy's house, a characteristic move in a novel in which houses (Tom's, Gatsby's) and other dwelling places (Nick's bungalow, the unseen rooms above Wilson's garage, Myrtle's New York apartment) are so important in mapping a social, psychological and erotic geography. Terms which a more conventional romantic narrative might apply to Daisy herself are transferred to her house: it is her house which is 'beautiful' and has 'an air of breathless intensity' and 'a ripe mystery'. Although the 'air of breathless intensity' is attributed to the fact that Daisy lives there, it is not so much her presence which produces that 'air' but the casualness with which she inhabits her dwelling, takes it for granted.

Moreover, although Gatsby, after his first visits with other officers from Camp Taylor, goes to the house alone, it is not the sense of being on his own there with Daisy, and the romantic and erotic opportunities it might offer, which seem to arouse his imagination so much as the idea of the house as a place for a more general, collective engagement with aesthetic, romantic and erotic contemplation. The use of plural rather than singular nouns helps to convey this more general idea: Gatsby does not think of *a* bedroom, of Daisy's bedroom, as he might if his primary aim were to possess Daisy; he thinks instead of bedrooms; of activities rather than activity; of romances rather than romance; of 'their presence' – the presence of the many men who had loved Daisy – rather than his own presence; of 'shades' and 'echoes' and 'emotions' which do not seem to be his alone. Gatsby imaginatively peoples Daisy's house with past, future and potential guests. In a sense, it is these intimations of Daisy's house which he will try to draw out and make explicit in his own West Egg palace, making it a mansion of many rooms and corridors, filled with 'gay and radiant activities' and new romances.

The up-to-dateness and aliveness of the romances at which the house hints is stressed by the adjectives 'fresh' and 'breathing' and by their similarity to 'this year's shining motor-cars' and 'dances whose flowers were scarcely withered'. The yoking of the images of new automobiles and flowers is another example of Fitzgerald's romantic modernism: flowers, an ancient lyrical image, are linked with new cars, a symbol of twentieth-century technology and consumption. A further source of Gatsby's excitement is that many men have already loved Daisy; it increases her 'value' in his eyes that she has been an object of desire for other men and he feels their presence in the house. In this sense, his desire for Daisy is what René Girard calls mimetic or imitative desire; he wants her because others have wanted her, his desire mimics theirs. 'Value' is a key word here and the question of value is implicitly active throughout *Gatsby*: what constitutes value? In speaking of Daisy's 'value' here, what kind of value is it? Is it, for example, the value of a commodity or an intrinsic value?

The extract goes on to emphasize that Gatsby himself, as this stage of his life, has no value in economic terms; he is 'penniless'. The image of the 'invisible cloak' presents him as a mythical figure, protected by his army uniform, but only temporarily. Insofar as he is a mythical figure, he is not wholly virtuous; indeed, the adverbs 'ravenously' and 'unscrupulously', applied to his possession of Daisy, and the fact that he 'took' her because he had no real right to 'touch' her, mark him as a predator. He has not deliberately claimed to be a millionaire, but he has not made his true financial and social status clear to Daisy. The passage emphasizes his isolation, his lack of a secure family background and his subordination to the Army.

Nick suggests that Gatsby had 'intended, probably, to take what he could and go'; as the adverb 'probably' indicates, Nick puts this forward as an inference, a likelihood rather than a certainty. But this is a further example of a Fitzgeraldian sentence whose import changes markedly after the dash. The language of the first part of the sentence is cynical and ruthless; the second part stresses 'commitment' and ends with the term 'grail', which is, in medieval legend, the cup or platter which Christ used at the Last Supper and in which Joseph of Arimathea received Christ's blood. Finding the grail is the traditional aim of a knight's quest. So by the end of the sentence quasi-religious, chivalric connotations have displaced the initial implications of cynicism and ruthlessness. Gatsby can no longer go without looking back. Daisy 'vanishes' – like the 'invisible cloak' mentioned earlier, the verb 'vanishes' has mythical, fairy-tale connotations, suggesting a magical and inexplicable disappearance. But she vanishes into a substantial rather than spiritual world: 'her rich house' – we see the emphasis on Daisy's house again – 'her rich full life', the repetition of the adjective 'rich' reinforcing the linking of Daisy with wealth, but not of a merely material kind. Once more Fitzgerald employs a dash to considerable effect, creating a momentary suspense as to what Daisy's disappearance left Gatsby with before giving an emphatic negative: 'nothing'. This echoes the last word of the previous chapter, when Daisy has again vanished into her rich house, this time the one she shares with Tom, and left Gatsby – again there is a dash to create a momentary suspense – 'watching over nothing' (p. 139).

Although the account of Daisy leaving Gatsby with 'nothing' in Louisville occurs later in the novel than the description of him 'watch-ing over nothing' outside Tom and Daisy's house on the night after Myrtle's death, the Louisville experience happens earlier in the sequence of events when they are rearranged chronologically. Viewed in that sequence, Daisy's first disappearance, in Louisville, foreshadows her last, in East Egg. But the first disappearance does not, in fact, leave Gatsby with nothing; as the next sentence tells us. 'He felt married to her, that was all.' The simplicity of the clause 'he felt married to her', followed by the apparent disclaimer in the offhand, diminishing phrase, 'that was all', make the whole sentence a masterly example of understatement. For it is clear that something momentous has occurred. Particularly when linked up with the earlier mention of the 'grail', the idea that Gatsby feels 'married' to Daisy transforms what might otherwise seem an act of casual, predatory sex into a sacrament, a religious ceremony or ritual which is a channel for divine grace. It is worth recalling here that Fitzgerald was brought up as a Roman Catholic and that, even though he forsook the faith after his twenty-first year, a sense of the sacramental quality of marriage, even without the formal ceremony, might well have stayed with him.

It is thus Gatsby who is 'breathless' and 'betrayed', as if *he* were the victim of a predator, when he and Daisy meet again two days later. Her mouth is described as 'curious' and 'lovely'; 'curious' here may carry a trace of its secondary meaning as a euphemism for 'erotic' or 'pornographic', relating to the physical consummation of their relationship. The focus then shifts from her mouth to her voice, and her voice is linked to wealth, reinforcing Gatsby's famous observation earlier in the novel (but later in chronological time): 'Her voice is full of money' (*GG* 115). In the concluding sentence of this extract, Fitzgerald yokes romantic terms – 'youth and mystery' – with economic ones – 'wealth', the simile of 'like silver', the invocation, in contrast to Daisy, of 'the poor'. Wealth is seen as ambivalent, as both imprisoning and preserving, as reifying people, turning them into things ('silver') but also as offering safety and pride. The description of Daisy here might seem to exemplify another famous Fitzgerald quotation, from the story 'The Rich Boy' (1926): 'The rich are different from you and me' (*AM* 1). In 'The Snows of Kilimanjaro' (1936), Ernest Hemingway met this claim with the mocking riposte: 'Yes, they have more money.' But Fitzgerald suggests that the difference is not merely quantitative but a change in the quality of existence. It is not necessarily wholly positive: wealth imprisons, turns flesh to silver, cools the heat of struggle. But nor is it wholly negative: wealth preserves, creates a kind of value and beauty and permanence, transcends human labour and effort.

It is also significant that in this passage Fitzgerald incorporates the further element of 'the freshness of many clothes'. We can link this to other key references in *Gatsby* to clothes, which serve both as means of, and metaphors for, identities and transformations, crucial costumes for performing and sustaining desired roles. To have an exiguous wardrobe is a sign of emotional or material poverty, like George Wilson, whose 'dark suit' is 'veiled' with 'white ashen dust' (*GG* 28); like Gatsby 'in a torn green jersey and a pair of canvas pants' on the afternoon he meets Dan Cody (*GG* 94–5); like Gatsby in his army uniform because he cannot afford to buy any civilian clothes when he encounters Wolfshiem after the First World War (ironically, the uniform which cloaked his penury in wartime Louisville blazons it forth in peacetime New York). These meagre garments contrast with Myrtle's changes of garb in the course of one Sunday afternoon from spotted dark blue crêpe-de-chine to brown figured muslin to elaborate, cream-coloured chiffon, made possible by Tom's money; with Dan Cody's purchase of 'a blue coat, six pairs of white duck trousers, and a yachting cap' for Gatsby when Cody takes the young man on to his yacht (*GG* 96); with the sartorial abundance Gatsby displays to Daisy when he first shows her round his house: 'massed suits and dressing-gowns and ties, and his shirts, piled like bricks [gold bricks, perhaps] in stacks a dozen high' (*GG* 89); the shirts he produces in profusion for Daisy.

This passage subtly and persuasively shows the intricate intermeshing of economic and erotic desire, of material, emotional and spiritual values. Those values also intermesh in the relationship of Dick and Nicole in *Tender*; the next passage we shall consider exemplifies this.

Marriage and Money: *Tender is the Night*, pp. 175–8

How do you do, lawyer. We're going to Como tomorrow for a week and then back to Zurich. That's why I wanted you and sister to settle this, because it doesn't matter to us how much I'm allowed. We're going to live very quietly in Zurich for two years and Dick has enough to take care of us. No, Baby, I'm more practical than you think – It's only for clothes and things I'll need it … Why, that's more than – can the estate really afford to give me all that? I know I'll never manage to spend it. Do you have that much? Why do you have more – is it because I'm supposed to be incompetent? All right, let my share pile up then. … No, Dick refuses to have anything whatever to do with it. I'll have to feel bloated for us both. … Baby, you have no more idea of what Dick is like than, than – Now where do I sign? Oh, I'm sorry.

… Isn't it funny and lonely being together, Dick. No place to go except close. Shall we just love and love? Ah, but I love the most, and I can tell when you're away from me, even a little. I think it's wonderful to be just like everybody else, to reach out and find you all warm beside me in the bed.

… If you will kindly call my husband at the hospital. Yes, the little book is selling everywhere – they want it published in six languages. I was to do the French translation but I'm tired these days – I'm afraid of falling, I'm so heavy and clumsy – like a broken roly-poly that can't stand up straight. The cold stethoscope against the heart and my strongest feeling 'Je m'en fiche de tout.' – Oh, that poor woman in the hospital with the blue baby, much better dead. Isn't it fine there are three of us now?

… That seems unreasonable, Dick – we have every reason for taking the bigger apartment. Why should we penalize ourselves just because there's more Warren money than Diver money. Oh, thank you, cameriere, but we've changed our minds. This English clergyman tells us that your wine here in Orvieto is excellent. It doesn't travel? That must be why we have never heard of it, because we love wine.

The lakes are sunk in the brown clay and the slopes have all the creases of a belly. The photographer gave us the picture of me, my hair limp over the rail on the boat to Capri. 'Good-bye, Blue Grotto,' sang the boatman, 'come again soo-oon.' And afterward tracing down the hot sinister shin of the Italian boot with the wind soughing around those eerie castles, the dead watching from up on those hills.

… This ship is nice, with our heels hitting the deck together. This is the blowy corner and each time we turn it I slant forward against the wind and pull my coat together without losing step with Dick. We are chanting nonsense:

'Oh-oh-oh-oh
Other flamingos than me,
Oh-oh-oh-oh
Other flamingos than me – '

Life is fun with Dick – the people in deck chairs look at us, and a woman is trying to hear what we are singing. Dick is tired of singing it, so go on alone, Dick. You will walk differently alone, dear, through a thicker atmosphere, forcing your way through the shadows of chairs, through the dripping smoke of the funnels. You will feel your own reflection sliding along the eyes of those who look at you. You are no longer insulated; but I suppose you must touch life in order to spring from it.

Sitting on the stanchion of this life-boat I look seaward and let my hair blow and shine. I am motionless against the sky and the boat is made to carry my form onward into the blue obscurity of the future, I am Pallas Athene carved reverently on the front of a galley. The waters are lapping in the public toilets and the agate green foliage of spray changes and complains about the stern.

✳ ... We travelled a lot that year – from Woolooware Bay to Biskra. On the edge of the Sahara we ran into a plague of locusts and the chauffeur explained kindly that they were bumble-bees. The sky was low at night, full of the presence of a strange and watchful God. Oh, the poor little naked Ouled Naïl; the night was noisy with drums from Senegal and flutes and whining camels, and the natives pattering about in shoes made of old automobile tires.

But I was gone again by that time – trains and beaches they were all one. That was why he took me travelling but after my second child, my little girl, Topsy, was born everything got dark again.

... If I could get word to my husband who has seen fit to desert me here, to leave me in the hands of incompetents. You tell me my baby is black – that's farcical, that's very cheap. We went to Africa merely to see Timgad, since my principal interest in life is archeology. I am tired of knowing nothing and being reminded of it all the time.

... When I get well I want to be a fine person like you, Dick – I would study medicine except it's too late. We must spend my money and have a house – I'm tired of apartments and waiting for you. You're bored with Zurich and you can't find time for writing here and you say that it's a confession of weakness for a scientist not to write. And I'll look over the whole field of knowledge and pick out something and really know about it, so I'll have it to hang on to if I go to pieces again. You'll help me, Dick, so I won't feel so guilty. We'll live near a warm beach where we can be brown and young together ...

... This is going to be Dick's work house. Oh, the idea came to us both at the same moment. We had passed Tarmes a dozen times and we rode up here and found the houses empty, except two stables. When we bought we acted through a Frenchman but the navy sent spies up here in no time when they found that Americans had bought part of a hill village. They looked for cannons all through the building material, and finally Baby had to twitch wires for us at the Affaires Étrangères in Paris.

No one comes to the Riviera in summer, so we expect to have a few guests and to work. There are some French people here – Mistinguett last week, surprised to find the hotel open, and Picasso and the man who wrote *Pas sur la bouche*.

… Dick, why did you register Mr and Mrs Diver instead of Doctor and Mrs Diver? I just wondered – it just floated through my mind – you've taught me that work is everything and I believe you. You used to say a man knows things and when he stops knowing things he's like anybody else, and the thing is to get power before he stops knowing things. If you want to turn things topsy-turvy, all right, but must your Nicole follow you walking on her hands, darling?

This extract relates, in fragmented form, key experiences of Nicole's in the first years of her married life with Dick. These experiences include the financial settlement she makes before her marriage to Dick; her honeymoon; the birth of her first child, Lanier, and her second, Topsy; her two mental breakdowns; her extensive travels with Dick; and their discovery of the deserted village on the French Riviera where they will build the Villa Diana. The extract covers a considerable time span – about three-and-a-half years – and its geographical sweep is wide: Lake Como in Italy; Zurich in Switzerland; Orvieto in Italy; the island of Capri, Woolooware Bay (actually in Australia, though Matthew J. Bruccoli suggests Fitzgerald might have used the name because he thought it sounded North African); Biskra in Algiers; Timgad, a ruined city of the Roman Empire in North-East Algeria; and the French Riviera. Nicole's life in these years is a journey through key European sites and into reminders of other, more ancient cultures: Imperial Rome (Timgad) and Africa.

The extract consists of an interior monologue, though paragraphs 1–4, 7 and 11–14 might more precisely be called semi-dialogues, in the sense that we hear Nicole's words and they seem to be directed to other people, but we do not hear the words of those whom she is supposedly addressing; we infer what they might be saying from her remarks and responses, though in some cases she does not seem to be actually speaking to someone but rather addressing them inside her head (as in paragraph seven in the passage which starts 'You will walk differently alone'). In other cases, it is not always clear whether she is actually speaking or merely thinking what she might say (does she, for example, ask Dick 'why did you register Mr and Mrs Diver instead of Doctor and Mrs Diver?' or merely formulate the question in her mind?). Nicole's most prominent interlocutor in these semi-dialogues is Dick; others include her sister, Baby Warren, a lawyer, a waiter, and nurses or doctors at hospitals where Nicole is a patient.

Much of the monologue is in the present tense and this gives an effect of immediacy, even if it is not always evident whether Nicole is supposed to be actually experiencing the events represented or vividly remembering them. There are some shifts into other tenses: for example, into the past tense in the ninth paragraph, which opens 'We travelled a lot that year' and gives a sense of looking back on and summarizing a set of experiences; or into the future tense, for instance after Nicole's second breakdown when she thinks 'I'll look over the whole field of knowledge and pick out something and really know about it', an intention that shows her desire for knowledge and her optimism but which we know, from the rest of the novel, that she will never fulfil, at least with Dick.

A significant strand of imagery in the excerpt relates to Nicole's images of her body as it is affected by money, pregnancy and childbearing. In the first paragraph, Nicole, discussing the pre-nuptial financial settlement with the lawyer and Baby Warren, uses the adjective 'bloated', which is used metaphorically to mean a bodily excess which symbolizes excessive wealth, as in the cliché phrase 'bloated capitalist' (we could link it up with the image of 'the round belly of the continent' in the account of Nicole's shopping spree examined earlier in this chapter). During Nicole's first pregnancy, she likens herself, in a vivid simile in the third paragraph, to 'a broken roly-poly that can't stand up straight'; a roly-poly is a rocking doll which is weighted so that it comes back to an upright position, but returning to an upright position is precisely what Nicole feels she cannot do at this stage. Her later image, in the fifth paragraph, of the slopes of the landscape having 'all the creases of a belly' may suggest her sense of the way in which childbearing has altered the intimate regions of her body, marked her with the signs of experience.

One other metaphor relating to body images occurs at the end of the excerpt, when Nicole says (this is one of those instances when it is uncertain whether she actually says it, or merely imagines saying it, to Dick): 'If you want to turn things topsy-turvy, all right, but must your Nicole follow you walking on her hands, darling?' Here Nicole expresses her reluctance to join Dick in turning things upside down and, significantly, employs an image of acrobatic performance which links up with Dick on the flying rings at Harvard or lifting a man on his shoulders while standing on a board towed by a boat. Nicole implies that Dick has a desire for this kind of exhibitionistic athletic display which she does not share and this marks a difference between them which will widen in the later scene, discussed in chapter 5 of this book, in which Dick tries to lift a man on a tow-board.

At the end of the fifth paragraph, the Italian landscape is personified, drawing on the familiar comparison of the shape of Italy on the map to the shape of a foot – 'the hot sinister shin of the Italian boot' – and it takes on a Gothic threatening quality; the castles are 'eerie'; the wind soughs, making a moaning, whistling or rushing sound; it seems that the dead are watching from the hills. This description has an ominous aspect, perhaps indicating a deterioration in Nicole's psychological state. But in the next paragraph but one, Nicole takes on a mythic quality in her own mind, looking seaward like a sailor in an ancient epic, and seeing herself 'motionless against the sky' and as a figurehead of Pallas Athene, the ancient Greek goddess of wisdom, the arts and just war. (We can link this with the association between the Owl-Eyed Man and Minerva, which we discussed in chapter 2 – Minerva is the ancient Roman name for Pallas Athene.) It is significant that Nicole uses a metaphor rather than a simile when she invokes Pallas Athene: that is, she does not say 'I am *like* Pallas Athene', but 'I *am* Pallas Athene', thus effecting a more complete identification between the two terms of the comparison, a momentary fusion between herself and a goddess from ancient myth. The sentence then comes back to reality, so to speak, by suggesting that this image of Pallas Athene is not the goddess herself but its artistic representation on the figurehead of a ship. The mythical moment can only be sustained in art, not in life. There is perhaps a link here with 'Ode on a Grecian Urn' by Fitzgerald's favourite poet, John Keats, which contrasts the stasis of art with the onward movement of life: art preserves but also freezes. The mythical gives way to the mundane and returns Nicole to the temporal world which interweaves matrimony, motherhood, madness and money in a mesh which she finds entrapping as well as sometimes enabling.

The subject of money recurs four times in the extract, at strategic points in the Divers' marriage: in the first paragraph, when the lawyer and Baby are drawing up Nicole's marriage settlement; in the fourth paragraph, when Nicole argues that they should take another apartment after their son's birth; in the tenth paragraph, after their daughter's birth and Nicole's second breakdown; and in the eleventh paragraph where it seems they have 'bought' – that significant verb – the empty houses at Tarmes. Each of these four references to money marks a shift in power relations between Nicole and Dick in regard to money. At first Nicole asserts to the lawyer and Baby that 'Dick has enough to take care of us'. After the birth of Lanier, she is calling Dick 'unreasonable' because of his apparent refusal to use Nicole's money to take a larger apartment; she sees this as a way of penalizing themselves and specifically draws attention to her family's economic superiority: 'there's more Warren money than Diver money'. After Topsy's birth and her second breakdown, Nicole is more insistent: 'We must spend my money and have a house – I'm tired of apartments and waiting for you' (the implication here perhaps is 'waiting for you to earn some money'). And the following paragraph makes it clear that Nicole has won the battle; it was Warren money that made it possible to purchase Tarmes (chapter 6 of *Tender* has already told us that Tarmes was an 'ancient hill village', six of whose 'peasant dwellings' have been combined to make the Divers' Villa Diana and four demolished to make its garden (*TN* 35, 36)).

Conclusions

These four extracts display a range of approaches to writing about money. The first two passages, from *Gatsby* and *Tender*, respectively, make use of a favourite Fitzgeraldian technique, the list, although this is not set out in an itemized format but woven into continuous prose. In the first passage, the list is of Myrtle's purchases; in the second passage, there are two lists of purchases – Rosemary's and Nicole's – and a third list of a different kind which itemizes some of the machines and people who produce Nicole's wealth. The list of Myrtle's purchases is woven into a passage that, by its use of active verbs of which Myrtle is the subject, demonstrate her empowerment as a consumer. It may be that Nick invites us to view Myrtle's shopping spree as vulgar; but there is a genuinely exhilarating and liberating aspect to it, particularly if we consider how it contrasts with the 'unprosperous' world of Wilson's garage (*GG* 27). This empowerment, however, also has an ironic dimension: we are not told directly where Myrtle's money comes from, but we know its source is Tom: she is defined at the start of the extract as 'his girl', a kind of possession, and we are aware that her power to purchase commodities is due to her own status as a sort of commodity. The first passage also implies that the profit motive can operate throughout society, from a street dog salesman to John D. Rockefeller. It shows, moreover, how natural objects may be commodified: Myrtle's body, the glowing sunshine, the dogs who are the street-seller's stock-in-trade.

The second passage contrasts the attitudes towards money of Rosemary and Nicole; Rosemary shares with her mother an attitude which Fitzgerald defines as 'middle-class': the idea that the money which you spend is earned by your own hard work: and Rosemary's list of purchases is short, practical and austere. Nicole's attitude shows no trace of middle-class thrift and her list of purchases is a long and extravagant assemblage of heterogeneous objects, some for herself and some for her friends. If a reader can take a sort of pleasure in Nicole's purchases, it is offset by a sense of profligacy and the explicit awareness of the sources of her wealth which the other list in the second paragraph provides: this is a list of the components of a system in which human labour and technology both function as a means to produce profit.

The third passage employs another key Fitzgerald technique, which is especially important in *Gatsby*: the interfusion of idealistic, quasi-religious, erotic and economic language to suggest how money can take on symbolic significance and combine with desire. Daisy's house gives a sense of beauty, intensity, mystery, radiance. richness; her 'value' rises for Gatsby because many men have already loved her; Gatsby takes her 'ravenously and unscrupulously' but finds he has 'committed himself to the following of a grail'; Daisy is idealized and reified, turned into a thing, 'gleaming like silver', but thus elevated socially and aesthetically 'above the hot struggles of the poor'. The fourth passage we have considered deploys an interior monologue, stream-of-consciousness technique to portray, in vivid fragments, the early years of a marriage in which money bulks large because the wife has so much more of it than the husband: it shows how, amid a variety of incidents which includes the birth of two children, extensive foreign travel, the publication of Dick's book and two mental breakdowns, the issue of money returns and eventually influences their choice of a house and a way of life.

All these passages exemplify a key theme of Fitzgerald's work: the ambivalence of money. It cannot simply be denounced as the root of all evil or sidelined as a merely material adjunct to emotional or ethical life. It is both empowering and constricting, corrupting and uplifting. Money is powerful in that it can enable and shape human behaviour (especially through consumption but also through the pursuit of profit) and can inform the dynamics of close relationships. It manifests itself in a range of forms, from the need that forces people to toil for low wages in factories, shops and plantations, to the immediate financial resources required to make purchases from shops over and above the necessities of life, to the capital which can buy the house in which people pursue their dreams of the good life, to the wealth that can vastly widen the range of life choices (but may also, as with Dick in *Tender*, prove enervating). Money may be bound up with the highest ideals and aspirations but can also endanger them when it is linked with moral impercipience.

Both *Gatsby* and *Tender* imply a key distinction between money which is earned and money which is unearned. Tom, Nicole and Daisy have been born into wealth, take it for granted, and feel entitled to it; Gatsby and Dick have not and do not. Gatsby gets his money by criminal means, but these entail effort: those moments in the novel when he is summoned to the phone hint at the complex demands of sustaining his criminal rackets. Dick has to rely mainly on Nicole's money to support their luxurious lifestyle, and after their separation he has to work as a provincial doctor. Nick appears to hover in between those who must and those who need not work, but he hardly seems a hotshot bond salesman and presumably relies on his father's financial support throughout his stay in New York; he does not, however, appear to be wealthy enough not to have to bother about work at all. It is being born into the kind of wealth which frees people from the need to work that, in Fitzgerald's perspective, makes the rich different: as 'The Rich Boy' puts it: 'They think, deep in their hearts, that they are better than we are because we had to discover the compensations and refuges of life for ourselves.' It is this sense of superiority, linked with but not negated by the potential for moral corruption that wealth also brings, which interests Fitzgerald. Moreover, the passage from 'The Rich Boy' suggests, the sense of superiority which results from being born into wealth can survive financial decline and disaster: 'Even when [the rich] enter deep into our world or sink below us, they still think that they are better than we are' (*AM* 1–2).

In both *Gatsby* and *Tender* financial disaster, in the shape of the 1929 Wall Street Crash, is imminent. *Gatsby*'s readers in the first four years of the novel's existence might not have foreseen this; but after that it formed an almost unavoidable element of the novel's context. This was true from the start for *Tender*, which came out in 1934. Subsequent experiences of boom and bust – most recently the one which culminated in the banking crisis of 2008 – are also likely now to feed into our experience of both novels. Perhaps they should be required reading for economists. But, as ever in Fitzgerald's treatment of money, it is not merely a question of making the point that bubbles of wealth will inevitably burst and bring disaster. Do we believe, for example, that the Buchanan or Warren fortunes would inevitably have been wholly wiped out in the Wall Street Crash? In historical reality, some fortunes were, but others, though reduced, survived, and the same has been true of subsequent crashes. The shadows of the Wall Street Crash and of later crashes which now fall across *Gatsby* and *Tender* highlight their exploration of the way in which money, when combined with the distorted sense of values it can encourage, can bring not only a financial loss but also a moral loss which may precede and is ultimately more traumatic than the financial one: an exchange in Fitzgerald's short story 'Babylon Revisited' (1931) encapsulates the same insight:

> 'I heard that you lost a lot in the crash.'
> 'I did,' and he added grimly, 'but I lost everything I wanted in the boom.'   (*TAR* 340).

Both Gatsby and Dick lose everything they wanted in the boom.

Methods of Analysis

- We examined the kinds of sentences used in the extracts, looking at their length and structure and, where appropriate, suggesting how these contributed to their meaning (e.g. the sentences in *Gatsby* in which Myrtle is the subject of all the finite verbs, thus highlighting her role as active agent; the long sentence describing Nicole's purchases and the labour which makes them possible in *Tender*).
- We discussed the diction – the choice of words – and focused on words that seemed significant (e.g. the adverbs used of Myrtle's manner of speaking in *Gatsby*; the aesthetic and religious connotations of the term 'grace' in *Tender*).
- We identified significant examples of imagery (e.g. 'this year's shining motor-cars' in *Gatsby*; 'the round belly of the continent' in *Tender*).
- We considered the way in which Fitzgerald uses lists (e.g. in the account of Myrtle's and Rosemary and Nicole's shopping expeditions).
- We explored Nicole's interior monologue, its shifts of tense, and its use of semi-dialogue in which words seemed to be addressed to other people whose replies are not given in the text.
- We drew attention to significant *intratextual* links (e.g. between the phrase 'the freshness of many clothes' and other references to clothes in *Gatsby*; between the acrobatic image of Dick turning things topsy-turvy and his attempt later in the novel to lift a man on a tow-board).

- We pointed out important *intertextual* links (e.g. the reference to the Grail legend in *Gatsby*; the possible link between Nicole's self-identification as Pallas Athene in *Tender* and Keats's 'Ode on a Grecian Urn').
- We highlighted the commodification of natural phenomena (especially the dog) in the first *Gatsby* extract and suggested that this could be seen in an ecocritical perspective.
- We traced the attitudes to money, consumption and value evident in the passages (e.g. Daisy's 'value' for Gatsby, the contrast between Rosemary and Nicole's view of spending).

Suggested Work

Examine the two following passages. The first is the description of Gatsby's parties which opens chapter two of the novel. This is an even more extravagant kind of conspicuous consumption than that of Myrtle and Nicole, since Gatsby gets no material goods as a result of his expenditure on his parties (and the one good that he desires, Daisy, never wanders into them and dislikes the one she does attend). Money is never directly mentioned in this passage but the glamour of Gatsby's parties is not due only to their spectacular display but also to the awareness, even if unarticulated, that they cost an incalculable amount, that Gatsby's bankroll appears infinite. The second passage is the scene in which Nicole's sister, Beth 'Baby' Warren, attempts, as Dick puts it to himself with inner hilarity, 'to buy Nicole a doctor' (in the shape of himself), not with a direct offer of money but with a suggestion that Nicole's father could use his influence at the University of Chicago to further Dick's academic career.

Analyse the style of these passages, try to sum up the nature of the way in which money enters implicitly and explicitly into each of them, and explore how they may link up with wider aspects of contemporary society (the uses of money for spectacular display, the way in which it may enter into the supposedly altruistic spheres of medicine and the academy).

[a] *Gatsby.* 'There was music from my neighbour's house … ' to 'The party has begun … ' (*GG* 41–2)

[b] *Tender.* 'It was exciting up on the mountain … ' to '"I'll take a look around."' (*TN* 167–9)

4

Gender

Fitzgerald's success as a novelist was bound up with his representations of women. *McCall's Magazine* (October 1925) dubbed him 'the man who discovered the flapper' and the *Louisville Courier* (30 September 1928) called him the 'Creator of Modern Girl Types' *(RE* 132, 112). But he also created notable male characters – Gatsby, Tom Buchanan, Dick Diver, Tommy Barban – in a tumultuous era in which both female and male gender roles, among many other things, were shifting and changing dramatically. Both *Gatsby* and *Tender* portray worlds in which (some) women are more emancipated to an extent but remain restricted in many ways, and where emancipation brings other problems, not least through the insecurity it may arouse in men. Men themselves are uncertain of their masculine identities and may become unduly aggressive or passive. In our first extract, we return to an earlier stage of the dinner party at Tom Buchanan's house which we visited in chapter 2 of this book and see how men and women are shown there.

Blocked Energies: *The Great Gatsby*, pp. 12–15

And so it happened that on a warm windy evening I drove over to East Egg to see two old friends whom I scarcely knew at all. Their house was even more elaborate than I expected, a cheerful red-and-white Georgian Colonial Mansion, overlooking the bay. The lawn started at the beach and ran towards the front door for a quarter of a mile, jumping over sundials and brick walks and burning gardens – finally when it reached the house drifting up the side in bright vines as though from the momentum of its run. The front was broken by a line of french windows, glowing now with reflected gold and wide open to the warm windy afternoon, and Tom Buchanan in riding clothes was standing with his legs apart on the front porch.

He had changed since his New Haven years. Now he was a sturdy straw-haired man of thirty, with a rather hard mouth and a supercilious manner. Two shining arrogant eyes had established dominance over his face and gave him the appearance of always leaning aggressively forward. Not even the effeminate swank of his riding clothes could hide the enormous power of that body – he seemed to fill those glistening boots until he strained the top lacing, and you could see a great pack of muscle shifting when his shoulder moved under his thin coat. It was a body capable of enormous leverage – a cruel body.

His speaking voice, a gruff husky tenor, added to the impression of fractiousness he conveyed. There was a touch of paternal contempt in it, even toward people he liked – and there were men at New Haven who had hated his guts.

'Now, don't think my opinion on these matters is final,' he seemed to say, 'just because I'm stronger and more of a man than you are.' We were in the same senior society, and while we were never intimate I always had the impression that he approved of me and wanted me to like him with some harsh, defiant wistfulness of his own.

We talked for a few minutes on the sunny porch.

'I've got a nice place here,' he said, his eyes flashing about restlessly.

Turning me around by one arm, he moved a broad flat hand along the front vista, including in its sweep a sunken Italian garden, a half acre of deep, pungent roses, and a snub-nosed motor-boat that bumped the tide offshore.

'It belonged to Demaine, the oil man.' He turned me around again, politely and abruptly. 'We'll go inside.'

We walked through a high hallway into a bright rosy-coloured space, fragilely bound into the house by french windows at either end. The windows were ajar and gleaming white against the fresh grass outside that seemed to grow a little way into the house. A breeze blew through the room, blew curtains in at one end and out the other like pale flags, twisting them up toward the frosted wedding-cake of the ceiling, and then rippled over the wine-coloured rug, making a shadow on it as wind does on the sea.

The only completely stationary object in the room was an enormous couch on which two young women were buoyed up as though upon an anchored balloon. They were both in white, and their dresses were rippling and fluttering as if they had just been blown back in after a short flight around the house. I must have stood for a few moments listening to the whip and snap of the curtains and the groan of a picture on the wall. Then there was a boom as Tom Buchanan shut the rear windows and the caught wind died out about the room, and the curtains and the rugs and the two young women ballooned slowly to the floor.

The younger of the two was a stranger to me. She was extended full length at her end of the divan, completely motionless, and with her chin raised a little, as if she were balancing something on it which was quite likely to fall. If she saw me out of the corner of her eyes she gave no hint of it – indeed, I was almost surprised into murmuring an apology for having disturbed her by coming in.

The other girl, Daisy, made an attempt to rise – she leaned slightly forward with a conscientious expression – then she laughed, an absurd, charming little laugh, and I laughed too and came forward into the room.

'I'm p-paralysed with happiness.'

She laughed again, as if she said something very witty, and held my hand for a moment, looking up into my face, promising that there was no one in the world she so much wanted to see. That was a way she had. She hinted in a murmur that the surname of the balancing girl was Baker. (I've heard it said that Daisy's murmur was only to make people lean toward her; an irrelevant criticism that made it no less charming.)

At any rate, Miss Baker's lips fluttered, she nodded at me almost imperceptibly, and then quickly tipped her head back again – the object she was balancing had obviously tottered a little and given her something of a fright. Again a sort of apology rose to my lips. Almost any exhibition of complete self-sufficiency draws a stunned tribute from me.

I looked back at my cousin, who began to ask me questions in her low, thrilling voice. It was the kind of voice that the ear follows up and down, as if each speech is an arrangement of notes that will never be played again. Her face was sad and lovely with bright things in it, bright eyes and a bright passionate mouth, but there was an excitement in her voice that men who had cared for her found difficult to forget: a singing compulsion, a whispered 'Listen', a promise that she had done gay, exciting things just a while since and that there were gay, exciting things hovering in the next hour.

In the first paragraph of this extract, a description of Tom's house and garden prefaces the introduction of Tom himself, as if the man who once dominated the football pitch is now subordinate to the place where he lives. The long sentence which describes the lawn takes what might merely be an inert metaphor in the verb 'ran' and, so to speak, runs with it, developing and extending it; the lawn not only runs but also jumps and has an impetus which does not stop even on reaching the house but modulates – Fitzgerald's dash marks the change of pace – into a slower, more casual motion. It is almost as if the garden takes on something of the energy, force and pace which Tom possessed in his glory days as a football player. The french windows glow with reflected gold: this image is both artistically appealing and an allusion to Tom's wealth; it demonstrates the interfusion of aesthetics and money which recurs in the novel.

In contrast to the energy of the lawn and the visual appeal of the house exterior, Tom himself is a static figure; he wears riding clothes but he is standing rather than in the saddle. Nick sets him in a time perspective by stating he has changed since his days at Yale, but he does not seem to have changed for the better, and Nick gives an unattractive impression of him. Whereas the windows of his house are gold and open to the afternoon, Tom is straw-haired and his hard mouth and supercilious manner suggest closure and defensiveness. His 'shining' eyes might seem at first to echo the glow of his house windows; but the potentially positive connotations of 'shining' are checked by the immediately following adjective, 'arrogant'. His eyes make him look as though he is always aggressive.

At the start of the second paragraph, Tom has simply been called 'sturdy', but Fitzgerald now elaborates the description of Tom's physique. He begins, however, in an interestingly indirect way, by drawing attention to the effeminacy of Tom's attire, even as his phrasing negates it: 'Not even the effeminate swank of his riding clothes could hide the enormous power of that body.' Although on one level this highlights the power of Tom's body by contrast with his 'effeminate' clothes it also, at the outset, casts a faint doubt upon his masculinity, even carries a hint of cross-dressing. The passage does go on, however, to stress Tom's physical size and strength: the noun 'body' is used itself three times in two sentences, emphasizing Tom's corporeal being. Its size and strength are reinforced by the adjectives 'enormous' (used twice) and 'great' and by the nouns 'power' and 'pack' (the latter also perhaps suggests a hunting pack and alludes to Tom's predatoriness, especially in regard to women). The sense that he strains the top lacing of his boots increases the sense of power, suggesting a vital force that is seeking to burst its boundaries. The description here has sexual, phallic connotations and symbolizes how Tom's sexual energies press upon the constraints of marriage and escape into affairs. The term 'leverage' could also have phallic connotations: we could make an intratextual link here with the use of the noun 'lever' near the end of chapter 2, where the lift boy's warning to McKee, '"Keep your hands off the lever"' (*GG* 39), might seem a coded warning against making sexual advances to Nick. Following hard on these hints, the adjective 'cruel' conveys the idea that sexual energies may take sadistic form and stresses the power of Tom's body to do harm.

The focus then shifts from Tom's physique to his voice, 'a gruff husky tenor', a further mark of masculinity which will contrast to Daisy's voice when it is evoked a little later in the extract. Tom's power over Nick is conveyed in the way in which he moves him about, turning him around by one arm and turning him around again. His hand gesture takes in his possessions – the garden, the roses, the motor-boat – but these seem inappropriate to his physique: the garden is sunken rather than salient, the roses have feminine connotations and the motor boat is personified as snub-nosed, short and turned-up, implying a curtailment of phallic power. Tom's ownership of a partly feminized domain boosts his masculinity; but the feminine attributes of that domain also threaten his partial emasculation.

Tom and Nick then walk into a zone more firmly marked as feminine; it is 'bright', an adjective strongly associated with Daisy later in the passage, and 'rosy-coloured', taking up the feminine associations of the garden roses. Tom's entry into this zone is a kind of symbolic sexual penetration which both reasserts his masculinity and risks absorption into the feminine. This zone could also be called liminal (from the Latin root 'limen', meaning 'threshold'); it is on the threshold, at the frontier between exterior and interior, 'fragilely bound into the house', where 'the fresh grass outside ... seemed to grow a little way into the house' and the windows are still open (crossing this space three months later, on the night after Myrtle's death, Nick will come to the pantry window through which he sees Tom and Daisy together and grasps how firmly they have excluded Gatsby; the liminal zone is then the threshold between the last vestiges of Gatsby's fairy-winged dream and the hard rock of reality). At this point, there are Homeric, epic echoes in the references to the 'wine-coloured' rug and the breeze making a shadow like wind on the sea. But these ancient traces of heroic masculine adventure seem ironic in this contained and feminized room which annuls masculine energy, though it represents a containment of feminine energy too. It could be seen here as a liminal zone between masculinity and femininity.

As Tom was static when Nick first saw him on the front porch, the two women (unnamed at this point) are also static, although their dresses are in motion. The couch on which they lie is 'enormous'; as this adjective was applied to Tom's physique in the second paragraph of this extract, it suggests that, while women occupy the couch, it is a man who supports them. An undercurrent of the cruelty earlier epitomized by Tom's body recurs in the words 'whip', 'snap' and 'groan', even though these now describe the wind's effect rather than Tom himself. It is almost as if the wind turns sadistic when confined in a domestic interior. When Tom shuts the rear door, its 'boom' symbolizes the attempt to impose his masculine presence.

Fitzgerald uses the simile of 'an anchored balloon' to describe the particular kind of stasis which the couch seems to manifest and he takes up this image again later in the paragraph, in the simile of the two women having 'just been blown back in after a short flight round the house' and the final metaphor of them ballooning slowly to the floor. This partly comic allusion to what was, by the 1920s, an older form of aerial travel, the hot-air balloon, locates the women in a slightly retrograde zone, as if they had not quite caught up with modernity and its new transport technologies. Later events in *Gatsby* reinforce the idea that they are technologically behind the times. While the younger Daisy, in Louisville, had her own 'little white roadster' (*GG* 73), her attempt to control a piece of cutting-edge technology (Gatsby's car) proves lethal. Jordan drives so close to some workmen that her car's fender flicks one man's coat buttons. The account of the wind, like that of Tom's garden, suggests that there is a lot of natural energy around but that the two young women, like Tom, are cut off from it, locked in stasis. The adjective 'caught', applied to the wind once Tom has shut the door, gives a sense of entrapment, as if the two women are also 'caught' within a space which Tom commands. But that space seems ultimately to command Tom as well.

The sense of stasis persists when the younger woman is described as 'completely motionless' and makes no response to Nick, although she does not seem idle since she gives the impression that she is balancing something on her chin with difficulty. A little later in the extract, she is called 'the balancing girl' and, in the light of what we learn about her in the rest of the novel, this might serve as a metaphor of the balancing act she has to perform as a relatively autonomous woman in a man's world. Daisy tries to rise but never makes it, laughing instead and saying 'I'm p-paralysed with happiness.' The term 'paralysed', which the slight stammer marked by the dash highlights, is on one level merely a manner of speaking, but it does reinforce the idea of stasis and make it more negative. In a sense, Daisy is indeed 'paralysed' by her situation as a woman and Tom's wife. The younger woman, Miss Baker, might seem similarly entrapped but the 'complete self-sufficiency' Nick identifies makes her appear detached from the situation, as if her entrapment is only temporary.

If Tom is primarily defined by his body, Daisy is primarily defined by her voice. Nick does not lavish on Daisy's body the elaborate epithets he gives Tom's. He does describe her face but in general lyric terms: 'sad', · 'lovely', 'passionate' and, repeated three times, 'bright': we can make an intertextual link here between the recurrence of this last adjective and its prominence in the late Romantic poetry of Algernon Charles Swinburne (for example, 'the brown bright nightingale amorous' in the Chorus of *Atalanta in Calydon*). Swinburne exemplified a kind of poetry that Modernist poets vigorously repudiated as vague and imprecise and Fitzgerald combined a fondness for Romantic vocabulary with a Modernist quest for precision. He goes on to apply further lyric terms to Daisy's voice – 'low' and 'thrilling' – and to call each speech it delivers 'unique', but he does not stop there. He then likens that voice, in a musical simile, to 'an arrangement of notes that will never be played again'. Here the act of attention that Daisy's voice arouses is aesthetic and ungendered; the ear – preceded, significantly, by a definite article rather than a gendered pronoun – follows i⊢ ⌐and down as it might follow a pattern of notes. But the next s⁄ at 68 words, the longest in the extract – identifies Dais⁄

terms of its effect upon men and makes it a complex phenomenon which incorporates 'excitement', memorability, 'a singing compulsion' and a 'promise' that she had done and would do 'gay, exciting things'; this 'promise' sets the appeal of the voice in the context of time and action, relating it to past and future and to doing things. These 'things' are erotic but not exclusively so; they stand for a more generalized excitement. It will be left to Gatsby to identify one other quality that pervades Daisy's voice: it is 'full of money' (*GG* 115).

The extract gives a sense of blocked energies in both men and women. In the extract from *Tender* we shall now consider, Nicole is shown emerging from Dick's dominance but falling under the sway of Tommy Barban.

Under Whose Sway?: *Tender is the Night*, pp. 313–15

Nicole did not want any vague spiritual romance – she wanted an 'affair'; she wanted a change. She realized, thinking with Dick's thoughts, that from a superficial point of view it was a vulgar business to enter, without emotion, into an indulgence that menaced all of them. On the other hand, she blamed Dick for the immediate situation, and honestly thought that such an experiment might have a therapeutic value. All summer she had been stimulated by watching people do exactly what they were tempted to do and pay no penalty for it – moreover, in spite of her intention of no longer lying to herself, she preferred to consider that she was merely feeling her way and that at any moment she could withdraw ...

In the light shade Tommy caught her up in his white-duck arms and pulled her around to him, looking at her eyes.

'Don't move,' he said. 'I'm going to look at you a great deal from now on.'

There was some scent on his hair, a faint aura of soap from his white clothes. Her lips were tight, not smiling and they both simply looked for a moment.

'Do you like what you see?' she murmured.

'Parle français.'

'Very well,' and she asked again in French. 'Do you like what you see?' He pulled her closer.

'I like whatever I see about you.' He hesitated. 'I thought I knew your face but it seems there are some things I didn't know about it. When did you begin to have white crook's eyes?'

She broke away, shocked and indignant, and cried in English:

'Is that why you wanted to talk French?' Her voice quieted as the butler came with sherry. 'So you could be offensive more accurately?'

She parked her small seat violently on the cloth-of-silver chair cushion.

'I have no mirror here,' she said, again in French, but decisively, 'but if my eyes have changed it's because I'm well again. And being well perhaps I've gone back to my true self – I suppose my grandfather was a crook and I'm a crook by heritage, so there we are. Does that satisfy your logical mind?'

He scarcely seemed to know what she was talking about.

'Where's Dick – is he lunching with us?'

Seeing that his remark had meant comparatively little to him she suddenly laughed away its effect.

'Dick's on a tour,' she said. 'Rosemary Hoyt turned up, and either they're together or she upset him so much that he wants to go away and dream about her.'

'You know, you're a little complicated after all.'

'Oh no,' she assured him hastily. 'No, I'm not really – I'm just a – I'm just a whole lot of different simple people.'

Marius brought out melon and an ice pail, and Nicole, thinking irresistibly about her crook's eyes, did not answer; he gave one an entire nut to crack, this man, instead of giving it in fragments to pick at for meat.

'Why didn't they leave you in your natural state?' Tommy demanded presently. 'You are the most dramatic person I have known.'

She had no answer.

'All this taming of women!' he scoffed.

'In any society there are certain – ' She felt Dick's ghost prompting at her elbow but she subsided at Tommy's overtone:

'I've brutalized many men into shape but I wouldn't take a chance on half the number of women. Especially this "kind" bullying – what good does it do anybody? – you or him or anybody?'

Her heart leaped and then sank faintly with a sense of what she owed Dick.

'I suppose I've got – '

'You've got too much money,' he said impatiently. 'That's the crux of the matter. Dick can't beat that.'

> She considered while the melons were removed.
> 'What do you think I ought to do?'
> For the first time in ten years she was under the sway of a personality other than her husband's. Everything Tommy said to her became part of her forever.

The first paragraph of the extract offers a subtle and complex analysis of Nicole's thoughts and feelings at this crucial moment in her life and marriage. With a mixture of sympathy and detachment, it evokes the interplay between Nicole's desire to act on her own initiative, to achieve a degree of autonomy, and the influences of Dick, of Tommy and of the behaviour of others which she has witnessed. The opening sentence focuses on what Nicole wants, on her rejection of the vaguely spiritual for an 'affair', a 'change'. The next sentence starts by pursuing Nicole's perceptions – 'She realized' – but the narrator then interpolates a participial phrase which indicates Dick's continued influence: 'thinking with Dick's thoughts' (it recalls the merging between Dick and Nicole symbolized in their early fusion of their forenames into 'Dicole' (*TN* 116)). Dick's thoughts, as Nicole interprets them, offer an aesthetic and moral appraisal of her intention: it is 'vulgar' because it is without emotion and it menaces 'all of them'. But this view is also seen as 'superficial' (it is not quite clear here whether this evaluation comes from Dick or Nicole).

The phrase 'On the other hand' introduces opposing considerations: Nicole blames Dick for the immediate situation – because he has gone off in pursuit of Rosemary Hoyt – and 'honestly thought that such an experiment [an 'affair', a change] might have a therapeutic value'. This seems to be Nicole's own 'honest' thought and, in prescribing therapy for herself, it is as if she is starting to take over the healing role that Dick had played for her before and to some extent during their marriage. But the idea of an affair as therapy sits uneasily with the earlier realization, based on Nicole's idea of what Dick would think, that an affair would be an 'indulgence' that threatened them all. In using the term 'therapeutic', Nicole participates in a wider cultural discourse that developed in the first part of the twentieth century in which the idea of 'therapy' can offer a licence for actions which might, in an ethical perspective, seem wrong and harmful.

The following sentence develops this sense of Nicole seeking a licence for dubious behaviour by suggesting how she has been 'stimulated' (the verb perhaps implies sexual as well as more general excitation) by 'watching people do exactly what they were tempted to do and pay no penalty for it'. She has witnessed a world in which it seems possible to yield to temptation with impunity. Ironically, she is herself living proof of the damage which may flow from this attitude: yielding to temptation and suffering no penalty is precisely what her father did when he committed incest with her; and although an extramarital affair is not a similarly heinous crime, it could be that, in adopting such an attitude, she is truly becoming 'Daddy's Girl', assuming her inheritance as her father's daughter.

The sentence and paragraph conclude by indicating two further aspects of Nicole; that she has formed the intention of 'no longer lying to herself' but that she is doing so insofar as she prefers to believe that she is merely feeling her way at present with Tommy, that she can withdraw at any time. The psychological process here is akin to what the French philosopher, novelist, short-story writer, playwright and essayist Jean-Paul Sartre, in his philosophical work *Being and Nothingness* (1943), would call 'mauvaise foi', bad faith, in which one pretends to oneself that one is not letting something happen even when one really knows that one is. The paragraph ends, not with a full stop, but with leader dots, as we move from an analysis of Nicole's thoughts and feelings to an evocation of her embrace with Tommy, related through a mixture of narrative description, still from Nicole's point of view, and dialogue.

Tommy's embrace of Nicole takes place 'in the light shade'; here the adjective 'light' primarily means 'relatively low in intensity', but if we stress another of its meanings, 'the natural agent that stimulates sight and makes things visible', the phrase 'light shade' becomes almost an oxymoron, a contradiction in terms. It is as if Nicole were entering into a frontier zone between light and shadow which symbolizes the moral ambiguity of her actions and the way in which she combines a lucid awareness of what she is doing with a denial of it. The sense of a paradoxical interplay between light and darkness, in which the conventional positive and negative associations of each element are partly mingled and interchanged, is echoed in the disconcerting moment in which Tommy, pulling Nicole closer and examining her face, asks when she began to have 'white crook's eyes'. White, the conventional colour of virtue and purity, is coupled here with crime.

Initially 'shocked and indignant' at Tommy's remark, Nicole then tries to convert it into a moment of self-definition and self-affirmation. She has no mirror by which she can visually check Tommy's claim and recognize or misrecognize herself; but she asserts that if her eyes have changed it is because she is 'well again', and this possibly means she has returned to her 'true self'. She defines this 'true self', however, as both crooked and determined by heredity: her 'grandfather was a crook' and she is 'a crook by heritage'. She omits her father here but he too, who abused her as a child, surely takes his place in her criminal lineage. So both her psychological health and her autonomy seem deeply compromised by statements which employ the first-person pronoun 'I' only to suggest the extent to which she is determined by heredity. There seems to be no easy escape for Nicole from definitions offered or imposed by others: from Dick she has moved to her family and to Tommy.

Although Dick is physically absent from this exchange between Nicole and Tommy, he is very much present in Nicole's mind and in the dialogue. We have already been told of Nicole 'thinking with Dick's thoughts'; Tommy himself raises the question of Dick's whereabouts, though without realizing its significance, and Nicole indicates that Dick is with, or dreaming about, Rosemary Hoyt. When Nicole starts to object to Tommy's denunciation of the 'taming of women', she feels 'Dick's ghost prompting at her elbow' – though the image of him as a 'ghost' is an ominous sign that he is no longer alive for her as he once was and a premonition of how his presence in her life, and in the world, will diminish as the novel proceeds (the term 'ghost' is applied to a diminished, emasculated husband in *Gatsby*, when Myrtle walks through Wilson 'as if he were a ghost' (*GG* 28)).

Despite Dick's absent presence, however, Tommy increasingly displaces him and makes remarks which mount a challenge to him. The image which describes Nicole's irresistible preoccupation with Tommy's comment on her captures the power of that challenge: 'he gave one an entire nut to crack, this man, instead of giving it in fragments to pick at for meat'. It is not clear here whether it is Dick whom Nicole thinks of as giving her fragments to pick at for meat, but this is possibly the case. The image suggests Tommy's capacity to challenge and define Nicole and to treat her as a person who can crack 'a whole nut'. The notion of Tommy giving Nicole the 'whole nut' also bears a sexual implication – 'nuts' is slang for testicles – which perhaps suggests, by contrast, a deterioration in Dick's sexual performance which contrasts with his youthful self-image as a 'big stiff' (*TN* 130). When Tommy asks Nicole why 'they' did not leave her in her 'natural state', he implicitly criticizes Dick as the primary tamer of Nicole. Though Dick's ghost prompts her to defend 'taming' in terms of a proper conformity to social conventions, she does not carry it through, and the sentence breaks off, in that kind of aposiopesis, that sudden breaking off of a sentence marked by a dash, which is often significant in Fitzgerald. Tommy goes on to denounce 'kind' bullying in a more explicit attack on Dick, referred to as 'him' – 'what good does it do anybody? – you or him or anybody?' Nicole's attempts to assert herself increasingly break down at this stage of her dialogue with Tommy: she 'subsides' at 'Tommy's overtone' and her heart, after leaping, sinks faintly.

The emergence of Tommy's remark on Nicole's money somewhat resembles that of Gatsby's comment that Daisy's voice is 'full of money'. In *Gatsby*, Nick, trying to define the peculiar quality of Daisy's voice, says 'It's full of – ', but does not complete the sentence, either because he cannot find the words or because Gatsby interrupts him (or perhaps a mixture of both). It is Gatsby who then takes over and makes an emphatic pecuniary diagnosis: 'Her voice is full of money' (*GG* 115). In *Tender*, it is Nicole, rather than Nick, who starts a statement which she does not complete – 'I suppose I've got – ' – and Tommy who 'impatiently' interrupts to say 'You've got too much money.' He then extends this into another observation of her husband – 'Dick can't beat that' – which is, on one level, a put-down of his rival for Nicole but also a shrewd appraisal of Dick's situation which confirms what we already know, for example from Nicole's interior monologue, analysed in chapter 3: backed by the Warren family fortune, Nicole's economic power over Dick is invincible. After Tommy's remark, Nicole's attempts to assert herself or state her own (or Dick's) case collapse into submission to Tommy's guidance 'What do you think I ought to do?' By the end of the extract, Dick no longer subordinates her, but Tommy does. Later that afternoon, they drive to a small shore hotel and make love, sealing the new, and inequitable, bond between them.

The relationship between Nicole and Tommy thus reaches a kind of consummation which will eventually turn into marriage. If it seems that Nicole will still be dominated by her husband, she appears likely to acquire at least slightly more autonomy than in her relationship with Dick with its persistent doctor–patient element. In *Gatsby*, the relationship between Nick and Jordan is much more fraught than between Nicole and Tommy, as the next passage for analysis shows.

Lies and Driving: *The Great Gatsby*, pp. 58–9

For a while I lost sight of Jordan Baker, and then in midsummer I found her again. At first I was flattered to go places with her, because she was a golf champion, and everyone knew her name. Then it was something more. I wasn't actually in love, but I felt a sort of tender curiosity. The bored haughty face that she turned to the world concealed something – most affectations conceal something eventually, even though they don't in the beginning – and one day I found what it was. When we were on a house-party together up in Warwick, she left a borrowed car out in the rain with the top down, and then lied about it – and suddenly I remembered the story about her that had eluded me that night at Daisy's. At her first big golf tournament there was a row that nearly reached the newspapers – a suggestion that she had moved her ball from a bad lie in the semi-final round. The thing approached the proportions of a scandal – then died away. A caddy retracted his statement, and the only other witness admitted that he might have been mistaken. The incident and the name had remained together in my mind.

Jordan Baker instinctively avoided clever, shrewd men, and now I saw that this was because she felt safer on a plane where any divergence from a code would be thought impossible. She was incurably dishonest. She wasn't able to endure being at a disadvantage and, given this unwillingness, I suppose she had begun dealing in subterfuges when she was very young in order to keep that cool, insolent smile turned to the world and yet satisfy the demands of her hard, jaunty body.

It made no difference to me. Dishonesty in a woman is a thing you never blame deeply – I was casually sorry, and then I forgot. It was on that same house-party that we had a curious conversation about driving a car. It started because she passed so close to some workmen that our fender flicked a button on one man's coat.

'You're a rotten driver,' I protested. 'Either you ought to be more careful, or you oughtn't to drive at all.'

'I am careful.'

'No, you're not.'

'Well, other people are,' she said lightly.

'What's that got to do with it?'

'They'll keep out of my way,' she insisted. 'It takes two to make an accident.'

'Suppose you met somebody just as careless as yourself.'

'I hope I never will,' she answered. 'I hate careless people. That's why I like you.'

Her grey, sun-strained eyes stared straight ahead, but she had deliberately shifted our relations, and for a moment I thought I loved her. But I am slow-thinking and full of interior rules that act as brakes on my desires, and I knew that first I had to get myself definitely out of that tangle back home. I'd been writing letters once a week and signing them: 'Love, Nick,' and all I could think of was how, when that certain girl played tennis, a faint moustache of perspiration appeared on her upper lip. Nevertheless there was a vague understanding that had to be tactfully broken off before I was free.

Every one suspects himself of at least one of the cardinal virtues, and this is mine: I am one of the few honest people that I have ever known.

Jordan Baker is the most emancipated woman in *Gatsby*; she has no family (apart from an aged aunt) and, unlike Daisy and Myrtle, no husband, she appears to be free of financial worries, and she is a sporting celebrity, enjoying the kind of kudos that had once been Tom's. Nick, by contrast, is the most passive man in the novel – even the 'anaemic' Wilson (*GG* 27) explodes in violent vengeance after his wife's death. Both Jordan and Nick thus diverge from, and implicitly challenge, gender stereotypes. As the narrator, however, Nick is able to exercise a certain kind of power over all the other characters and to reassert his masculine authority and identity, most notably, in this extract, when he makes a generalization which impugns the honesty of women while exempting them from condemnation: 'Dishonesty in a woman is a thing you never blame deeply.'

Despite this patronizing exculpation of female dishonesty, Nick judges Jordan harshly. The diction of the extract shows this; it applies a range of adjectives to her which have derogatory connotations, especially when used of women. Six of them denote aspects of her physical appearance: her face is 'bored' and 'haughty'; her smile is 'cool' and 'insolent'; and her body is 'hard' and 'jaunty'. As a driver, she is 'rotten' and 'careless'. The most damning adjective of all, amplified by an adverb which insists on the immutability of the ascribed trait and implicitly likens it to a disease, is 'incurably dishonest'. But Nick offers only two pieces of anecdotal evidence for this verdict. The first, witnessed by Nick himself, is that Jordan 'lied' about the borrowed car she left out in the rain. The other evidence, swollen by rumour but supported by only two witnesses who back-pedalled on their original assertions, is that Jordan moved her ball from 'a bad lie' in the semi-final of her first big golf tournament. The noun 'lie' in the second piece of evidence reinforces the negative meaning of the verb 'lied' in the first. Although 'lie' in this context means, not an intentional untruth, but 'the position in which something [in this case a golf ball] comes to rest', the similarity in sound and spelling between 'lied' and 'lie' creates a near-fusion between the two terms and strengthens the sense of Jordan's dishonesty. The application of the adjective 'bad' to 'lie' strengthens this further, giving the impression that Jordan had not only moved her ball from 'a bad lie' but had also, in doing this, perpetrated 'a bad lie'. But both pieces of evidence remain shaky and hardly add up to proof of incurable dishonesty.

The denigration of Jordan is also evident in the references to cars and driving which figure significantly in this passage. In *Gatsby*, cars and driving are both empowering and potentially lethal and feature as symbols of character and the conduct of life. One element of this passage which exemplifies the exchange of conventional male/female attributes between Nick and Jordan is that Jordan is behind the wheel, not Nick (though Nick has a car – appropriately, given his evasive tendencies, 'an old Dodge' (*GG* 9) – we never hear of him driving any car in the novel). But for Nick, Jordan's relationship to cars also demonstrates her negative traits. Her carelessness is exemplified first of all by her leaving a borrowed car out in the rain and her dishonesty, as we have already remarked, by her lying about it. It is more vividly demonstrated by the incident, at the same house-party, in which she is driving (presumably the same borrowed car), and passes so close to some workmen that the car's fender flicks a button on one man's coat. In the ensuing dialogue, Jordan initially asserts that she is a 'careful' driver but implicitly acknowledges she is a 'careless' one when Nick challenges her. Despite Nick's challenge, however, Jordan is still in control of the situation, still metaphorically as well as literally behind the wheel, and her last comment, 'That's why I like you', has an effect which Nick sums up by a driving metaphor: she had intentionally 'shifted' their relations (in a usage which is mainly North American, the verb 'to shift' can mean to change gear in a car, and 'shift', as a noun, means a gear lever or gear-changing mechanism; later in the novel, just before the fateful exchange of cars for the journey to New York, Tom asks Gatsby if his car is 'standard shift' (*GG* 115)). But although Nick inwardly responds to Jordan's shift of their relations into another gear, thinking momentarily that he loves her, he does not follow it up, employing a car-related metaphor to describe his inhibitions when he calls himself 'full of interior rules that act as *brakes* on my desires' (my emphasis).

Nick judges Jordan to be dishonest and dangerous but a slight shift of perspective might make her look dashing and daring, possessing characteristics that might more conventionally have been ascribed to men in the 1920s. By contrast, Nick is – as Jordan flatteringly implies at the end of their dialogue – careful. Too careful, perhaps, to emerge as a figure of full-blooded masculinity. Again, the diction is telling: Nick is 'flattered' to accompany Jordan 'because she was a golf champion'. Being the escort of a sporting champion might seem, especially in the 1920s, more the role of a woman than a man. Nick feels 'a sort of tender curiosity' towards Jordan and feeling tender might also look more a feminine than a masculine trait. Moreover, Nick's curiosity has an element of patronising voyeurism which might indeed seem characteristic of the kind of male gaze to which women are subjected, but which also emphasizes Nick's role as the passive observer. Jordan cannot bear to be 'at a disadvantage', whereas Nick seems almost permanently in this state, except when he withdraws into his judgemental, recording role. Although Nick reports and implicitly reproves Jordan's lie about the borrowed car and her alleged cheating in the golf tournament, he does not appear to ask for her version of these incidents but to accept them unquestioningly as proof positive of her dishonesty. His affirmation that he himself is 'honest' seems belied by his acknowledgement that he still insincerely signs his letters 'Love, Nick' to the girl back home with whom he has 'a vague understanding' but of whom he wants to be free (*GG* 59).

If Nick's masculinity is uncertain throughout *Gatsby*, Dick Diver in *Tender* seems, in his younger days, an epitome of graceful manliness, tall, strong, handsome, intelligent and sensitive. But his drinking and the decline of his marriage lead him to the public humiliation portrayed in the next passage, when he tries to perform an athletic feat he had once accomplished with ease.

Dick's Debacle: *Tender is the Night*, pp. 303–5

Swimming away, Nicole saw that the cloud of Dick's heartsickness had lifted a little as he began to play with Rosemary, bringing out his old expertness with people, a tarnished object of art; she guessed that with a drink or so he would have done his stunts on the swinging rings for her, fumbling through stunts he had once done with ease. She noticed that this summer, for the first time, he avoided high diving.

Later, as she dodged her way from raft to raft, Dick overtook her.

'Some of Rosemary's friends have a speed boat, the one out there. Do you want to aquaplane? I think it would be amusing.'

Remembering that once he could stand on his hands on a chair at the end of a board, she indulged him as she might have indulged Lanier. Last summer on the Zugersee they had played at that pleasant water game, and Dick had lifted a two-hundred-pound man from the board onto his shoulders and stood up. But women marry all their husbands' talents and naturally, afterwards, are not so impressed with them as they may keep up the pretense of being. Nicole had not even pretended to be impressed, though she had said 'Yes' to him, and 'Yes, I thought so too.'

She knew, though, that he was somewhat tired, that it was only the closeness of Rosemary's exciting youth that prompted the impending effort – she had seen him draw the same inspiration from the new bodies of her children and she wondered coldly if he would make a spectacle of himself. The Divers were older than the others in the boat – the young people were polite, deferential, but Nicole felt an undercurrent of 'Who are these Numbers anyhow?' and she missed Dick's easy talent of taking control of situations and making them all right – he had concentrated on what he was going to try to do.

The motor throttled down two hundred yards from shore and one of the young men dove flat over the edge. He swam at the aimless twisting board, steadied it, climbed slowly to his knees on it – then got on his feet as the boat accelerated. Leaning back he swung his light vehicle ponderously from side to side in slow, breathless arcs that rode the trailing side-swell at the end of each swing. In the direct wake of the boat he let go his rope, balanced for a moment, then back-flipped into the water, disappearing like a statue of glory, and reappearing as an insignificant head while the boat made the circle back to him.

Nicole refused her turn; then Rosemary rode the board neatly and conservatively, with facetious cheers from her admirers. Three of them scrambled egotistically for the honor of pulling her into the boat, managing, among them, to bruise her knee and hip against the side.

'Now you, Doctor,' said the Mexican at the wheel.

Dick and the last young man dove over the side and swam to the board. Dick was going to try his lifting trick and Nicole began to watch with smiling scorn. This physical showing-off for Rosemary irritated her most of all.

When the men had ridden long enough to find their balance, Dick knelt, and putting the back of his neck in the other man's crotch, found the rope through his legs, and slowly began to rise.

The people in the boat, watching closely, saw that he was having difficulties. He was on one knee; the trick was to straighten all the way up in the same motion with which he left his kneeling position. He rested for a moment, then his face contracted as he put his heart into the strain, and lifted.

The board was narrow, the man, though weighing less than a hundred and fifty, was awkward with his weight and grabbed clumsily at Dick's head. When, with a last wrenching effort of his back, Dick stood upright, the board slid sidewise and the pair toppled into the sea.

In the boat Rosemary exclaimed: 'Wonderful! They almost had it.'

But as they came back to the swimmers Nicole watched for a sight of Dick's face. It was full of annoyance as she expected, because he had done the thing with ease only two years ago.

The second time he was more careful. He rose a little, testing the balance of his burden, settled down again on his knee; then, grunting 'Alley oop!' began to rise – but before he could really straighten out, his legs suddenly buckled and he shoved the board away with his feet to avoid being struck as they fell off.

This time when the Baby Gar came back it was apparent to all the passengers that he was angry.

'Do you mind if I try that once more?' he called, treading water. 'We almost had it then.'

'Sure. Go ahead.'

To Nicole he looked white-around-the-gills, and she cautioned him: 'Don't you think that's enough for now?'

Nicole's perception of Dick in this extract has a largely detached quality, demonstrating both the gulf that has opened between them and the accelerating reversal in their roles: it is now Nicole, rather than Doctor Diver, who casts a diagnostic eye on their spouse; but it is a cold one apparently devoid of healing impulses. She uses the verb 'to play' to refer to Dick and Rosemary's conversation (to which she has been listening just prior to this extract), and she thus implies that Dick is engaging in a childish activity. In part, her attitude could spring from her envy of Rosemary's youthfulness (which she has registered with a shock shortly before this extract), and her jealousy of Rosemary's power to attract Dick. The term also represents, however, a limiting judgement on Dick. Nicole knows Dick well enough to see that, with Rosemary, he is 'bringing out his old expertness with people', but the adjective 'old' is a reminder that Dick himself is ageing and distinctly senior to Rosemary. The sense that Dick's 'expertness with people' is diminished is deepened by the image of it as 'a tarnished object of art'; this sounds like an authorial metaphor more than Nicole's own, a way of formulating her thoughts which she would not necessarily adopt herself, but it suggests that such expertness is a kind of aesthetic artefact – an 'object of art' – that has now lost brightness and lustre.

Nicole is also aware of Dick's drinking and his loss of physical strength and agility. In the passage about Dick's earlier life discussed in chapter 1, his skill on the flying rings as a Harvard student was one of the signs of his physical prowess. Now Nicole knows that if he tried to perform a similar feat he would be 'fumbling', a verb denoting a kind of clumsiness which has not been associated with the younger Dick. There is also a hint that he himself is aware of his waning physical agility: his avoidance of high diving, which, as his surname is 'Diver', suggests that he has renounced a defining aspect of himself. These markers of his loss of physical grace, strength and perhaps courage bode ill for the success of the feat he will soon try to perform and, more generally, for his ability to adjust to the current stage of his life.

When Dick suggests that they should go aquaplaning, Nicole 'indulged him as she might have indulged Lanier', their son, which deepens the implication, in the use of the verb 'to play' earlier in the extract, of a childish quality in Dick's behaviour. Two further examples of Dick's athletic feats are recalled: standing on his hands on a chair at the end of a board and, only last summer, lifting a two-hundred-pound man from the board onto his shoulders and standing up. This last feat not only shows the strength and agility Dick once possessed, but also symbolizes his capacity to support and raise the spirits of other people – a capacity crucial to his work as a psychiatrist, his cure of Nicole and his management of his American expatriate set.

Nicole sees Rosemary as stimulating Dick to try to perform the feat now. The stimulus is not simply Rosemary's physical attractiveness but her youth; Nicole compares it to the energy which 'the new bodies of her children' once released in Dick. The suggestion earlier in the passage that Dick's behaviour is childish is joined here by the implication that Dick has come to see youth as a source of fresh vigour and has developed a predatory, almost paedophiliac attitude towards it (when he was taken across a courtyard to the courtroom in Rome after hitting the plainclothes policeman, a crowd booed him, mistaking him for a native of Frascati in custody for the rape and murder of a 5-year-old girl; shortly afterwards, Dick said to his lawyer and Collis Clay, 'I want to make a speech … I want to explain to these people how I raped a five-year-old girl. Maybe I did … ' (*TN* 256)). If Dick, as suggested in chapter 2, has been a kind of self-sacrificing Christ figure with 'pieces of his own most personal self for everyone' (*TN* 89), he now seems to feed on youth to try to boost his own vitality, in a kind of vampirism. Nicole is conscious of the age gap which divides Dick and herself from the other, younger people in the boat and she is aware that Dick might once have worked to efface this but is no longer doing so because he needs all his energy and attention for the athletic feat he is about to try to perform.

The next paragraph builds up the suspense as Dick waits to take his turn. It starts with an account of how one of the young men gets control of the board and climbs on to it. When he back-flips into the water, a simile describes him as 'disappearing like a statue of glory', suggesting Dick will find him a hard act to follow. Nicole declines to take part, recognizing her limitations, and Rosemary rides the board with practical efficiency, refusing to try to show off, though still acting as a magnet for her admirers. Then Dick's turn comes. The narrator homes in again on Nicole, seeing her 'smiling scorn' (which might be visible to others) and then going inside her mind to specify the source of her irritation, Dick's 'physical showing-off for Rosemary'.

A short paragraph then describes, in a straightforward way, Dick and the young man making preparations for Dick's 'lifting trick'. It is worth noting here the verb 'knelt' that is used of Dick. On one level, this is the physical act Dick must perform in order to lift the man; but we may recall that, earlier in the novel, Nicole 'knelt' when she broke down in the bathroom (*TN* 125) and also that, in *Gatsby*, Myrtle 'knelt in the road' after Gatsby's car had fatally struck her (*GG* 131). In each case, there is a religious resonance, a sense that some sort of rite is being enacted: Myrtle kneels before the eyes of T.J. Eckleburg; Nicole kneels before the gods of violation and purification; Dick kneels before the gods of youth and masculinity. With Dick, there is also a sense that he needs to pray for success because it is unlikely he will achieve it with his own unaided efforts. The preparation for the 'lifting trick' also involves an initial obeisance before the man he would lift – he must bow to him before he can lift him – and a potentially sexualized physical intimacy as male neck and male crotch meet.

The point of view then becomes a collective one, that of 'the people in the boat, watching closely'. They perceive Dick's difficulties, and, we can infer, this increases his humiliation as he fails to lift the man and they both fall into the sea. Rosemary tries to protect Dick by saying they almost succeeded, but Nicole's merciless eye sees Dick's annoyance and understands the reason for it. Dick tries but fails again. In his second attempt, the phrase 'the balance of his burden' is used. In our discussion of Jordan Baker earlier in this chapter, we suggested that 'balance' could be a Fitzgeraldian metaphor for the proper conduct of life and the same might be true here: Dick is not only testing the balance of his burden on the tow-board but also in his current life, and in both cases he cannot lift it or withdraw in a dignified way from the attempt to do so. After his second failure to lift the man, Dick's anger is visible to all the passengers on the boat. He asks politely if he can try once more – despite his anger, his manners have not deserted him – but Nicole, seeing he looks tired and ill, speaks to him as if he were a child and also with something of the authoritarian quality which he showed towards her during the scene in the hotel bathroom witnessed by Rosemary. In the context of this stage of the novel, the question, 'Don't you think that's enough for now?' acquires a wider relevance; it could apply, not only to his self-destructive desire to persist in trying to perform the lifting trick, but also to his persistence in his relationship with Rosemary, his life on the Riviera, and his marriage to Nicole.

Conclusions

All the passages portray situations in which women and men are unable to find roles which release their better energies and qualities. Daisy is largely static, perhaps in a sense paralysed; her chief asset is her voice, but that is used to intrigue men rather than to articulate her own desires and plans. She enjoys a certain power over men, primarily through her voice, but remains in a marriage with Tom in which he has been flagrantly unfaithful from an early stage (the Santa Barbara chambermaid) and is likely to be again (at the Gatsby party she and Tom attend, she sees him trying to make out with a girl who is 'common but pretty' (*GG* 102)). Jordan Baker, as a golf champion with no family except an aged aunt, enjoys a greater degree of freedom than Daisy or Nicole, but has to perform a difficult balancing act and comes under the regulatory gaze of Nick who condemns her after a summary trial. Nicole takes the initiative in moving out of a deteriorating relationship with Dick; but it is possible that Dick may have anticipated and even planned this, and she ditches Dick only to fall under the dominance of Tommy.

Tom Buchanan is the epitome of the physically powerful male but his strength has no positive outlet; he no longer plays sports; he does not seem to have been to war (unlike Nick and Gatsby); his huge house and garden offer him no sphere for action and although he shows them off as an extension of himself, they seem rather to dominate him. They symbolize his possession of the feminine but also threaten him with feminization. Nick, for much of *Gatsby*, is a passive voyeur who is unable to rise to the challenge that Jordan implicitly poses and can only condemn her and finally reject her. In *Tender*, Tommy Barban finds scope for his energies in war but his martial exploits seem detached from any higher purpose – he is fighting less for a cause than for the sake of fighting. Dick is humiliated in his attempt at masculine display and at proving he can still support other human beings; literally and symbolically, he fails to keep his balance and falls, a half-man more than a double man.

The four passages contribute to the exploration throughout Fitzgerald's fiction of uncertainties in regard to the roles of men and woman and the definitions of masculinity and femininity. They provide vivid and sensitive explorations of female aspiration and partial autonomy but show the ways in which it is constricted by social pressures and male and female anxieties. They are also sensitive to masculine insecurities and humiliations. They show a world in which the appeal of sharply defined and differentiated male and female roles and identities remains strong but in which attempts to enforce them prove damaging for both men and women. Fitzgerald's novels imply an ideal of balance between masculine and feminine qualities (within and between individuals) but strongly register the difficulties of realizing this ideal within the kinds of society they portray.

Methods of Analysis

- We examined the kinds of sentences used in the extracts, looking at their length and structure and, where appropriate, suggesting how these contributed to their meaning (e.g. the long sentence in *Gatsby* describing the momentum of Tom's lawn; the sentence in *Tender* where the insertion of a participial phrase into the rendering of Nicole's thoughts indicates Dick's continued influence upon her).
- We discussed the diction and focused on words that seemed significant (e.g. the derogatory adjectives applied to Jordan in *Gatsby*; the use of the term 'fumbling' to suggest Dick's physical decline in *Tender*).

- We identified significant examples of imagery (e.g. the automobile metaphors of 'shifts' and 'brakes' in *Gatsby*; the image of Dick's 'expertise with people' as a 'tarnished object of art' in *Tender*).
- We drew attention to significant *intratextual* links (e.g. between the nouns 'lever' in the extract and 'leverage' in chapter 2 of *Gatsby*; between the 'swinging rings' in this extract and the 'flying rings' in Book 2, chapter 1 of *Tender*).
- We pointed out important *intertextual* links (e.g. between the use of the word 'bright' in *Gatsby* and in Swinburne's poetry; between the image of Dick as a 'ghost' in *Tender* and the image of Wilson as a 'ghost' in *Gatsby*).
- We traced the representations of gender and gender relationships evident in the extracts (e.g. the sense of blocked energies in men and women in *Gatsby*; Nicole's move from the sway of Dick to the sway of Tommy in *Tender*).

Suggested Work

Examine the two following passages. The first, from *Gatsby*, is a portrayal of a vital female and a vapid male – Myrtle and George Wilson. The passage conveys the material poverty of the Wilsons but sharply contrasts Wilson's lack of substance and spark with Myrtle's strong physical presence and smouldering energy. The second, from *Tender*, is the reunion in Rome between Dick and Rosemary Hoyt, who, as a young film star, is economically independent, like Jordan Baker. Dick has been 'the ideal by which [she] measured other men', but she has to adjust to the man he now is and finally consummates the relationship which 'had begun with a childish infatuation on a beach'.

Analyse the style of these passages, try to sum up the gender positions and interrelations they portray, and explore how they may link up with wider aspects of contemporary society (the lack of outlets for a woman like Myrtle, of material and emotional support for a man such as George; the combination of independence and vulnerability in relatively emancipated young woman like Jordan (who, we infer, is hurt by Nick's rejection of her) or Rosemary).

[a] *Gatsby.* 'I followed him over a low whitewashed railroad fence ... '
     to ' ... just as George Wilson emerged with two chairs from his
     office door' (*GG* 27–9)

[b] *Tender.* '"Tell me the truth about you," he demanded.' to ' ... what
     had begun with a childish infatuation on a beach was accomplished
     at last'. (*TN* 230–3)

5

Trauma

Both *Gatsby* and *Tender* are marked by the international trauma of the First World War; in *Gatsby*, Gatsby and Nick are veterans of that war and in *Tender*, Dick, Abe North (also a veteran) and Rosemary visit a Somme battlefield. The novels are also marked by physical and psychological trauma as it impacts on individuals: physically, there is the breaking of Myrtle's nose by Tom Buchanan in *Gatsby* and the breaking of Dick's nose and rib by the Italian police in *Tender*; the shooting of Jules Peterson and the beating to death of Abe North in *Tender*; the mutilation and death of Myrtle in *Gatsby* when Gatsby's car, driven by Daisy, hits her; and the murder of Gatsby and the suicide of Wilson in *Gatsby*. Psychologically, *Gatsby* shows the title character's despair (as Nick imagines it) after his loss of Daisy, and the grief of Wilson after Myrtle's death and of Nick after Gatsby's death; while *Tender* depicts the reawakening of Nicole's memories of her father's incestuous rape by the bloodied bedclothes she sees after Peterson's murder, and Dick's final knowledge that he has lost Nicole.

An analysis of Fitzgerald's style in his accounts of these traumas demonstrates its economy and power, its capacity to convey violence, death and loss in an unsparing but understated way. We begin with Myrtle's death in *Gatsby*.

Blood in the Dust: *The Great Gatsby*, pp. 131–2

The 'death car' as the newspapers called it, didn't stop; it came out of the gathering darkness, wavered tragically for a moment, and then disappeared around the next bend. Mavromichaelis wasn't even sure of its colour – he told the first policeman that it was light green. The other car, the one going towards New York, came to rest a hundred yards beyond, and its driver hurried back to where Myrtle Wilson, her life violently extinguished, knelt in the road and mingled her thick dark blood with the dust.

Michaelis and this man reached her first, but when they had torn open her shirtwaist, still damp with perspiration, they saw that her left breast was swinging loose like a flap, and there was no need to listen for the heart beneath. The mouth was wide open and ripped a little at the corners, as though she had choked a little in giving up the tremendous vitality she had stored so long.

*

We saw the three or four automobiles and the crowd when we were still some distance away.

'Wreck!' said Tom. 'That's good. Wilson'll have a little business at last.'

He slowed down, but still without any intention of stopping, until, as we came nearer, the hushed, intent faces of the people at the garage door made him automatically put on the brakes.

'We'll take a look,' he said doubtfully, 'just a look.'

I became aware now of a hollow, wailing sound which issued incessantly from the garage, a sound which as we got out of the coupé and walked toward the door resolved itself into the words, 'Oh, my God!' uttered over and over in a gasping moan.

'There's some bad trouble here,' said Tom excitedly.

He reached up on tiptoes and peered over a circle of heads into the garage, which was lit only by a yellow light in a swinging metal basket overhead. Then he made a harsh sound in his throat, and with a violent thrusting movement of his powerful arms pushed his way through.

The circle closed up again with a running murmur of expostulation; it was a minute before I could see anything at all. Then new arrivals deranged the line, and Jordan and I were pushed suddenly inside.

Myrtle Wilson's body, wrapped in a blanket, and then in another blanket, as though she suffered from a chill in the hot night, lay on a work-table by the wall, and Tom, with his back to us, was bending over it, motionless. Next to him stood a motor-cycle policeman taking down names with much sweat and correction in a little book. At first I couldn't find the source of the high, groaning words that echoed clamorously through the bare garage – then I saw Wilson standing on the raised threshold of his office, swaying back and forth and holding to the doorposts with both hands. Some man was talking to him in a low voice and attempting, from time to time, to lay a hand on his shoulder, but Wilson neither heard nor saw. His eyes would drop slowly from the swinging light to the laden table by the wall, and then jerk back to the light again, and he gave out incessantly his high, horrible call:

'Oh, my Ga-od! Oh, my Ga-od! Oh, Ga-od! Oh, my Ga-od!'

This extract starkly conveys the mutilation and death of Myrtle and Wilson's grief. In the first section, Nick describes a key event he himself has not witnessed by drawing on testimony at the inquest into Myrtle's death and on newspaper reports. It exemplifies one of the ways in which Fitzgerald overcomes a key limitation of a novel with only one main first-person narrator; that such a novel, if it is to remain probable, can only describe what the narrator sees and experiences. It is, however, possible to supplement this with the accounts of others, mediated through the narrator, and this is Fitzgerald's technique in *Gatsby*. Here, Michaelis, the young Greek who runs the café in the valley of ashes, and who serves as Wilson's primary comforter after Myrtle's death, is the main eyewitness. The extract begins with Nick taking a phrase from newspaper accounts, 'the death car', which is both a kind of journalistic cliché and a reinforcement of a key strand in the novel – the destructive as well as liberating power of the automobile. The emergence of this 'death-car' from 'the gathering darkness' seems deeply ominous. The actual impact of the car upon Myrtle is not described – we are told that it 'wavered tragically' and only the adverb suggests something very bad has happened. Michaelis's uncertainty about the car's colour is an aspect of the wider uncertainty which surrounds the whole event (it is left to the African American witness, the 'pale well-dressed Negro', to identify the car's colour correctly as 'yellow' (*GG* 133)). But the initial ambiguity about the car's colour does not extend to its driver; while Nick will later guess that Daisy rather than Gatsby was behind the wheel, no one else makes this suggestion, at least publicly.

After the evasive statement that the car 'wavered tragically', the passage continues to soft-pedal by stating that the other car 'came to rest', a rather roundabout and dignified way of saying that it stopped; it suggests a projectile reaching the end of its trajectory but implies a disciplined rather than desperate surcease of motion. In the context, the word 'rest' also hints at the familiar tombstone inscription 'Rest in Peace'. It is only with the verb 'hurried' that the pace of the passage accelerates, and the first explicit sense of the brutality of the impact and of its lethal consequence is given in the words 'her life violently extinguished'. 'Extinguished' is a term most usually applied to fires and suggests a certain fiery quality in the living Myrtle, who seemed, when Nick first met her, 'as if the nerves of her body were continually smouldering' (*GG* 28). The verb 'knelt', with its religious associations of praying, implies that she is paying unwilling homage to the strange god of this place, Dr T.J. Eckleburg (we observed in the previous chapter how 'knelt' is also used of Dick on the tow-board and we shall see, in our analysis of the second extract in this chapter, how it is also used of Nicole). The adjectives 'thick' and 'dark' powerfully convey the viscous quality of Myrtle's blood, and we can make an intertextual link here between the noun 'dust' and the phrase 'earth to earth, ashes to ashes, dust to dust' in the burial service in the Book of Common Prayer (1662), which calls to mind the ashes in the valley which surrounds her.

The paragraph that follows is unusually graphic and physical for Fitzgerald (compare the indirect description of the dead Gatsby, to be discussed later in this chapter). Although it is a sense of medical emergency which makes Michaelis and the male driver of the New York-bound car tear open Myrtle's shirtwaist, their action is also a kind of violation; in another context, it could look like sexual assault. The description of the shirtwaist as 'still damp with perspiration' brings across the corporeal aliveness and sexual potential which Myrtle possessed until a few moments ago. But any hope that she may have survived is cancelled by the sight of the breast, which still retains its erotic and maternal associations but is now partly dissociated from the totality of a body, as in a cubist painting, and has a mechanical rather than vital motion: 'swinging loose like a flap'. This sight prevents the two men from making any closer physical contact with Myrtle and serves as a metonymy for her deadness.

The focus then shifts from breast to mouth, wide open but silent (contrast this muteness with Myrtle's volubility in chapter 2 of *Gatsby*). The sense of the violence of her death is intensified by the terms 'ripped', suggesting a forcible tearing and applying to her torn breast as well as to her mouth, and 'choked', implying obstruction of the throat and the state of speechlessness produced by strong emotion. Both these terms convey not only the violence of Myrtle's death but also the constriction of her life; the diminishing phrase 'a little', which follows both 'ripped' and 'choked', poignantly indicates the limited scope of her last, desperate dash for freedom which has ended in fatality rather than fulfilment. The final simile reminds us of Myrtle's huge energies, with its invocation of a 'tremendous vitality' which has been stored, only to be given up in death; the verb 'giving up' is an echo of the phrase 'give up the ghost', meaning to die or to stop functioning, to yield up the spirit.

The first two paragraphs of the extract make it unequivocally clear, before Nick himself sees the body, that Myrtle is dead, and they graphically convey her mutilation. The narrative then shifts from Nick's paraphrase of the inquest testimony to Nick's own eyewitness (and earwitness) account. At first Tom does not plan to stop and it is only when he sees 'the hushed, intent faces of the people at the garage door' that he brakes 'automatically', an adverb suggesting, at this stage, a merely reflex, unthinking response. He expresses a voyeuristic desire to 'take a look', but it is the sense of hearing rather than sight which is activated initially and marks Nick's first direct mention of his own reactions. Nick hears a 'hollow', 'wailing' and 'incessant' sound which only becomes audible as a repeated 'Oh, my God!' as they approach the garage door. The prospect of 'bad trouble' excites Tom, who still does not feel personally involved. It is only when he looks over the head of the crowd that he himself responds with a primal noise – 'a harsh sound in his throat' – and uses his physical strength to push through the crowd.

Although the reader already knows that Myrtle is dead, the actual sight of the body still comes as a shock, because we share in its impact on Nick and Tom. Characteristically, Nick does not describe his own feelings but concentrates first of all on a clear description of what he sees. The first sentence of the paragraph might issue from an impersonal, third-person narrator. The simile 'as though she suffered from a chill in the hot night' is an effective one because it does suggest the sort of reason that Myrtle, from what we have previously seen of her liking for creature comforts, might have had for wrapping blankets around herself if she were still alive: it poignantly summons up her living image to set against her dead one. Nick's attention is then captured again by the 'high, groaning words' – words now rather than inarticulate noise – which he can hear but whose source he cannot initially locate. Then sound is followed by the sight of Wilson: the present participles which describe Wilson's actions – 'standing', 'swaying', 'holding' – give the sense that he is engaged in incessant, repetitive motion to match his incessant, repetitive words of distress. The man who is trying to comfort him is similarly engaged in repeated if less constant actions: 'talking', 'attempting' to lay a hand on his shoulder. But it is made clear that Wilson is obsessed with only one thing.

The phrase 'laden table', which could in other circumstances refer to a table loaded with good things, with food for feasting, takes on an ironic dimension here, since the table is 'laden' only with the deadweight of Myrtle's corpse (the same adjective will be applied to Gatsby's corpse on the pneumatic mattress in his swimming pool, as we shall discuss later in this chapter). The adverb 'incessantly' is repeated to convey the seeming endlessness of Wilson's call. When Nick renders this call in direct speech, 'God' splits into two syllables, and the first syllable – 'Ga' – is also that of Gatsby's name. The portrayal of Wilson's grief is an unremitting representation of acute, ongoing trauma which needs some kind of closure.

The second example of trauma we shall consider, from *Tender*, also involves the aftermath of a violent death, the murder of Jules Peterson, and the reawakening of the incest trauma of Nicole Diver.

Blood on the Bed: *Tender is the Night*, pp. 123–6

The body, as Dick lifted it, was light and ill-nourished. He held it so that further hemorrhages from the wound would flow into the man's clothes. Laying it beside the bed he stripped off the coverlet and top blanket and then opening the door an inch, listened – there was a clank of dishes down the hall followed by a loud patronizing 'Mer*ci*, Madame,' but the waiter went in the other direction, toward the service stairway. Quickly

Dick and Nicole exchanged bundles across the corridor; after spreading this covering on Rosemary's bed, Dick stood sweating in the warm twilight, considering. Certain points had become apparent to him in the moment following his examination of the body; first, that Abe's first hostile Indian had tracked the friendly Indian and discovered him in the corridor, and when the latter had taken desperate refuge in Rosemary's room, had hunted down and slain him; second, that if the situation were allowed to develop naturally, no power on earth could keep the smear off Rosemary – the paint was scarcely dry on the Arbuckle case. Her contract was contingent upon an obligation to continue rigidly and unexceptionally as 'Daddy's Girl.'

Automatically Dick made the old motion of turning up his sleeves though he wore a sleeveless undershirt, and bent over the body. Getting a purchase on the shoulders of the coat he kicked open the door with his heel, and dragged the body quickly into a plausible position in the corridor. He came back into Rosemary's room and smoothed back the grain of the plush floor rug. Then he went to the phone in his suite and called the manager-owner of the hotel.

'MacBeth? – it's Doctor Diver speaking – something very important. Are we on a more or less private line?'

It was good that he had made the extra effort which had firmly entrenched him with Mr MacBeth. Here was one use for all the pleasingness that Dick had expended over a large area he would never retrace ...

'Going out of the suite we came upon a dead Negro ... in the hall ... no, no, he's a civilian. Wait a minute now – I knew you didn't want any guests to blunder on the body so I'm phoning you. Of course I must ask you to keep my name out of it. I don't want any French red tape just because I discovered the man.'

What exquisite consideration for the hotel! Only because Mr MacBeth, with his own eyes, had seen these traits in Doctor Diver two nights before, could he credit the story without question.

In a minute Mr MacBeth arrived and in another minute he was joined by a gendarme. In the interval he found time to whisper to Dick, 'You can be sure the name of any guest will be protected. I'm only too grateful to you for your pains.'

Mr MacBeth took an immediate step that may only be imagined, but that influenced the gendarme so as to make him pull his mustaches in a frenzy of uneasiness and greed. He made perfunctory notes and sent a telephone call to his post. Meanwhile with a celerity that

Jules Peterson, as a business man, would have quite understood, the remains were carried into another apartment of one of the most fashionable hotels in the world.

Dick went back to his salon.

'What *hap*pened?' cried Rosemary. 'Do all the Americans in Paris just shoot at each other all the time?'

'This seems to be the open season,' he answered. 'Where's Nicole?'

'I think she's in the bathroom.'

She adored him for saving her – disasters that could have attended upon the event had passed in prophecy through her mind; and she had listened in wild worship to his strong, sure, polite voice making it all right. But before she reached him in a sway of soul and body his attention focussed on something else: he went into the bedroom and toward the bathroom. And now Rosemary, too, could hear, louder and louder, a verbal inhumanity that penetrated the keyholes and the cracks in the doors, swept into the suite and in the shape of horror took form again.

With the idea that Nicole had fallen in the bathroom and hurt herself, Rosemary followed Dick. That was not the condition of affairs at which she stared before Dick shouldered her back and brusquely blocked her view.

Nicole knelt beside the tub swaying sidewise and sidewise. 'It's you!' she cried, ' – it's you come to intrude on the only privacy I have in the world – with your spread with red blood on it. I'll wear it for you – I'm not ashamed, though it was such a pity. On All Fools Day we had a party on the Zurichsee, and all the fools were there, and I wanted to come dressed in a spread but they wouldn't let me – '

'Control yourself!'

' – so I sat in the bathroom and they brought me a domino and said wear that. I did. What else could I do?'

'Control yourself, Nicole!'

'I never expected you to love me – it was too late – only don't come in the bathroom, the only place I can go for privacy, dragging spreads with red blood on them and asking me to fix them.'

'Control yourself. Get up – '

Rosemary, back in the salon, heard the bathroom door bang, and stood trembling: now she knew what Violet McKisco had seen in the bathroom at Villa Diana. She answered the ringing phone and almost cried with relief when she found it was Collis Clay, who had traced her to the Divers' apartment. She asked him to come up while she got her hat, because she was afraid to go into her room alone.

Rosemary has summoned Dick urgently into her bedroom where she has found the body of the Swedish African Jules Peterson, an unsuccessful entrepreneur who has been the victim in what Dick, just before this extract begins, has called, with casual, dismissive, belittling racism 'only some nigger scrap'. But the brief description of the body as 'light and ill-nourished' at the start of the extract conveys the pathos of Jules's life and death. Dick's apparent priority is to save Rosemary's reputation by getting Peterson's corpse out of her bedroom but he seems to fail to realize the impact the bloodstained coverlet and sheet may have on Nicole – or perhaps, on some level, he is perpetrating an act of aggression against his wife/patient. His concern for Rosemary and lack of consideration for Nicole mark a stage in the decline of his marriage and perhaps in his own deterioration. The bloodied bedclothes plunge Nicole once more into crisis, reawakening the original trauma of her rape by her father and also activating her present jealousy by suggesting that Dick may just have taken Rosemary's virginity. This in turn is a traumatic moment for Rosemary, who sees and hears with her own eyes Nicole's hitherto concealed craziness. The passage is notable for its contrast between the rational narrative prose which depicts Dick's swift actions and the vivid associative discourse of Nicole, which has a potent surrealistic logic of its own as it wells up from deep and damaged levels of her being.

The first paragraph has the pace and directness of a thriller. Told in the third person from Dick's point of view, it shows Dick thinking and acting swiftly and decisively. Nicole seems to function with great efficiency in the exchange of coverlets and blankets, but she says nothing and the narrator does not admit the reader to her point of view, so we can only imagine her feelings and thoughts. The description of Dick's thoughts at this point focuses first of all on his analysis of why Peterson was killed and how he got into Rosemary's bedroom, and then on the urgency of protecting Rosemary from possible scandal and the cancellation of her contract. He calls to mind the real-life case of the popular comedy film star Roscoe 'Fatty' Arbuckle (1887–1933), whose career was destroyed when he was tried for the manslaughter of a young starlet, Virginia Rappe, even though, after three trials, he was eventually acquitted. Rosemary has to continue as 'Daddy's Girl', a title which, in this context, relates not only to her public image but also to her relationship with

Dick: he acts here as Rosemary's protective father. But there is another 'Daddy's Girl' whom he seems to forget: Nicole.

The extract goes on to show Dick's continued command of the situation: he puts the body in the corridor, smoothes Rosemary's rug which has been ruffled by the corpse being dragged over it, and phones the manager who has the ominous name 'MacBeth'. In making the call, Dick announces himself as 'Doctor' Diver, assuming the mantle of the medical practitioner. Dick congratulates himself on the effort he has made to get into MacBeth's good books, and there is a brief point-of-view shift to MacBeth himself, which indicates that the hotel manager unquestioningly believes Dick's story because he has already seen for himself Dick's considerateness. MacBeth arrives in a minute and a gendarme arrives within another minute: if taken literally, these would be improbable speeds, but they are examples of hyperbole, of deliberate exaggeration which is not meant to be taken literally, and they function to suggest a slightly magical quality in the way in which Dick's decisive and swift management seems to resolve a potentially nightmarish situation. The motif of speed is continued in the use of the archaic or literary term 'celerity' for swiftness of movement and the narrator jokes grimly that Peterson would have 'quite understood' the swiftness with which his corpse was moved to another apartment 'of one of the most fashionable hotels in the world' – a phrase which sets up an ironic contrast between the opulence of Peterson's surroundings and his malnourishment and poverty.

When Dick, having worked his magic, returns to Rosemary, their exchange has a witty, sophisticated quality – there is no sense of sympathy for Peterson. Rosemary's question – 'Do all the Americans in Paris just shoot at each other all the time?' – refers to the earlier incident in chapter 19 when Dick, Rosemary and others were seeing Abe off and a man was shot at the entrance to a Pullman car (*TN* 95). Dick responds facetiously – 'This seems to be the open season' – but his next question, 'Where's Nicole?' could suggest that he is experiencing anxiety about his wife, apparently for the first time in this situation. Rosemary replies that she thinks Nicole is 'in the bathroom', a location that links up with the bathroom in the Villa Diana that Violet McKisco visited at the end of chapter 7 in Book 1 (*TN* 45, 46) and saw a scene which clearly made a large impression on her but which she did not, at that point, reveal.

There is then, in this extract, a switch to Rosemary's point of view, which shows her idolatry of Dick for rescuing her from disaster. The diction here takes on a romantic, quasi-religious quality: 'saving'; 'prophecy'; 'wild worship'; 'soul'. But as Rosemary moves towards Dick – presumably for an embrace – she registers his shift of attention and his own movement towards the bathroom. As in the scene in *Gatsby* which we have just discussed, at the garage immediately after Myrtle's death, the initial emphasis is on hearing rather than sight; acute human distress is first announced through sound. To begin with, as in *Gatsby*, no precise words emerge: there is a sense of increasing volume – 'louder and louder' – and the adjectives and nouns used to describe the sound are abstract, suggesting a phenomenon which words cannot specify exactly: 'a verbal inhumanity'; 'the shape of horror'. But the passage does strongly convey how the sound, like some monstrous, quasi-supernatural figure, moves into and takes over the whole apartment: forceful verbs denote its movements – 'penetrated', 'swept'; precise names identify the orifices and apertures through which it passes – 'the keyholes and the cracks in the doors'; there is a sense of something that can change its shape and split itself up in order to get through any kind of space, however minimal, and which can then reform. It seems a palpable but not wholly material horror, like the visitations of evil evoked in Fitzgerald's first novel *This Side of Paradise* (1920) (*TP* 102–6) and in the story 'A Short Trip Home' (1927) (*TR* 273–93, esp. 289–92). After the thriller element which has just preceded it, it is a kind of excursion into a modern gothic mode, in which horror emerges, not in an old castle or mansion but in 'one of the most fashionable hotels in the world'.

The next paragraph stays with Rosemary's point of view and her own temporary interpretation of the situation – that Nicole has fallen and injured herself in the bathroom. The narrator then indicates that Rosemary has got it wrong but does not instantly give the right answer, delaying the resolution of the puzzle with the formal, slightly arch beginning of the next sentence: 'That was not the condition of affairs.' But the verb 'stared' suggests that the sight is unexpected and compelling, even though Dick prevents Rosemary from staring for long. At this point a different Dick emerges; he is no longer graceful and considerate, but uses his body aggressively, like Tom Buchanan pushing through the crowd in Wilson's garage after Myrtle's death. Rosemary is 'shouldered' back and her view 'brusquely blocked'. The words imply an element of coercion in Dick's concealment of Nicole's condition, not only in this instance but also more generally.

With her view thus impeded, Rosemary has only had a brief glimpse of Nicole, but it is nonetheless significant: 'Nicole knelt by the tub swaying sidewise and sidewise.' We can compare this with how, in *Gatsby*, Myrtle 'knelt' in the road after being hit by the car, mingling her blood with the dust (*GG* 131). Both passages make a link between kneeling, trauma and blood, with their religious associations. The present participle 'swaying' is used to describe Nicole's movements as it is of Wilson's 'swaying back and forth and holding to the garage doorposts' in his garage after Myrtle's death. With Nicole, as with Wilson, the participle suggests the incessant, repetitive quality of the movements; the accumulation of alliterative 's' sounds in *Tender* reinforces this. But the primary emphasis on sound, on what Rosemary hears, remains; the exchange between Dick and Nicole is rendered in dialogue.

In contrast to the verbal repetition of Wilson, with his reiterations of 'Oh my Ga-od', Nicole's words are much more varied, working with a vivid associative logic whose leading motif is the 'spread with red blood on it'. This is what seems to have reawakened her original incest trauma. Nicole appears to conflate three situations: the original trauma; the All Fools' Day party when she was in the clinic on the Zurichsee; and their present situation, which involves two sources of trauma: the dead Jules Peterson and the possibility that Dick may have taken Rosemary's virginity. Nicole sees the bathroom as the only place in which she can achieve privacy, free from the attentions of a figure who is either her father or Dick, or sometimes both at once. A part of her seems to want to blazon forth her original trauma – to wear a spread – but she has been forbidden to do so and told to wear a domino – a loose cloak worn with a mask for the upper part of the face. The apparent implication here is that she has been barred from publicly articulating and acknowledging her original trauma and forced to mask it, to put on a disguise in order to avoid damaging her family by scandal.

Compared to Nicole's driven but vivid discourse, what we hear of Dick's contribution to the dialogue consists chiefly of imperatives: 'Control yourself', twice repeated, and 'Get up – .' It is a coercive, authoritarian approach which lacks empathy. Possibly it is due to

Rosemary's presence and Dick's desire to protect her – and to maintain Rosemary's image of himself and his marriage which might, if disrupted, make him less attractive to her. But it may also indicate that Nicole's demands have drained Dick; that he has heard all this, or something like it, before and can no longer respond in a sympathetic and resourceful way; that he is, quite simply, tired of being Nicole's doctor and nurse as well as her husband. This dialogue contrasts sharply with the exchange between Dick and Nicole which Rosemary overheard five years before, in Book 1, chapter 12, just before her shopping expedition with Nicole, when husband and wife avowed their passion for each other and arranged to meet to make love later that day (we discussed this in chapter 3). Here their dialogue is at cross-purposes and shot through with mistrust and anger.

We shift back to Rosemary's point of view, as the 'bang' of the bathroom door cuts short the dialogue between Dick and Nicole. The adjective 'trembling' is the first sign of the effect on Rosemary of what she has seen and heard – as when she overheard Dick and Nicole arranging to make love, an intimate revelation impacts initially on her body. An explicit link is made to the enigma of what 'Violet McKisco had seen in the bathroom at Villa Diana': this enigma is now resolved, but painfully. The phone call from Rosemary's admirer, Collis Clay, is a relief. She is glad that he will accompany her into her room, which she fears to enter alone because when she last did so she found a corpse, and the scene in the bathroom has now shaken her further.

This extract shows both Nicole and Rosemary experiencing multiple traumas. For Nicole, it is the reactivation of her original incest trauma; the ongoing trauma of having to conceal that original trauma from the world (to wear a domino, a mask); and the fresh trauma of the bloodied bedclothes. For Rosemary, it is the trauma of finding Peterson's corpse in her room, on her bed, and the trauma of the discovery of the distress behind the bright façade of Nicole's public mask and the Divers' marriage. Dick, caught between two traumatized women, loses his grace and resourcefulness and becomes physically boorish (roughly blocking Rosemary's view) and orally authoritarian (ordering Nicole to control herself in a situation where she seems to have lost the capacity to do so). The extract moves with remarkable effectiveness from a thriller mode (Dick's deft management of the body) to a romantic mode

(Rosemary's adoration of Dick for saving her) to a modern gothic mode (the inhuman sound that takes possession of the hotel suite), to a realist mode which strongly conveys the effect of trauma on language (Nicole's associative discourse) and on the body (Rosemary's trembling). Falling as it does at the end of the first section of the book as originally published, the passage makes a powerful contribution to the overall themes and emotional impact of *Tender*.

We will now explore a third example of trauma, this time from *Gatsby*.

Death of a Dream: *The Great Gatsby*, pp. 153–4

At two o'clock Gatsby put on his bathing-suit and left word with the butler that if anyone phoned word was to be brought to him at the pool. He stopped at the garage for a pneumatic mattress that had amused his guests during the summer, and the chauffeur helped him to pump it up. Then he gave instructions that the open car wasn't to be taken out under any circumstances – and this was strange, because the front right fender needed repair.

Gatsby shouldered the mattress and started for the pool. Once he stopped and shifted it a little, and the chauffeur asked him if he needed help, but he shook his head and in a moment disappeared among the yellowing trees.

No telephone message arrived, but the butler went without his sleep and waited for it until four o'clock – until long after there was anyone to give it to if it came. I have an idea that Gatsby himself didn't believe it would come, and perhaps he no longer cared. If that was true he must have felt that he had lost the old warm world, paid a high price for living too long with a single dream. He must have looked up at an unfamiliar sky through frightening leaves and shivered as he found what a grotesque thing a rose is and how raw the sunlight was upon the scarcely created grass. A new world, material without being real, where poor ghosts, breathing dreams like air, drifted fortuitously about … like that ashen, fantastic figure gliding toward him through the amorphous trees.

The chauffeur – he was one of Wolfshiem's protégés – heard the shots – afterwards he could only say that he hadn't thought anything much about them. I drove from the station directly to Gatsby's house and my rushing anxiously up the front steps was the first thing that alarmed anyone. But they knew then, I firmly believe. With scarcely a word said, four of us, the chauffeur, butler, gardener, and I hurried down to the pool.

There was a faint, barely perceptible movement of the water as the fresh flow from one end urged its way toward the drain at the other. With little ripples that were hardly the shadows of waves, the laden mattress moved irregularly down the pool. A small gust of wind that scarcely corrugated the surface was enough to disturb its accidental course with its accidental burden. The touch of a cluster of leaves revolved it slowly, tracing, like the leg of transit, a thin red circle in the water.

It was after we started with Gatsby toward the house that the gardener saw Wilson's body a little way off in the grass, and the holocaust was complete.

In the first three paragraphs of this extract, Nick reconstructs the last hour of Gatsby's life; he does not state his sources, but his account is presumably based partly on evidence given by the butler and chauffeur at the inquest (perhaps supplemented by newspaper reports) and partly on his own imaginative reconstruction of Gatsby's state of mind. These paragraphs provide a further example of how Fitzgerald in *Gatsby*, while using a first-person narrator, can describe convincingly events which that narrator has not directly experienced. Nick does not use the first-person pronoun 'I' in these paragraphs (indeed, he only uses it four times in the whole extract); he is effectively a third-person narrator. The opening sentence establishes a precise time – 'two o'clock' – indicates that Gatsby has changed into a bathing-suit, and suggests that he is still waiting for a phone call from Daisy. Gatsby pumps up the pneumatic mattress and orders that the open car should not be taken out under any circumstances, despite the damage to its front right fender.

Gatsby's instructions to the butler and chauffeur seem to be signs of a man still fully in control of his situation. But the change from the smart, vivid suits he usually wears into a bathing-suit nonetheless seems significant: for the first time since he became 'Jay Gatsby', he has taken off his costume, shown more of what lies beneath, made himself more vulnerable; there is an echo of James Gatz, the underclad youth in 'a torn green jersey and a pair of canvas pants' he was before he met Dan Cody (*GG* 94–5). The slightly ritualistic quality of this change of clothing is reinforced by the pumping up of the pneumatic mattress; the literal meaning of 'pneumatic' here is 'containing air under pressure', but the adjective can also mean 'belonging or relating to spiritual existence'. The current online *Oxford English Dictionary* gives examples which range from Edward Benlowes's *Theophilia* (1652) – 'Then did of th' Elements Dust Mans Bodie frame / A perfect Microcosm, the Same / He quickned [*sic*] with a sparkle of Pneumatick Flame' – to the journal *30 Days in Church and World* (1993): 'The spirit, beyond "the prison of the rational and psychological world", is the place where "pneumatic" man dips directly into the divine.'

It is as if Gatsby, a figure of high artifice, is now performing a series of rites which bring him into closer contact with the primal elements and bear him up spiritually, exposing more of his body to the air, putting air into the mattress on which he will float on water. When he shoulders the mattress and stops to shift it a little, he faintly echoes Christ carrying the cross, a figure going to his martyrdom (we can recall here the earlier image of him as 'a son of God' who 'must be about His Father's business' (*GG* 95)). The shaking of his head means that his last gesture is one of negation; his refusal of help suggests that he must go on alone; and the adjective 'yellowing' conveys a sense of autumnal decay which symbolizes Gatsby's declining dream.

The next paragraph starts in an unequivocally factual mode, again presumably based on the butler's inquest evidence. Then, for the first time in the extract, the pronoun 'I' is used to preface what is clearly announced as a speculation – 'I have an idea.' At this point, we shift from a supposedly evidence-based account to one emerging from Nick's imaginative empathy with Gatsby. Nick initially presents the account as provisional: 'I have an idea ... perhaps ...'. The next sentence starts with 'If', which grammatically is a conjunction introducing a conditional clause – 'If that was true'. From this conditional premise, Nick draws what is offered as an inevitable conclusion – 'If that was true, he must have felt ... '. Although it is possible to imagine that Gatsby might have felt otherwise, we tend to accept Nick's speculation at this stage, because it corresponds to what we already know of Gatsby.

Nick evokes what he believes to be Gatsby's trauma; his loss of 'the old warm world', the price he has paid for his prolonged obsessive aspiration (the economic metaphor of 'price' is appropriate, given the way in which his obsession with Daisy was bound up with money). The use of the modal verb, the 'must have' formulation, continues at the start of the next sentence (the conditional has now dropped away) and makes Nick's account seem increasingly authoritative, so that the reader does tend to feel: yes, Gatsby must have felt like this. Gatsby's feelings here are presented in terms of vision, of what he saw, as if – making the link with the eyes on Dr T.J. Eckleburg's advert and the Owl-Eyed Man at Gatsby's party and funeral – he has put on a pair of glasses which now enable him to see clearly. But clear sight is painful. The adjectives build up the intensity: the sky is 'unfamiliar', the leaves 'frightening', the rose 'grotesque', the sunlight 'raw' and the grass 'scarcely created', as if this were some early, unsuccessful version of the Garden of Eden, or a botched attempt at one of those 'fast movies' showing natural growth which Nick mentions in chapter 1 (*GG* 9).

The final sentence of this paragraph dispenses with any suggestion that Nick's account of Gatsby's state of mind is speculative: by this time, Nick has fully identified with Gatsby; he has, in a sense, become Gatsby, and the reader is likely to feel wholly convinced by his evocation of Gatsby's feelings and perceptions. It seems that Gatsby experiences much more than mere disappointment after the collapse of his dream, descending to a kind of existential nadir which partly resembles that of Roquentin in Jean-Paul Sartre's novel *Nausea* (1938). The opening phrase of the sentence, 'A new world', echoes the founding moment evoked at the end of *Gatsby*: the discovery of 'the new world' when the Dutch settlers first arrived in America. But whereas that 'new world' seemed novel, natural, nurturing and maternal, a 'fresh green breast', this one lacks true being: it is 'material without being real', a place of ghosts who live on the air of dreams – the air of which Daisy's desertion has now deprived Gatsby. It is a kind of modern version of the ancient underworld of classical myth, the abode of the dead. This haunting, haunted general picture then returns, after the ellipsis, to the fantastic reality of the 'ashen, fantastic figure gliding toward him through the amorphous trees'. This is Wilson, but he is not named at this point; instead, the sentence draws on terms used in earlier descriptions of him and of the valley of ashes: of Myrtle 'walking through her husband as if he were a ghost' (*GG* 28); of the valley of ashes as 'a fantastic farm' (*GG* 26). The present participle 'gliding' conveys Wilson's smooth movements and the adjective 'amorphous' indicates that the trees now have a formless quality.

In the next paragraph, the narrative returns from empathic imaginative speculation to factual, evidence-based reconstruction, even though there is something odd about the nature of the evidence, given that the chauffeur seems less a chauffeur than an agent of Wolfshiem and that he hears but does not think much about the shots. Is this because he is used to shots, since he is really a gangster? But shouldn't a gangster be even more alert to them? Does his response indicate that he knew Gatsby might be getting killed and chose to ignore it because Gatsby had become a liability for Wolfshiem? The following sentence brings Nick back directly into the narrative, now describing events he himself has experienced; his drive back to Gatsby's house, his anxious rush up the steps, his journey with the chauffeur, butler and gardener to the pool.

The subsequent paragraph describes the discovery of Gatsby's body floating on the pneumatic mattress, but it adopts a technique of indirection: we are not told, in so many words, that Gatsby's dead body lay on the mattress and Nick's feelings are not mentioned; he never uses the first-person pronoun here. Taken by itself, the paragraph might be by an impersonal third-person narrator. To some extent, it has a lyrical, peaceful quality which belies the violent crime scene it describes: several of its adjectives and adverbs indicate minimal movements: 'faint'; 'little'; 'small', 'thin'; 'barely'; 'hardly'; 'scarcely'; 'slowly'. There is, however, a much stronger sense of movement in the description of how 'the fresh flow from one end [of the pool] urged its way toward the drain at the other', and the trajectory here seems to be one of endless renewal and decline, from 'fresh flow' to 'drain' and back again – a repetitive rather than progressive motion which can be linked with the novel's final image of human beings as boats moving forward only to be borne back endlessly into the past.

The adjective 'laden', however, strikes an ominous note, if we recall the earlier use of this adjective to describe the table in Wilson's garage which bore Myrtle's body, in the extract discussed earlier in this chapter. The repetition of the term 'accidental' recalls Myrtle's fatal accident and suggests, more generally, the arbitrary nature of Gatsby's death. Like the account of the world drained of meaning after the collapse of Gatsby's dream, it seems to suggest that sense of absurdity, of meaninglessness, that will later be a key motif of mid-twentieth-century existentialism. Then at the end of the sentence comes the term 'burden', which literally means 'a heavy load', and metaphorically signifies 'a cause of hardship, worry or grief'. If we make an intertextual link with Christian's heavy spiritual burden in John Bunyan's *Pilgrim's Progress* (1678–84), this suggests that Nick will hereafter bear the burden of Gatsby's memory and that the narrative we are reading is an attempt to come to terms with this.

The 'cluster of leaves', linking back to the 'yellowing trees' among which Gatsby earlier disappeared, reminds the reader that it is autumn. The 'thin red circle' might be merely the after-image of the leaves as they slowly revolve the mattress, but they also suggest blood. The simile 'the leg of transit' means the leg of a compass, and we might make a further intertextual link here with a famous compass image in 'A Valediction: Forbidding Mourning' by the seventeenth-century English metaphysical poet John Donne. There the image affirms the continued union of two lovers who are physically parted but remain inseparably joined by their love like the two legs of a compass. If this association is borne in mind here, it contrasts ironically with the failure of Gatsby's union with Daisy. In a sense, it does seem, when they first meet again, that this union has survived their five-year physical parting and that they have remained joined though apart, like the two legs of Donne's compasses; but their union does not long survive their coming together again after five years. It is significant that the 'leg' in this passage is singular, isolated.

The last paragraph, consisting of one 28-word sentence, brings chapter 8 of the novel to an end. Although describing an action in which he takes part – the carrying of Gatsby's body towards his house – Nick uses the first-person plural pronoun 'we' rather than the first-person singular 'I'. As in the previous paragraph, he says nothing about his own feelings and leaves the reader to infer them; and it may be that, if the union between Daisy and Gatsby had already been broken before Gatsby's death, that death itself breaks the union between Gatsby and Nick. Ironically, Nick's conveyance of Gatsby to the house may be the first time he touches Gatsby physically – and it is notable he refers here to 'Gatsby', as if he were still alive, rather than to 'Gatsby's body'. By contrast, he bluntly speaks of 'Wilson's body' in the concluding paragraph. In this paragraph, the word 'holocaust' does not carry the weight of black enormity it would bear after the Second World War but it did, in Fitzgerald's time, denote mass destruction and slaughter as well as retaining its meaning of a sacrificial offering – and there is a sense in which Gatsby, Wilson and Myrtle have been sacrificed to preserve the stability of Tom and Daisy's marriage.

We look finally in this chapter at the trauma, in *Tender*, of Dick's loss of Nicole.

Cutting the Cord: *Tender is the Night*, pp. 322–4

She wandered about the house rather contentedly, resting on her achievement. She was a mischief, and that was a satisfaction; no longer was she a huntress of corralled game. Yesterday came back to her now in innumerable detail – detail that began to overlay her memory of similar moments when her love for Dick was fresh and intact. She began to slight that love, so that it seemed to have been tinged with sentimental habit from the first. With the opportunistic memory of women she scarcely recalled how she had felt when she and Dick had possessed each other in secret places around the corners of the world, during the month before they were married. Just so had she lied to Tommy last night, swearing to him that never before had she so entirely, so completely, so utterly …

… then remorse for this moment of betrayal, which so cavalierly belittled a decade of her life, turned her walk toward Dick's sanctuary.

Approaching noiselessly she saw him behind his cottage, sitting in a steamer chair by the cliff wall, and for a moment she regarded him silently. He was thinking, he was living a world completely his own and in the small motions of his face, the brow raised or lowered, the lips set and reset, the play of his hands, she saw him progress from phase to phase of his own story spinning out inside him, his own, not hers. Once he clenched his fists and leaned forward, once it brought into his face an expression of torment and despair – when this passed its stamp lingered in his eyes. For almost the first time in her life she was sorry for him – it is hard for those who have once been mentally afflicted to be sorry for those who are well, and though Nicole often paid lip service to the fact that he had led her back to the world she had forfeited, she had thought of him really as an inexhaustible energy, incapable of fatigue – she forgot the troubles she caused him at the moment when she forgot the troubles of her own that had prompted her. That he no longer controlled her – did he know that? Had he willed it all? – she felt as sorry for him as she had sometimes felt for Abe North and his ignoble destiny, sorry as for the helplessness of infants and the old.

She went up putting her arm around his shoulder and touching their heads together said:

'Don't be sad.'

He looked at her coldly.

'Don't touch me!' he said.

Confused she moved a few feet away.

'Excuse me,' he continued abstractedly. 'I was just thinking what I thought of you – '

'Why not add the new classification to your book?'

'I have thought of it – "Furthermore and beyond the psychoses and the neuroses – "'

'I didn't come over here to be disagreeable.'

'Then why *did* you come, Nicole? I can't do anything for you any more. I'm trying to save myself.'

'From my contamination?'

'Profession throws me in contact with questionable company sometimes.'

She wept with anger at the abuse.

'You're a coward! You've made a failure of your life, and you want to blame it on me.'

While he did not answer she began to feel the old hypnotism of his intelligence, sometimes exercised without power but always with substrata of truth under truth which she could not break or even crack. Again she struggled with it, fighting him with her small, fine eyes, with the plush arrogance of a top dog, with her nascent transference to another man, with the accumulated resentment of years; she fought him with her money and her faith that her sister disliked him and was behind her now; with the thought of the new enemies he was making with his bitterness, with her quick guile against his wine-ing and dine-ing slowness, her health and beauty against his physical deterioration, her unscrupulousness against his moralities – for this inner battle she used even her weaknesses – fighting bravely and courageously with the old cans and crockery and bottles, empty receptacles of her expiated sins, outrages, mistakes. And suddenly, in the space of two minutes she achieved her victory and justified herself to herself without lie or subterfuge, cut the cord forever. Then she walked, weak in the legs, and sobbing coolly, toward the household that was hers at last.

Dick waited until she was out of sight. Then he leaned his head forward on the parapet. The case was finished. Doctor Diver was at liberty.

The excerpt starts by describing Nicole's sense of 'achievement' at having become Tommy Barban's lover, a 'mischief' rather than 'a hunter of corralled game'; 'mischief' can mean a person who engages in playful behaviour but it also has more serious connotations, of a person who causes harm or trouble (its root is the old French 'mischief' from 'meschever', 'come to an unfortunate end'). The implication is that Nicole has a sense of achievement because she has proved that she can not only engage in playful behaviour but also act in a way that can cause harm or trouble; she has already done the latter in one of her manic destructive bouts, for example in Book 2, chapter 15, when she grabs the steering wheel when Dick is driving and almost kills herself and her husband and children (*TN* 210–12), but now she is doing it in a conscious, controlled way. She is no longer pursuing things which have been made easily available to her and which she can secure with little sense of achievement; the image of her being 'no longer a hunter of corralled game' conveys this development. The phrase 'corralled game' is almost an oxymoron, a near-contradiction in terms, since 'game' denotes wild creatures while to be 'corralled' is to be penned.

The passage subtly traces how Tommy displaces Dick in Nicole's mind and feelings. There is a reference back to the time when 'her love for Dick was fresh and intact'; 'intact' is a key word in *Tender*, as we mentioned in chapter 1 of this book when we examined the description of the youthful Dick in which he tells himself, using the third person, that 'he must be less intact', and the narrator remarks, 'He knew that the price of his intactness was incompleteness' (*TN* 130). If we connect the uses of 'intact' here and in the account of Dick's earlier life, the implication emerges that Nicole's earlier 'intact' love for Dick may also have entailed a certain incompleteness. Nicole herself starts to slight that love, and the narrator then intrudes with what might seem today an outrageously sexist statement: that Nicole exemplifies 'the opportunistic memory of women'. This sweeping and derogatory generalization recalls Nick Carraway's remark in *Gatsby* that '[d]ishonesty in a woman is a thing you never blame deeply' (*GG* 58–9), but it is more intrusive because it comes, not from a first-person narrator whose opinions are necessarily partial, but with the authority of a third-person omniscient narrator. The narrator goes on to correct Nicole's opportunistic memory by reminding the reader 'how she had felt when she and Dick had possessed each other in secret places around the corners of the world' in the month prior to their marriage, suggesting both the intense, intimate privacy of their relationship (glimpsed by Rosemary when she overheard their assignation to make love) and its peripatetic nature ('around ... the world'). This reminder cues the narrator's use of the verb 'lied' to describe how she told Tommy that their lovemaking was the best she had ever experienced – another example of 'dishonesty in a woman'. We can make an intertextual link between the use of the verb 'lied' in this context and its use in Shakespeare's Sonnet 138 which plays on 'lie' as deliberate untruth and 'lie' in the sense of having sex: 'Therefore I lie with her and she with me / And in our faults by lies we flattered be.'

The ellipses and paragraph break at this stage of the extract stress the redirection of Nicole's thoughts and her physical turn towards Dick's work-house. We then see Dick from Nicole's point of view; he is momentarily the unaware object of her gaze. It is another example of the role-reversal which occurs in Book 3 of *Tender*; Nicole is now in the position of the doctor observing the patient, interpreting his signs and symptoms. We are not given access to Dick's thoughts and feelings, but to Nicole's inferences about them and her view of his physical movements. The image of 'his own story spinning out inside him' suggests that these thoughts and feelings are taking a narrative form, but it is no longer a story which he and Nicole share, or to which the reader is privy. The extent of his inner turmoil is suggested, however, by the clenching of his fists and the 'expression of torment and despair' whose 'stamp' lingers in his eyes when it has passed. A further sign of the role-reversal, the change in the balance of power, is that Nicole now, almost for the first time, feels sorry for him. An insight into the way she once saw him is provided by the images of 'an inexhaustible energy, incapable of fatigue'.

An example of free indirect discourse is provided by the start of the sentence 'That he no longer controlled her – did he know that? Had he willed it all?' In direct discourse, in an interior monologue for instance, this would be: 'That he no longer controls me – does he know that? Did he will it all?' In indirect discourse, it would be: 'She reflected that he no longer controlled her and wondered whether he knew it and whether he had willed it all.' But the sentence is neither fully direct nor fully indirect. In this way it gives the reader the impression of coming closer to the texture of Nicole's thoughts than indirect discourse would while retaining the sense of a third-person narrator. Nicole's thought itself is an interesting one, suggesting that in some way Dick may have been responsible for what has now happened; his task was to cure Nicole and, in curing her, he has now lost her. The paragraph concludes by stressing her sympathy for Dick in a way that indicates how reduced he has become; he is now on a par with the hapless Abe North and with helpless children and elderly people.

We then move outside Nicole's mind to a description of an externally observable event: Nicole's putting her arm around Dick's shoulder and touching their heads together. This contact, intended to comfort, contrasts ironically with their passionate premarital contacts which the narrator has recently recalled. A sharp dialogue follows, in which Dick rejects Nicole's offered comfort and Nicole suggests she should be added as a case study to his book – the book which still awaits completion. As if confirming that her cure is complete, he declares that he can do nothing for her any more and that he is trying to save himself. Nicole takes this up provocatively, suggesting he desires to save himself from her 'contamination' – as if she were a disease – and Dick's response is an icy retreat into professional jargon. Nicole retaliates with fundamental accusations: that he is a coward and a failure and wants to blame her for it. Dick does not reply, perhaps because he recognizes the justice of her indictment, and also possibly because he sees that her capacity to indict him – to diagnose the moral and existential malaise of the man who was once her doctor – demonstrates that she has achieved autonomy and no longer needs him. But Dick's inner consciousness is not directly represented at this stage; we return to Nicole's point of view to witness her inner battle.

First Nicole starts to feel the 'hypnotism of his intelligence'; 'hypnotism' suggests a Svengali-like manipulation which is counteracted by the word 'intelligence' with its implications of the conscious and the rational and then by the word 'truth', with its image of rock-like, geological substrata against which she is powerless. The very long 117-word sentence that follows suggests the fierceness of her inner struggle and uses grammatical parallelism (in this case, the repetition of phrases starting with the preposition 'with') to bring together various aspects of her character and Dick's. There is an accumulation of disparate elements which recalls the list of Nicole's purchases in the extract considered in chapter 3 of this book: 'small, fine eyes'; 'plush arrogance of a top dog'; 'nascent transference to another man'; 'accumulated resentment of years'; 'money'; 'faith that her sister disliked him and was behind her now'. The sentence moves on to pit three aspects of Nicole against three aspects of Dick in a series of oppositions: 'her quick guile against his wine-ing and dine-ing slowness, her health and beauty against his physical deterioration, her unscrupulousness against his moralities'.

A metaphor for Nicole's inner weapons, 'old cans and crockery and bottles', follows; this evokes so vividly the kind of row in which people throw things at each other that it may momentarily be difficult to remember that all this is happening inside Nicole's head, that objects are not actually being hurled. But the sentence then extends the metaphor: the old cans, crockery and bottles are 'empty receptacles of her expiated sins, outrages, mistakes', as if she is clearing out her past as one might clear a cluttered pantry. The subsequent sentence declares Nicole's triumph and ends with the image of 'cut[ting] the cord forever', suggesting that, like a baby whose umbilical cord is severed, she has parted from the husband who was both her good father and also a sort of mother who nurtured her until she could be properly born. The last sentence of the paragraph drives home her victory. The argument, particularly the one that has just taken place within her, has left her physically weak in the legs and in tears; but the adverb 'coolly' which prefaces 'sobbing' indicates that the tears are not for searing unhappiness but for an emotional upset over which she is gaining control. The end of the sentence makes it clear she now possesses the household which she once shared with Dick. It is the final move in the struggle to determine what kind of house they would live in which had begun early in their marriage, with their arguments about whether Nicole's money should be used to pay for their residences.

In the last paragraph, which concludes the chapter, the point of view switches back to Dick; but we still see him mainly from the outside and gain no access to his thoughts and feelings. Compared to the long, complex sentences of the previous paragraph, the sentences here are short and simple, with no subordinate clauses. In contrast to the tumult of inner activity inside Nicole's head, only two of Dick's actions are described: one is passive – waiting until Nicole has gone; the other is minimally active – leaning his head forward on the parapet. Otherwise, as with Nick's response to Gatsby's death, we are left to infer Dick's feelings, and this perhaps makes the passage more eloquent. The two last sentences are both true and ironic: the case is finished because Dick has healed Nicole and in that respect has been a successful 'Doctor'; but this 'case' cannot simply be filed away and forgotten like a satisfactorily concluded medical case; it has entailed both the loss of his professional identity and the deeply traumatic personal loss of Nicole. Moreover, the 'liberty' he now enjoys is of an empty, purposeless kind since, like Gatsby on his last afternoon, he has lost the woman who gives his life meaning and has nothing else.

Conclusions

All these passages offer powerful accounts of trauma. They achieve their effects by a variety of means but detachment, indirection and understatement are especially important. For instance, the mutilation of Myrtle, the removal of Jules Peterson's corpse, and the laden mattress in the swimming pool which bears Gatsby's body are described in a detached way that omits explicit emotion. We imaginatively infer the feelings the bodies produce rather than hearing about them directly. In the case of the impact of Myrtle's death on Wilson, or of the reactivation of Nicole's incest trauma, the omission of emotional description suggests that rational language cannot articulate such deep wounds: only an almost ritualistic lament (Wilson) or a frantic burst of free association (Nicole) can begin to be adequate to the situation, and these are more powerful because they erupt in a context of disciplined prose. Gatsby's despair, as imagined by Nick, is rendered with almost philosophical precision. The finality of Dick's loss of Nicole is suggested to us indirectly, as we see him through Nicole's eyes and, when alone, in terms of a brief but eloquent physical gesture.

Fitzgerald is one of the great modern explorers of trauma in his fiction. He is concerned with ways in which people may be damaged physically and psychologically, through the oppression of others (Myrtle, Nicole) and also through the unintended consequences of their own idealism and aspiration (Gatsby and Dick). He develops a way of writing about trauma which is more powerful because it involves indirection, detachment and understatement. If he is a romantic modernist, he is also, in this respect, a classical writer: his concision and lack of emotional display in his most painful scenes echo an ancient Greek or Roman taciturnity and restraint (as some other Modernist work did). In their engagements with trauma, both *Gatsby* and *Tender* could be called modern tragedies.

A question that runs through both novels – implicitly in *Gatsby*, explicitly in *Tender* – is: what modes of healing are available for those who have suffered trauma but still live? We could say that Nick's writing of Gatsby's story is an attempt at self-healing and exemplifies the salving power of art – but we do not know whether Nick's composition cures him or merely prefaces his retreat into provincial obscurity (like Dick). In the modern world, the psychiatrist and psychotherapist represent an alternative mode of healing, which Dick – Doctor Diver – initially embodies. But once Dick marries Nicole and moves into moneyed leisure, he also becomes a kind of artist trying to fashion the lives of his wife and friends. This helps to heal Nicole but leaves Dick bereft. We can compare and contrast Dick's bereft state with Gatsby's after the death of his dream. Gatsby has also been a kind of artist (though perhaps a bad one, as our first chapter suggested) who has tried to fashion an earthly paradise in which the attainment of Daisy will be the crowning glory. When the collapse of this grandiose scheme leaves him bereft, Wilson solves the problem of what to do next (Gatsby's death could be a kind of suicide; wouldn't a combat-hardened ex-soldier and ruthless gangster always be alert to the possibility of armed ambush and well able to defend himself if he wanted to?). But Dick, it seems, is a survivor; he has to go on living and must come to terms with his loss. Both *Gatsby* and *Tender* address the issue of the proper response to trauma and of how, and to what extent, it can be healed.

Methods of Analysis

- We examined the kinds of sentences used in the extracts, looking at their length and structure and, where appropriate, suggesting how these contributed to their meaning (e.g. the sentence in *Gatsby* starting with 'If' which speculates on Gatsby's state of mind on the last afternoon of his life; the 117-word sentence in *Tender*, with its grammatical parallelisms, which describe Nicole's feelings and thoughts in the build-up to her final breach with Dick).

- We discussed the diction and focused on words that seemed significant (e.g. 'ripped' and 'choked' in the description of the dead Myrtle; 'intact' in relation to Nicole in *Tender*).

- We identified significant examples of imagery (e.g. in *Gatsby* the image of Myrtle's breast 'swinging loose like a flap'; the metaphor of Nicole cutting the cord which binds her to Dick in *Tender*).

- We drew attention to significant *intratextual* links (e.g. between the phrase 'the death car' and the motif in *Gatsby* of the automobile as destructive as well as liberating; between Rosemary's sight of Nicole in the hotel bathroom and the hitherto enigmatic scene witnessed by Violet McKisco in the Villa Diana bathroom).

- We pointed out important *intertextual* links (e.g. in *Gatsby* between the noun 'dust' in the graphic description of the dead Myrtle and the phrase 'dust to dust' in the Book of Common Prayer; between the 'leg of transit [compass]' in the description of the floating mattress bearing Gatsby's body and the compass image in John Donne's poem 'A Valediction: Forbidding Mourning').

- We traced the representations of trauma evident in the extracts, noting Fitzgerald's capacity for direct, graphic presentation (e.g. in the description of the dead Myrtle) and his more frequent technique of indirection and understatement (e.g. in the accounts of Nick finding Gatsby's body or Dick's final severance from Nicole).

Suggested Work

Examine the two following passages, both of which portray physical trauma: the breaking of Myrtle's nose by Tom Buchanan and the breaking of Dick's nose and rib in a beating in Italy. Analyse the way in which the immediate physical trauma is evoked and consider its implications for the characters and themes of the novel. For instance, when Tom breaks Myrtle's nose, what does this say about the nature of his relationship with her (and with Daisy)? What does Dick's arrest and beating suggest about the kind of person he has become?

[a] *Gatsby*. From 'Myrtle pulled her chair close to mine ... ' to 'Taking my hat from the chandelier, I followed.' (*GG* 38–9)

[b] *Tender*. From 'There was dirty water in the gutters ... ' to 'The men went out, a door clanged, he was alone.' (*TN* 244–6)

6

Endings

This chapter looks at the endings of *Gatsby* and *Tender*, comparing and contrasting their style and significance and considering how each ending reconfigures the narrative which precedes it and reinforces, amplifies and clarifies key themes. In each ending, a dramatized scene involving two characters which refers back to major elements of the earlier narrative is followed by a concluding commentary. The first passages for analysis are these dramatized scenes, and the two final passages are the concluding commentaries which bring both novels to an end – though leaving many questions reverberating in the reader's mind. We begin with Nick's chance meeting with Tom Buchanan in Fifth Avenue.

Dust in the Eyes: *The Great Gatsby*, pp. 169–70

One afternoon late in October I saw Tom Buchanan. He was walking ahead of me along Fifth Avenue in his alert, aggressive way, his hands out a little from his body as if to fight off interference, his head moving sharply here and there, adapting itself to his restless eyes. Just as I slowed up to avoid overtaking him he stopped and began frowning into the windows of a jewellery store. Suddenly he saw me and walked back, holding out his hand.

  'What's the matter, Nick? Do you object to shaking hands with me?'
  'Yes. You know what I think of you.'

'You're crazy, Nick,' he said quickly. 'Crazy as hell. I don't know what's the matter with you.'

'Tom,' I inquired, 'what did you say to Wilson that afternoon?'

He stared at me without a word, and I knew I had guessed right about those missing hours. I started to turn away, but he took a step after me and grabbed my arm.

'I told him the truth,' he said. 'He came to the door while we were getting ready to leave, and when I sent down word that we weren't in he tried to force his way upstairs. He was crazy enough to kill me if I hadn't told him who owned the car. His hand was on a revolver in his pocket every minute he was in the house – ' He broke off defiantly. 'What if I did tell him? That fellow had it coming to him. He threw dust into your eyes just like he did in Daisy's, but he was a tough one. He ran over Myrtle like you'd run over a dog and never even stopped his car.'

There was nothing I could say, except the one unutterable fact that it wasn't true.

'And if you think I didn't have my share of suffering – look here, when I went to give up that flat and saw that damn box of dog biscuits sitting there on the sideboard, I sat down and cried like a baby. By God it was awful – '

I couldn't forgive him or like him, but I saw that what he had done was, to him, entirely justified. It was all very careless and confused. They were careless people, Tom and Daisy – they smashed up things and creatures and then retreated back into their money or their vast carelessness, or whatever it was that kept them together, and let other people clean up the mess they had made ...

I shook hands with him; it seemed silly not to, for I felt suddenly as though I were talking to a child. Then he went into the jewellery store to buy a pearl necklace – or perhaps only a pair of cuff buttons – rid of my provincial squeamishness for ever.

This is Nick's final encounter with Tom Buchanan, notable for its concise narrative prose and dialogue, for supplying a key link in the chain of events that led to Gatsby's death, for Nick's unusual attempt at self-assertion, for his judgement of Tom and Daisy, and for its echoes (the necklace, the 'pair of cuff buttons') of earlier elements in the novel. It is set, not in East or West Egg, but in New York City itself, the place of excitement and opportunity conjured up earlier in the novel which has also become, by now, the place that Nick is rejecting to return to his Midwest home town. The particular part of New York in which it is set is also significant: the meeting takes place in Fifth Avenue, one of the most expensive shopping streets in the world, a symbol of riches and conspicuous consumption. It suggests that Tom has returned to his old world of wealth and the fact that he stops to look into the windows of a jewellery store implies that he is now the consumer rather than Myrtle – and Myrtle's expenditure on her shopping spree in chapter 2 was, we feel, humble by comparison with anything Tom might be likely to buy.

Initially, Nick is positioned as voyeur, seeing but unseen. Some of the characteristics with which Tom was endowed on their first reunion in the novel are reiterated here: Nick does not dwell on Tom's physique this time but one of the adjectives applied in this passage to his way of walking, 'aggressive', echoes the adverb used of the way in which his eyes give him 'the appearance of always leaning aggressively forward' (*GG* 12) in Nick's first description of him in chapter 1. His eyes are 'restless', recalling how they flashed about 'restlessly' as he and Nick stood on his porch on Nick's first visit (*GG* 13) and how, later that evening, he hovered 'restlessly' about the room when Nick was first talking to Daisy on that visit (*GG* 15). (Restlessness is a quality Tom shares with Nick, Jordan and Gatsby, who are all called restless at some point in the novel (*GG* 9, 23, 122); the adjective is also applied to the 'restless eye' which 'the constant flicker of men and women and machines' in New York satisfies (*GG* 57)). The position of Tom's hands, which makes them look as if they are ready 'to fight off interference', recalls 'the violent thrusting movement of his powerful arms' with which he pushed through the crowd around Myrtle's body (*GG* 132).

The apparent fighting readiness of Tom's hands changes to a gesture of greeting when he spots Nick and holds out his hand – which Nick initially refuses. A sharp dialogue ensues in which Nick, for the first time, expresses moral disapproval of Tom to his face and challenges him about what he said to Wilson on the afternoon of Gatsby's death. Nick begins to turn away, but Tom then grabs him. This imposition of physical authority is a repeated motif in the novel: on their first re-encounter at West Egg, Tom turns Nick around by one arm to survey the front vista and then to take him into the house (*GG* 13); later that evening he wedges his tense arm 'imperatively' under Nick's to 'compel' him on to the porch (*GG* 16); on the train to West Egg, he takes hold of Nick's elbow and 'literally force[s]' him from the carriage to go and meet Myrtle (*GG* 27). In their Fifth Avenue meeting, he seems once again to be taking charge of the situation, though this time he is at a moral disadvantage.

Tom confirms Nick's suspicion of how he sent Wilson off to hunt for Gatsby. When he attempts to justify what he did, he uses a metaphor which includes two key symbolic terms in the novel, 'dust' and 'eyes'. For example, in the first section of the novel, Nick speaks of the 'foul dust' that 'floated in the wake of [Gatsby's] dreams' (*GG* 8); in chapter 2, 'bleak dust' drifts over the valley of ashes (*GG* 26); and in chapter 7 Myrtle, kneeling in the road after Gatsby's car has struck her, mingles her blood with the dust. The eyes link up with Dr T. J. Eckleburg in the ophthalmologist's advertisement, with the Owl-Eyed Man at Gatsby's party and funeral, and with other references in the novel to eyes and to the difficulty of seeing clearly and accurately. But here it is Tom who has been, metaphorically, throwing dust in people's eyes. Tom's simile, which likens the way in which Gatsby supposedly ran over Myrtle to the way in which 'you'd run over a dog', links up with Myrtle's purchase of the dog in chapter 2 (an incident Tom will shortly recall) and indicates both the low value of animal life in the society Fitzgerald depicts and the way in which Myrtle, like the dog she bought, has become a commodity – though it is Tom, rather than Gatsby, who treats her in this way. Tom concludes his self-justifying statement by echoing the policeman's declaration at Wilson's garage, and his own earlier one, that Gatsby 'didn't even stop his car' (*GG* 133,135).

At this point, Nick's brief defiance of Tom collapses, with his claim that there is nothing he could say 'except the one unutterable fact that it wasn't true'. Here we might ask why Nick cannot say this. It may be out of loyalty to Gatsby, with the idea that Gatsby would not want his chivalrous act in shielding Daisy to be blazoned forth in a way that would sully her reputation. It may that he does not want to acknowledge that he failed to tell the truth to the police or give evidence at the inquest. But he offers no reason and thus plays his part in the conspiracy of Tom and Daisy to conceal the truth. Tom then launches into a sentimental recollection in which the sight of the box of dog biscuits reminded him of Myrtle in a way that reduced him to tears.

In the next paragraph, Nick inwardly takes the moral high ground, condemning Tom and Daisy – though not to Tom's face – for being careless and destructive and retreating from the consequences of their actions, without acknowledging that his own silence helped to cloak their retreat. He shakes hands with Tom, again adopting an inner attitude of superiority, but clearly, in a sense, backing down from his earlier refusal to do so. Tom then goes into the jewellery store and the two possible purchases which Nick suggests he might make echo earlier parts of the novel: the pearl necklace links with the string of pearls valued at $350,000 which Tom gave Daisy the day before their wedding (*GG* 74) and the 'pair of cuff buttons' recalls the '[f]inest specimens of human molars' which Wolfshiem was wearing as cuff buttons when Nick first met him (*GG* 70). Each of these cases showed the triumph of the commodity: Tom's gift marks his acquisition of Daisy and Wolfshiem's cuff buttons show human substance turned into sinister ornament.

Nick's closing comment that Tom was 'rid of my provincial squeamishness for ever' seems intended as a judgement on Tom and perhaps, more generally, on metropolitan life, rather than on Nick; his 'provincial squeamishness' is really, he implies, a form of moral superiority, the ethical consciousness which Tom and Daisy lack. But it does also indicate his defeat by Tom, by New York, by metropolitan life: he came to New York to be a 'bond' man but he has failed, in the city, to create the human and moral bonds which might have enabled him to stay there. Earlier in the novel, he has attributed 'provincial inexperience' to himself (*GG* 50); now he uses the term 'provincial' almost as a badge of pride, implicitly pitting provincial conscience against city corruption. But the term nonetheless marks his failure to impose himself upon the city, to grasp that vision of possibility seen from the Queensboro Bridge.

The next passage, from *Tender*, marks Dick's failure in the very place where he once triumphed: the beach in front of Gausse's Hotel.

Blessing the Beach: *Tender is the Night*, pp. 335–7

> He had seen them though, as they left their pavilion, and he followed them with his eyes until they disappeared again. He sat with Mary Minghetti, drinking anisette.

'You were like you used to be the night you helped us,' she was saying, 'except at the end, when you were horrid about Caroline. Why aren't you nice like that always? You can be.'

It seemed fantastic to Dick to be in a position where Mary North could tell him about things.

'Your friends still like you, Dick. But you say awful things to people when you've been drinking. I've spent most of my time defending you this summer.'

'That remark is one of Doctor Eliot's classics.'

'It's true. Nobody cares whether you drink or not – ' She hesitated, 'even when Abe drank hardest, he never offended people like you do.'

'You're all so dull,' he said.

'But we're all there is!' cried Mary. 'If you don't like nice people, try the ones who aren't nice, and see how you like that! All people want is to have a good time and if you make them unhappy you cut yourself off from nourishment.'

'Have I been nourished?' he asked.

Mary was having a good time, though she did not know it, as she had sat down with him only out of fear. Again she refused a drink and said: 'Self-indulgence is back of it. Of course, after Abe you can imagine how I feel about it – since I watched the progress of a good man toward alcoholism – '

Down the steps tripped Lady Caroline Sibley-Biers with blithe theatricality.

Dick felt fine – he was already well in advance of the day; arrived at where a man should be at the end of a good dinner, yet he showed only a fine, considered, restrained interest in Mary. His eyes, for the moment clear as a child's, asked her sympathy and stealing over him he felt the old necessity of convincing her that he was the last man in the world and she was the last woman.

… Then he would not have to look at those two other figures, a man and a woman, black and white and metallic against the sky …

'You once liked me, didn't you?' he asked.

'*Liked* you – I *loved* you. Everybody loved you. You could've had anybody you wanted for the asking – '

'There has always been something between you and me.'

She bit eagerly, 'Has there, Dick?'

'Always – I knew your troubles and how brave you were about them.' But the old interior laughter had begun inside him and he knew he couldn't keep it up much longer.

'I always thought you knew a lot,' Mary said enthusiastically. 'More about me than anyone has ever known. Perhaps that's why I was so afraid of you when we didn't get along so well.'

His glance fell soft and kind upon hers, suggesting an emotion underneath; their glances married suddenly, bedded, strained together. Then, as the laughter inside of him became so loud that it seemed as if Mary must hear it, Dick switched off the light and they were back in the Riviera sun.

'I must go,' he said. As he stood up, he swayed a little; he did not feel well any more – his blood raced slow. He raised his right hand and with a papal cross he blessed the beach from the high terrace. Faces turned upward from several umbrellas.

'I'm going to him,' Nicole got to her knees.
'No, you're not,' said Tommy, pulling her down firmly. 'Let well enough alone.'

This scene takes place on the day of Dick's departure from the Riviera; he is on the high terrace above the beach in front of Gausse's hotel. Just before this extract starts, Nicole has seen Dick from a distance and has remarked, in response to Baby Warren's comment that she thinks Dick 'might have the delicacy to go', that the beach 'is his place – in a way, he discovered it. Old Gausse always says he owes everything to Dick' (*TN* 335). It is Dick whose creative skills have made the beach and hotel into a fashionable spot.

The opening sentence of the extract indicates that Dick has also seen Nicole and Baby and watched them until they disappeared. He is sitting with Mary Minghetti – once Mary North – and the shift in the extract from the surname she now bears to the one by which he originally knew her suggests a kind of partial return to their earlier relationship which highlights the way in which the balance of power between them has changed. It is now Mary who conducts a kind of diagnosis of Dick. Mary refers to how, in resolving the awkward situation brought about by her cross-dressing prank with Lady Caroline Sibley-Biers, Dick had behaved as he used to – and Mary would like Dick to start behaving again like that all the time. But Dick is no longer in control of situations as he once was; this is indicated by his sense that it is fantastic that Mary can tell him about things, whereas once he would have already known them. Mary makes it clear to Dick that he behaves rudely and offensively when he is drunk and claims that 'I've spent most of my time defending you this summer' – a remark Dick satirically calls 'one of Dr Eliot's classics', suggesting that it was drawn from the *Harvard Classics*, the 55-volume set of classic books drawn up by Doctor Charles W. Eliot, the reforming president of Harvard University from 1869 to 1909; Dick is implying that Mary has perpetrated an earnest cultural cliché but he is also deflecting the import of her observation of the effect of drink upon his behaviour.

Dick accuses Mary and others of dullness, a judgement upon the expatriate set he once dominated which also implies that he was one who could make them shine. Mary retorts that Dick will no longer be nourished by 'nice' people if he makes them unhappy. When Dick asks whether he has been nourished, the question goes unanswered, but the reader might want to pursue it. In a sense, Dick has been fed, psychologically, by making people happy; in another sense, he has fed them, giving them 'pieces of his own most personal self' (*TN* 89), dissipating his energies upon those who often lack initiative and discipline themselves.

There is a then a shift of focus away from the dialogue to Mary's inner feelings, but the narrative voice-over indicates that she is not aware of them – she 'was having a good time though she did not know it' – and that it was only fear that had made her sit down with Dick; the nature of her fear is unspecified but it may be that she was afraid that Dick would start behaving badly if left to his own devices and that she joined him in order to try to prevent this. Mary persists in her diagnostic approach, accusing Dick of self-indulgence, but the appearance of Lady Caroline Sibley-Biers casts an ironic light on this charge, since Mary and Caroline were self-indulgent in the cross-dressing which might have led to an embarrassing court appearance if Dick had not intervened.

We then switch back to Dick's point of view and it is confirmed, in a slightly euphemistic, jocular, evasive way, that he has been drinking a lot already that day – he feels 'fine' but is already 'well in advance of the day', 'where a man should be at the end of a good dinner'. Nonetheless he can still behave sensitively towards Mary, showing his old finesse, taking 'a fine, considered, restrained interest' in her. His eyes are momentarily 'clear as a child's', a simile which contributes to the motif of vulnerable childhood innocence that recurs in the novel, but it is ironic in this context, applied to a man who has been so damaged by experience. The connotations of innocence dissolve as the imperative of the seducer steals over Dick, 'the old necessity of convincing [Mary] that he was the last man in the world and she was the last woman'. But the following short, one-sentence paragraph, with ellipses at the start and finish, shows that this is not only the revival of an old imperative, but a tactic to avoid looking at Nicole and Tommy. Neither is named here; they are first introduced as 'figures'; then identified in terms of a primal code of gender as 'a man and a woman'; and finally described as if they were modern sculptures, 'black and white and metallic', abstracted from the colour and fleshliness of humanity.

Dick seems to be seeking reassurance when he asks Mary if she once liked him, and she provides it in ample measure, recalling to him the Dick that once was. Dick presses the issue, suggesting, in what he perhaps knows to be a cliché, that there has always been 'something between' them, and Mary, like a fish, takes the bait, 'bit[es] eagerly'. But a part of Dick is pretending and, inside his mind, he can no longer take himself seriously. Moreover, there is a suggestion here – in the adjective 'old' applied to his 'interior laughter' – that this had always been the case to some extent, that there was always a self-division in which he performed the part of the attractive man but could inwardly laugh at himself. Whereas he could once have sustained the act, he knows now he cannot do so for long.

Mary also pays tribute to the way in which she always thought he knew a lot about people, knew more about her than anyone else, and that accounted for her fear of him when they disagreed. Dick responds with a glance that 'fell soft and kind upon hers'; the verb 'fell' here has a predatory element, as if used of a bird of prey (compare the last line of Tennyson's poem 'The Eagle': 'And like a thunderbolt he falls'). The adjectives 'soft' and 'kind' (used here as adverbs), and the implication of 'an emotion underneath' only partly counteract this. Their exchange of glances becomes a kind of proxy lovemaking, stressed by the verbs 'married', 'bedded' and 'strained together'; it is as if at this point Dick is not only trying not to notice Nicole and Tommy but also – inside his own head – to make Nicole jealous, to show, at least to himself, that although Nicole may no longer find him attractive, another woman from their old set does. But there is clearly a part of Dick which remains detached, which is laughing at himself, at his performance, at his metaphorical seduction of Mary with words and looks, and the interior laughter becomes so loud that he thinks Mary must hear it and – in a shift of metaphor from the aural to the visual – he switches off 'the light', the romantic and erotic glow he has cast upon them, and they return, not to darkness, but, in a paradox, to the Riviera sun. The metaphor here could recall Gatsby showing Daisy round his mansion and flipping on the light switch in chapter 5 of the earlier novel (*GG* 91); like Gatsby, Dick is still in control, but, in contrast to Gatsby, he is no longer providing illumination for the woman of his dream. Dick then quickly, decisively, says he must go, like a lover who does not want to linger after he has secured his objective and lost interest in the partner with whom he was 'strain[ing] together' a few minutes before.

When Dick stands up, he is no longer fully in control of his body – he sways slightly, and, as we saw with the distraught Wilson in *Gatsby* and the demented Nicole earlier in *Tender*, swaying can indicate intense, obsessive feeling in Fitzgerald. Dick no longer feels well, the alcohol and emotional stress taking their toll; his malaise emphasizes the physical decline of his body evident in his failure to perform the lifting trick which we discussed in the previous chapter and in the contrast between Nicole's 'health and beauty' and his 'physical deterioration' in the extract which we also examined in the previous chapter. The expression 'his blood raced slow' is another paradox: 'slow', used here as an adverb ('slowly'), seems to contradict the idea of speed in the verb 'to race'; but this does convey the contradiction in Dick's mind and body, the combination of physical excitement and sluggishness which mirrors his conflicted desires: to flee from, or stay on, the beach; to leave, or cleave to, Nicole.

Dick then blesses the beach with a papal cross. This act recalls the religious connotations in the image of the beach as a 'bright prayer mat' near the start of *Tender* and in Dick's quasi-Eucharistic provision of 'pieces of his own most personal self' (*TN* 89) in the account of the mobile party in chapter 18. It also links up with Fitzgerald's own description of Dick, in his notes for the novel, as 'a spoiled priest' (qtd *SG* 393). There is a non-ironic sense in which the beach has been Dick's holy place in which he has tried to create a small utopian community which is also an aesthetic object, a work of art. The faces which turn upwards from some umbrellas as Dick gives the beach his blessing demonstrate that he has not quite lost his capacity for the dramatic gesture which attracts attention, and that perhaps some people at least implicitly recognize him as a tutelary spirit of the place. It is the last of his acts relating to the beach. There is then a section break and a short final paragraph in which the scene switches to Nicole and Tommy: Nicole starts to get up as if in response to Dick's blessing – though only to her knees, recalling her posture in the bathroom when Rosemary saw her after the incident of the bloodstained spread – and declares that she is 'going to him', raising the possibility that, even at this last moment, their relationship might resume; but Tommy firmly stops her, confirming that he, not Dick, now controls her. The last word, 'alone', confirms Dick's isolation.

Both this passage from *Tender,* and the previous passage from *Gatsby* we considered, could serve as endings for their respective novels; but we now turn to the actual endings of those novels, first of all to *Gatsby.*

Beating On: *The Great Gatsby*, pp. 171–2

On the last night, with my trunk packed and my car sold to the grocer, I went over and looked at that huge incoherent failure of a house once more. On the white steps an obscene word, scrawled by some boy with a piece of brick, stood out clearly in the moonlight, and I erased it, drawing my shoe raspingly along the stone. Then I wandered down to the beach and sprawled out on the sand.

Most of the big shore places were closed now and there were hardly any lights except the shadowy, moving glow of a ferryboat across the Sound. And as the moon rose higher the inessential houses began to melt away until gradually I became aware of the old island here that flowered once for Dutch sailors' eyes – a fresh, green breast of the new world. Its vanished trees, the trees that had made way for Gatsby's house, had once pandered in whispers to the last and greatest of all human dreams; for a transitory enchanted moment man must have held his breath in the presence of this continent, compelled into an aesthetic contemplation he neither understood nor desired, face to face for the last time in history with something commensurate to his capacity for wonder.

And as I sat there brooding on the old, unknown world, I thought of Gatsby's wonder when he first picked out the green light at the end of Daisy's dock. He had come a long way to this blue lawn, and his dream must have seemed so close that he could hardly fail to grasp it. He did not know that it was already behind him, somewhere back in that vast obscurity beyond the city, where the dark fields of the republic rolled on under the night.

Gatsby believed in the green light, the orgastic future that year by year recedes before us. It eluded us then, but that's no matter – tomorrow we will run faster, stretch out our arms further … And one fine morning –

So we beat on, boats against the current, borne back ceaselessly into the past.

The extract starts in a matter-of-fact, mundane way, with a clear indicator of time – 'the last night' – and an example of the rhetorical device known as a 'zeugma' ('yoking') in which two items are joined by a verb or preposition, in this case the preposition 'with'. Items linked in this way may be different in meaning, and that is the case here: the packed trunk, a familiar metonymy of departure for travel, is linked with what could almost be seen as a sign of a renunciation of travel – the sale of Nick's car, the 'old Dodge' which is mentioned near the start of the novel (*GG* 9) but which we have never seen him drive. He has, for the moment at least, given up the automobile – that empowering but destructive form of modern transport which has been so crucial in *Gatsby* – and will presumably use an earlier form of transport, the train, to return to his native city where, it is implied, he will stay: this movement back to the Midwest is a reversal of his earlier outward trajectories, to Europe in the First World War and to New York in the spring of 1922.

Nick revisits Gatsby's now deserted house, seen as 'a huge incoherent failure' – it does not hang together. Insofar as the house is a symbol of Gatsby's dream, the terms 'incoherent' and 'failure' perhaps intimate the mission Nick will assume when he returns home: to write about Gatsby's dream in a way which will give it coherence and wrest from its failure a kind of success, making Gatsby an example of 'loser wins'. This sense of an incipient writing project is made more explicit in Nick's erasure of 'the obscene word' from Gatsby's white steps; this act could seem to prefigure how Nick will narrate Gatsby's story in a way that subdues its sordid and magnifies its sublime aspects. The white steps, their obscene inscription effaced, anticipate the white paper on which Nick will inscribe his narrative, while suggesting that the impression of virginal purity the paper gives is illusory, that it has already been written upon even if the script has now been erased. Here, as often elsewhere in *Gatsby*, 'white' suggests a state of apparent innocence which is already compromised: the 'white palaces' of East Egg (*GG* 11), the 'gleaming white' windows of the room in the Buchanan house where Daisy and Jordan sit in their 'white dresses' (*GG* 13, 17), the 'white girlhood' of Daisy and Jordan in Louisville (*GG* 24), the 'white roadster' Daisy owned there (*GG* 73), the 'white heaps and sugar lumps' of the buildings of New York City (GG 67). It is also possible to interpret 'white' here in racial terms, linking it with Tom's fears that 'the white race' will be 'utterly submerged' (*GG* 18): we do not know what the 'obscene word' is, but it could be a racist slur on Gatsby in terms of his inferred ethnic origins (Jewish, for example): in this case, Nick's effacement of the word could be a fundamentally racist attempt to reassert Gatsby's 'whiteness', his racial purity.

Nick then goes down to the beach and sprawls on the sand: there is a sense here that he has left the house, the artefact of human civilization, for more primal elements: sand, sea, darkness – there are hardly any artificial lights. The rising moon acts magically not to reveal but to dissolve the houses which are 'inessential' – a perhaps surprising adjective in a novel in which, as we observed in chapter 3, houses are very important. But the movement here seems to be away from surfaces to essences. The verb 'melt' has Shakespearean resonances, linking with Hamlet's desire, in his first soliloquy, that 'this too too solid [or sullied] flesh would melt' (1.12.29). But here it is not flesh which melts but its habitations – houses – and the barriers of time. In a more modern context, the 'melting away' of the houses suggests the 'dissolve' in film, the gradual blending of one image or scene into another. There is a rich sense of transformation in this passage which culminates in the evocation of 'the old island that once flowered here for Dutch sailors' eyes – a fresh, green breast of the new world'. The verb 'flowered' suggests, in the context of an uncultivated island, a natural process; but the term 'eyes' might make us pause, in a novel in which eyes do not always represent or foster clear vision.

The sentence moves on to convey freshness, greenness and the maternal and erotic image of the 'breast of the new world'. There is a contrast here with the mutilated breast of Myrtle after the accident, nearly severed from her body and moving mechanically, 'swinging loose like a flap' (*GG* 131). In contrast to Myrtle's breast, in which form has been severed from function, this breast of the new world is new and nurturing. But it also invites rapacity. It has been deforested to make way for human habitations such as Gatsby's house, but even in its lost arboreal days it 'pandered in whispers': 'to pander' means to gratify or indulge an immoral or distasteful desire or habit, and the sense of fostering the illicit in this verb is accentuated by the phrase 'in whispers', which suggests speaking furtively, as if afraid to be heard. So the apparent freshness and innocence of the new world was already compromised. But it did nonetheless have a brief idealistic moment; it may have been pandering, but it was doing so to 'the last and greatest of all human dreams'. For a moment which is marked as both brief and magical – 'transitory' and 'enchanted' – the continent 'compelled' people into an undesired 'aesthetic contemplation' – an awareness of beauty which did not entail a desire to possess it. It is also marked, however, as a moment which will not recur, which emerged then 'for the last time in history'. It is no longer possible for the world to offer something which is 'commensurate to man's capacity for wonder'. It is worth highlighting the rhythmic phrasing here, the use of the late Latin word 'commensurate' (rather than, say, equal) to mean 'corresponding in size and degree' and the way in which it alliterates with 'capacity'.

The phrase 'for the last time in history' fixes the moment in which it was still possible to find something commensurate to man's capacity for wonder firmly in the past, and this emphasis on the past runs through the rest of the passage. The next paragraph returns from the far to the recent past but does suggest that wonder was still possible for Gatsby when he 'first picked out the green light at the end of Daisy's dock'. With that, Nick suggests, 'his dream must have seemed so close that he could hardly fail to grasp it' – notice that he employs the 'must have' phrasing that he used in speculating on Gatsby's thoughts on the last afternoon of his life. But Nick intervenes to identify as an illusion Gatsby's belief that he might be about to realize his dream, emphasizing that 'it was already behind him'. Here Nick uses a spatial metaphor. It was 'already behind him, somewhere back in that vast obscurity beyond the city, where the dark fields of the republic rolled on under the night'. But he is talking about time and the history of the USA, as the mention of 'the republic' shows. The adjective 'dark' suggests that the history of 'the republic' may have its darker elements.

The next paragraph starts with an emphatic statement of Gatsby's belief in 'the green light'. Here, the meaning of the 'green light' does not only represent Daisy, but also 'the orgastic future that recedes year by year before us'. It is a future of wild excitement, of which sexual orgasm is the epitome, but it is 'receding', going away from us even as we move towards it. It eluded us in the past but this does not stop us believing in the possibility of attaining it if we make more effort, run faster and stretch further. The final phrase is an aposiopesis, a sentence breaking off with a dash, as if unable to specify the precise nature of the goal that might be reached 'one fine morning'. But it also cuts off the optimistic surge and we move into the short, one-sentence final paragraph.

This paragraph uses sailing metaphors: 'beat', 'boats', current'. To 'beat' is to sail into the wind, with repeated 'tacking' – changing course by turning a boat's head into and through the wind: the sense of sailing into the wind is reinforced by the idea of going 'against the current', and the sentence goes on to suggest that one is only going backwards. The sailing imagery indicates an attempted spatial movement, across water, but the sentence concludes with a marker of time, 'the past'. The sentence casts an ironic light on Gatsby's earlier claim that 'of course' one can repeat the past (*GG* 106). It asserts, not only that one *can* repeat the past, but also that one inevitably *does* repeat the past, not so much by trying to do so but in the very effort to go forward, to leave the past behind. The sentence also contends, however, that repeating the past does not involve going back to a time before things went wrong and choosing the road which will lead to fulfilment (as Gatsby hopes to do by going back to Daisy's house in Louisville and marrying her from there). Rather, repeating the past is a matter of reliving an endless cycle of expectation and disappointment. Here Nick mounts a challenge to the forward movement not only of America but also of Western civilization. In the nineteenth century, the speaker in Tennyson's poem *Locksley Hall* declared, 'Not in vain the distance beacons. Forward, forward let us range, / Let the great world spin for ever down the ringing grooves of change. / Thro' the shadow of the globe we sweep into the younger day; / Better fifty years of Europe than a cycle of Cathay' (Cathay was the name by which China was known to medieval Europe and a 'cycle' here means 'a series of events that are regularly repeated in the same order'); the implication of Nick's metaphors is that 'fifty years of Europe' – or the USA – may, in their fundamental pattern, involve the same regular repetition of events as 'a cycle of Cathay'.

This passage presents Gatsby as an image of American and human aspiration. It has a visionary quality as the 'inessential houses' melt away and the original Dutch settlers in the New World are evoked. But the passage also contains elements which suggest the limits of that aspiration and vision; for example, the use of the verb 'pandered', the sense, increasingly insistent as the passage moves to its conclusion, that the dream is already, and always, in the past, that life is cyclical rather than linear, that aspiration always carries us backwards as well as forwards. It is a peculiarly memorable piece of prose in its capacity to start from a specific place, time and person and make these representative of the history of a nation and, perhaps, of all human history. Its high rhetoric contrasts with the downbeat ending of *Tender*, to which we shall now turn.

Dying Fall: *Tender is the Night*, pp. 337–8

Nicole kept in touch with Dick after her new marriage; there were letters on business matters, and about the children. When she said, as she often did, 'I loved Dick and I'll never forget him,' Tommy answered, 'Of course not – why should you?'

Dick opened an office in Buffalo, but evidently without success. Nicole did not find out what the trouble was, but she heard a few months later that he was in a little town named Batavia, N.Y., practising general medicine, and later that he was in Lockport, doing the same thing. By accident she heard more about his life there than anywhere: that he bicycled a lot, was much admired by the ladies, and always had a big stack of papers on his desk that were known to be an important treatise on some medical subject, almost in process of completion. He was considered to have fine manners and once made a good speech at a public health meeting on the subject of drugs; but he became entangled with a girl who worked in a grocery store, and he was also involved in a lawsuit about some medical question; so he left Lockport.

After that he didn't ask for the children to be sent to America and didn't answer when Nicole wrote asking him if he needed money. In the last letter she had from him he told her that he was practising in Geneva, N.Y., and she got the impression that he had settled down with some one to keep house for him. She looked up Geneva in an atlas and found it was in the heart of the Finger Lakes section and considered a pleasant place. Perhaps, as she liked to think, his career was biding its time, again like Grant's in Galena; his latest note was post-marked from Hornell, N.Y., which is some distance from Geneva and a very small town; in any case he is almost certainly in that section of the country, in one town or another.

Compared to the conclusion of *Gatsby*, which magnifies its protagonist into a symbol of America and of universal human aspiration, and which returns, imaginatively, to the founding moment of American history, this is a very downbeat, diminuendo ending, what Fitzgerald called a 'dying fall' (qtd *SG* 437), taking the phrase from Shakespeare's *Twelfth Night* (1.1.4). Its subdued prose contrasts markedly with the sustained rhetoric of the finale of the earlier novel. The closing section of *Tender* conveys, in a quietly moving way, the dwindling of Dick's great promise into provincial obscurity and parochial scandal. The lack of precise detail ('Nicole did not find out what the trouble was', 'a lawsuit about some medical question', 'in one town or another') helps to reinforce this sense of obscurity (Dick no longer matters enough for the details to count). The passage is narrated from Nicole's point of view, which limits our knowledge of Dick's activities to what Nicole knows and means we can only infer Dick's thoughts and feelings.

Like the conclusion of *Gatsby*, the ending of *Tender* starts in a mundane, matter-of-fact way; it is made clear, however, that a decisive reconfiguration has occurred: Nicole has married Tommy, she speaks of her love for Dick in the past tense, and Tommy appears to feel that Dick is no threat – he does not demand that she forget Dick (a notable contrast to Gatsby here, who tries to insist, in vain, that Daisy deny that she ever loved Tom). The narrator then summarizes what Nicole learns of Dick's movements. He has returned to America, after his long sojourn in Europe, but he is now living the downside of the American Dream, rather than the heroic if inevitable failure evoked at the end of *Gatsby*. In the essay 'My Lost City' (1932), Fitzgerald famously remarked that he 'once thought there were no second acts in American lives' (*CU* 31) and this seems to be true of Dick; or rather, his second act is one which shows his decline and there is no triumphant third act in the offing. The young man who had passed with aplomb through major academic and metropolitan sites – Yale, Johns Hopkins, Vienna, Zurich, Paris – now lives in a series of little towns of successively diminishing size in New York State: Buffalo, Batavia, Lockport, Geneva (there is an ironic contrast with the major European city that is its namesake). He no longer follows a career as a psychiatrist but practises general medicine. This in itself might be an honourable choice, a conscious rejection of the big time for a life of provincial virtue; but in Dick's case, it does not quite look like that.

Nicole learns more about his life in Lockport than anywhere else 'by accident' – a phrase which suggests that she does not make any systematic inquiries into her ex-husband's activities (and we might ask, echoing Tommy Barban's question, 'Why should she?'; it is clear that the Dick phase of her life is over). Dick clearly retains his power to charm, even if he exercises it in a smaller field, but his gesture towards the completion of a major book has an element of pathos; it is 'almost in process of completion'. The slightly unusual phrasing here is telling; it combines elements of two more common phrases – 'almost complete' and 'in process of completion', each of which marks a more definite and advanced stage than Dick has reached. His book is neither 'almost complete' nor 'in the process of completion' but about to reach the stage where it would be 'in process of completion'; one feels, however, that reaching this stage will be indefinitely postponed, that Dick's book will never be finished, like Mr Casaubon's *Key to All Mythologies* in George Eliot's *Middlemarch* (1871–2). In his new life in America, Dick's manners also impress and he seems to make a contribution to public health concerns. But the suggestion that he might have turned into a worthy small-town citizen is compromised by a whiff of scandal: his involvement with 'a girl who worked in a grocery store'. The girl's occupation as a grocery store worker is, implicitly, an ironic echo of the novel's earlier invocation of Ulysses S. Grant, 'lolling in his general store in Galena' (*TN* 132); it looks as though Dick, in this later phase of his life, has not escaped the humble lot symbolized by the general store but embraced it in his search for female company and that he now seeks women much lower down the social scale than the upper-crust Nicole or even the Hollywood star Rosemary. In itself, this might be a good sign that he is choosing a partner for her intrinsic worth rather than her social status; but the term 'girl' suggests that Dick is continuing his pursuit of younger women, an activity that seems more dubious and predatory the older he grows.

Finally, Dick appears to lose interest in his children and to ignore Nicole's offer of money – an offer which recalls the economic imbalance which ran through their courtship and marriage and which was vividly evident in Nicole's interior monologue, discussed in chapter 3 of this book. Dick continues to practise medicine and seems to be living with a woman, but no further details are vouchsafed. Nicole likes to think that there may be a third act in his life, that his career is biding its time, like Grant's in Galena. Following on from the implicit ironic echo in the previous paragraph of the novel's earlier reference to Grant, this is an explicit ironic echo of the same reference and recalls the narrator's reassurance, at that previous point in the novel, that Dick, like Grant in his general store in Galena, 'is ready to be called to an intricate destiny' (*TN* 132). The novel has now traced that 'intricate destiny', but, in contrast to Grant, Dick has not found triumph and fame but defeat and obscurity. His latest letter is from 'a very small town', Hornell, but his exact whereabouts are no longer worth specifying; he is 'in that section of the country, in one town or another'.

Conclusions

We will aim here to sum up the results of our analyses in the earlier chapters of this book and in this chapter and offer a brief final assessment of Fitzgerald's achievement in *Gatsby* and *Tender*.

Beginnings

Fitzgerald uses an indirect, elaborate approach at the start of *Gatsby* and *Tender*, and thus establishes a narrative strategy, a way of telling a story,

for both novels; neither will release information about
and themes in a straightforward way but will use indirection,
chronological scrambling to sharpen the reader's curiosity at crucial p
Later passages from each novel present characters and events in a m
direct way but this is still not wholly straightforward. This indirect
approach to narrative is not merely an intriguing technique but a
correlative of the problems the characters experience in knowing and
understanding themselves, other people, and the worlds in which
they move. Gatsby and Dick appear to embody idealist and romantic
aspirations which are also bound up with American national identity and
the 'American Dream' and the novels in which they appear explore the
difficulty of realizing these aspirations and this dream in the fragmented
social order of the modern world.

Society

Fitzgerald portrays this fragmented social order through the microcosm of
the party in which people mix together but may also play out unresolved
tensions and fail to communicate. All the parties in both novels are
attempts at human sociability in a society in which the bonds of family
and traditional community have been weakened, but they are riven by a
range of tensions. For all their flaws, however, Gatsby's huge parties and
the Divers' smaller parties have artistic and utopian aspects; they create
temporary, fragile structures in which people can, at moments, enjoy
heightened existences. Both Gatsby and Dick are, in a sense, artists
and idealistic rulers of their small domains. We can link these parties
with the artistic and political projects of the earlier twentieth century
which tried to create new forms to release and intensify positive human
potentials but which sometimes brought forth demons. In the kind
of fragmented social order that the parties symbolize, money takes on
particular importance as a way of shaping identities and relationships.

money
– rela.

Money

The ambivalence of money is a crucial Fitzgerald theme. In his work, it
is both liberating and confining, corrupting and elevating. Money may

est ideals and aspirations but endangers
ioral awareness. Fitzgerald is fascinated by
ned and unearned money, and especially
is view, being born into wealth makes the
a sense of superiority which can survive
ich also makes them morally vulnerable. We
by and *Tender* in the shadow of the 1929 Wall
ald is not simply saying that boom leads to
bust; his more point is that the possession of money opens up
the possibility of a ethically and aesthetically richer life but may lead
to a human loss which is more fundamental than the financial one. In
Gatsby and *Tender*, this human loss is especially evident when money,
or the lack of it, enters into gender roles and relationships.

Gender

Gender roles and relationships were shifting and changing in Fitzgerald's
world and he offers vivid and perturbing portrayals of characters whose
masculinity and femininity can no longer be taken for granted. Daisy
Buchanan is deeply dissatisfied but can see no escape from her lot.
Jordan Baker is independent but isolated, falling for a man who is not
her measure. Nicole Diver emerges from abuse to a kind of autonomy
but still finally submits to an overly dominant male. Tom Buchanan
can find no outlet for his huge physical energies except in philandering,
racism and petty violence. Nick Carraway is a passive voyeur who fails
in relationships with women and yields to more dominant males. Dick
Diver seems at first to be a superman but fails to realize his potential.
Tommy Barban is aggressively macho but lacks a real cause for which
to fight. This kind of uncertainty about gender roles and relationships
plays a major part in the traumas both novels explore.

Trauma

Fitzgerald is strongly aware of the immediate and longer-term impact
of physical and psychological trauma and he focuses on such traumas

in *Gatsby* and *Tender*, often using indirect means to bring them home to us. The two novels are deeply marked by loss, violence and death and face them unflinchingly; but they are also intensely alert to sources of energy and beauty and convey a sense of life's potentials. *Gatsby* and *Tender* show that some traumas are immitigable and bear the stamp of tragedy; but those who survive them may be able to come to terms with them through articulating them (as Nick does in *Gatsby*) or through forming new relationships (as Nicole and even Dick do in *Tender*). Both novels implicitly pose the question of how to end narratives of trauma in ways that will release energy for continued life; and this question is bound up with how the novels themselves end.

Endings

As we have seen in this chapter, *Gatsby* and *Tender* each provide scenes which could serve as the endings of the novels in which they occur: Nick's meeting with Tom in Fifth Avenue, Dick's departure from the beach. But the novels do not in fact end there but go on to provide passages in narrative and discursive prose which, explicitly in the case of *Gatsby*, implicitly in the case of *Tender*, suggest the import of all that has gone before. In the light of the novels' concern with trauma, this extension of endings relates to the problem which was emerging in psychoanalysis in Fitzgerald's time, of how to terminate the analytic process, and which trauma studies and therapy today might formulate as how, after a traumatic experience, to achieve closure. The endings of *Gatsby* and *Tender* each offer a kind of closure, though in a different key: in *Gatsby* there is an exalted, exhilarating sense of an endlessly repeated, ever-unsuccessful struggle; in *Tender*, there is a subdued sense of the 'dying fall' which follows the failure of high aspirations. Both these perspectives acknowledge and assimilate loss and look beyond it to a clear-eyed continuance of life.

We can relate the exalted ending of *Gatsby* to a famous Fitzgerald observation in an undated letter to his daughter when he spoke of:

> the thing that lies behind all great careers, from Shakespeare's to Abraham Lincoln's, and as far back as there are books to read – the sense that

life is essentially a cheat and its conditions are those of defeat, and that the redeeming things are not 'happiness and pleasure' but the deeper satisfactions that come out of struggle.   (*CU* 306)

We can relate the subdued ending of *Tender* to an equally famous Fitzgerald maxim in his 1936 essay 'Handle with Care': 'the natural state of the sentient adult is a qualified unhappiness' (*CU* 84).

Fitzgerald's achievement as a novelist, at its highest in *Gatsby* and *Tender*, depends on the quality of his prose and the insights it conveys. As his friend and fellow-author John O' Hara remarked, in a letter to another writer who emerged in the 1930s and would go on to win the Nobel Prize for Literature, John Steinbeck: 'Fitzgerald was a better just plain writer than all of us put together. Just words writing' (qtd *SG* 567). But Fitzgerald's achievement also depends on the ways in which that prose is woven into broader fictional structures and how his combinations of style and form, certainly in *Gatsby* and *Tender*, succeed in grasping the polarities of life, the Everlasting Yea and the Everlasting Nay (as the Victorian sage Thomas Carlyle called them), and holding them, for transitory, enchanted moments, in equipoise before, like the figures on Keats's Grecian Urn shaking off stasis, like the pioneering Dutch sailors breaking from their compelled contemplation, they surge into activity again, with everything, good and bad, that this entails.

PART II

THE CONTEXT AND THE CRITICS

7

F. Scott Fitzgerald: Life and Works

Scott Fitzgerald was a man of many parts which seem difficult to reconcile. He was a self-destructive drunk and a prolific, hard-working and highly talented professional writer who, in his 20-year career, produced four complete novels, one major work-in-progress, about 150 short stories, around 30 articles and essays, a substantial set of notebooks, and a sheaf of correspondence. He wanted to be 'one of the greatest writers who have ever lived', but much of his creative energy went into commercial fiction and film scripts that were never produced. He was almost always in debt, but managed not only to support himself but also to pay for his wife's prolonged stays in costly mental hospitals and his daughter's private schooling and elite university education at Vassar. He lived with his wife for only ten years, all of them fraught, but he never divorced her and Scott and Zelda have joined the pantheon of great lovers in literary history and popular culture. He rarely saw his daughter as she grew up, but his letters to her show a caring father intensely concerned for her moral welfare and cultural development and ready to share his deepest reflections with her. He led an itinerant life, with few possessions, and never owned a permanent home, but he usually dwelt in some style in high-class hotels or in large and comfortable rented houses or apartments with servants. He often behaved appallingly but he could also be funny, gracious and charming.

Always attractive to women, he was anxious about his virility and sensitive to hints that he might have homosexual inclinations. Physically slight and fairly short (about five foot seven), he frequently got into fights (in which he usually came off worst). Sometimes seen as intellectually lightweight, the bibliographies he drew up for the 'College of One' he created for Sheilah Graham and the references scholars have traced in his fiction indicate a formidably wide range of reading and a mind remarkably alive to key intellectual currents of his time. Finding instant fame with his first novel, *This Side of Paradise* (1920), he seemed a forgotten man by the late 1930s. Since his death in 1940, at the age of 44, he has become more famous than ever, a cultural icon who glows across time.

Francis Scott Key Fitzgerald was born in St Paul, Minnesota on 24 September 1896, the first and only son of Edward Fitzgerald and Mary (known as Mollie) McQuillan. Death shadowed his birth: three months before, the two girls who would have been his sisters had died at the ages of 1 and 3. The speaker in the semi-autobiographical 'Author's House' (1936) sees this as the moment at which he started to be a writer; this suggests that Fitzgerald, at the age of about 40, had come to regard writing as a destiny decided in the womb and determined by loss. He was named after a distant ancestor, a second cousin thrice removed, Francis Scott Key (1779–1843) who, in 1814, had written a song called 'The Star-Spangled Banner'. In view of Fitzgerald's ability to express major themes of American history and national identity in his work, his forenames would seem especially appropriate after 1931, when America adopted Key's song as its national anthem. The Keys were part of the lineage of seventeenth-century Maryland families from which Fitzgerald's paternal grandmother, Cecilia Ashton Scott, descended. Nothing definite is known of his paternal grandfather, Michael Fitzgerald, though the surname suggests Irish origins, but Philip F. McQuillan, Fitzgerald's maternal grandfather, was undoubtedly of Irish extraction, born in County Fermanagh; in the USA, he married the daughter of an Irish immigrant carpenter, Louisa Allen, and built up a successful wholesale grocery business. On his death at the age of 43 in 1877, he left a then-large legacy of $266,289.49 to his five surviving children, of whom Mollie was the eldest. Mollie thus brought money to her marriage with Edward Fitzgerald, while her husband brought what Fitzgerald later called the 'series of reticences and obligations that go under the poor old shattered word "breeding"' (qtd *SG* 26). Both Fitzgerald's parents were practising Catholics and reared him in the faith.

If Edward Fitzgerald possessed breeding, he lacked commercial acumen. Less than two years after Scott's birth, in April 1898, his furniture factory, the proudly named American Rattan and Willow Works, failed and he went to work as a wholesale salesman for Proctor and Gamble in Buffalo, New York State (the town which is the first stop on Dick Diver's descent to obscurity after his return to the USA at the end of *Tender*). In January 1901, the Fitzgeralds moved to Syracuse, New York where Annabel, Scott's only sister to survive infancy, was born in July that year (another sister born in Buffalo in 1900 had lived no more than an hour). The Fitzgerald family returned to Buffalo in September 1903.

When Scott reached the age of 11, another shadow fell across his life; in March 1908, Proctor and Gamble dismissed 55-year-old Edward Fitzgerald, leaving him, his son later believed, 'a broken man' (qtd *SG* 23) . In the summer of that year, the Fitzgeralds came back to St Paul. Due perhaps to financial difficulties, Scott and Annabel went to live with their maternal grandmother, Louisa McQuillan, in Laurel Avenue and their parents stayed with a friend on Summit Avenue. Edward worked with little success as a wholesale grocery salesman from the real-estate office of his brother-in-law. It was not until April 1909 that the Fitzgeralds lived together as a family again, first at Louisa McQuillan's while she was abroad, and then, from September 1909, in Holly Avenue.

In September 1908, Fitzgerald had entered a boys' private school, St Paul Academy, and just over a year later, in October 1909, he was published for the first time. A short story, 'The Mystery of the Raymond Mortgage', appeared in the school magazine, *St Paul Academy Now & Then*. Three further stories would feature in the magazine during his time at St Paul. In August 1911, he wrote his first play, a one-act drama called *The Girl From Lazy J.*, which was put on, not at school, but in the Summit Avenue home of the Elizabethan Dramatic Club, named after its organizer, Elizabeth Magoffin; Fitzgerald took the lead role. But his poor scholarly performance at St Paul Academy made his family decide to send him to the Catholic Newman School in Hackensack, New Jersey.

Fitzgerald started at Newman in September 1911. His first year was unhappy but he was able to convert a humiliation on the football field, which made him look like a coward, into a kind of triumph by writing a poem called 'Football' which appeared in the Christmas 1911 issue of the school magazine, the *Newman News*. In 'Author's House' (1936), Fitzgerald recalled that this 'made me as big a hit with my father as if I had become a football hero'. He felt that it taught him a larger lesson – writing could compensate for failure: 'if you weren't able to function in action you might at least be able to tell about it, because you felt the same intensity – it was a back door way out of facing reality' (*AA* 234–5). While he was at Newman, the school magazine also featured three of his short stories. Moreover, he wrote two full-length plays which were put on by the Elizabethan Drama Club back in St Paul: *The Captured Shadow* (August 1912), which would later feature in the Basil Duke Lee story with the same title, first published in 1928; and *The Coward* (August 1913).

Fitzgerald's most significant human encounter at Newman occurred in November 1912 when he met Father Sigourney Fay, a former Episcopalian bishop who had converted to Roman Catholicism. Fay, then aged 37, was a wealthy, cultivated man who liked and encouraged Fitzgerald. In his first novel, *This Side of Paradise* (1920), Fitzgerald drew an appreciative portrait of Fay in the character of Monsignor Darcy. Fay introduced Fitzgerald to the 27-year-old Anglo-Irish writer, diplomat and Catholic convert Shane Leslie, who then seemed, Fitzgerald remembered, 'the most romantic figure I had ever known' because he had sat at Tolstoy's feet, swam with Rupert Brooke and been 'a young Englishman of the governing classes' when Britain was at the height of its imperial power (qtd *SG* 42). Leslie would later recommend 'The Romantic Egotist', an earlier version of *This Side of Paradise*, to Scribner's; Fitzgerald would dedicate his second novel, *The Beautiful and Damned* (1922), to Leslie.

Fitzgerald scraped into Princeton University in September 1913; his poor performance in the entrance exams meant he would have to take make-up exams in some subjects. But he loved the Princeton ambience: in an essay published in 1927, he rhapsodized the university as 'the loveliest riot of Gothic architecture in America, battlement linked on to battlement, hall to hall, arch-broken, vine-covered – luxuriant and lovely over two square miles of green grass' (*AA* 93). His hopes of football glory were quickly dashed – he was 'not big enough (or good enough)' (*CU* 70) – but he turned to his 'back door way' out of reality, writing material for the *Princeton Tiger*, the *Nassau Literary Magazine* (known as the *Nassau Lit*) and the Triangle Club, which produced an annual musical comedy written by students and took it on tour in the Christmas vacation. The Club held a competition each year to select the script to be staged and Fitzgerald's book and lyrics for *Fie! Fie! Fi-Fi!* won this in 1914. Fitzgerald also formed significant friendships with two other students who were editors of the *Nassau Lit* and budding writers: John Peale Bishop, who would become a poet, essayist and novelist, and Edmund Wilson, who would emerge as one of America's leading men of letters and whom Fitzgerald would call, in his 1936 essay 'Pasting it Together', his 'intellectual conscience' (*CU* 79).

Fitzgerald neglected his academic work, however, and this took its toll when he failed a make-up exam in coordinate geometry and was, in consequence, forbidden to undertake the 3,500-mile Christmas tour of *Fie! Fie! Fi-Fi!* He returned to his home city for the vacation and it was there, on 4 January 1915, that he met 16-year-old Ginevra King and fell for her; she was beautiful, rich and widely admired. When he returned to Princeton, he bombarded her with letters at a rate she found difficult to reciprocate. Academically, he passed enough courses to enable him to remain at Princeton for his sophomore (second) year and he had two great social successes: on 26 February 1915 he was elected secretary of the Triangle Club, which almost guaranteed that he would be president in his senior (fourth) year, provided he stayed at the university; and in March he became a member of Cottage, one of the most prestigious student eating clubs at Princeton.

But the spectre of academic failure continued to stalk him. At the start of his junior (third) year, in the autumn of 1915–16, he flunked the make-up exam in qualitative analysis and was thus banned from holding campus offices. This scuppered his hope of the presidency of the Triangle Club and again debarred him from its Christmas tour, though he contributed to the lyrics of the production for that year, *The Evil Eye*, and a striking photograph of him in drag, as a chorus girl, was used in publicity, attracting fan letters from men. But in November he was diagnosed with malaria (possibly a tubercular attack) and dropped

out of Princeton for the rest of that academic year. The Princeton
record stated that 'Mr Fitzgerald was required to withdraw from the
University January 3, 1916 for scholastic deficiencies' but in May,
Dean Howard McClennan, at Fitzgerald's request, supplied an open
letter saying he had withdrawn voluntarily 'because of ill-health' (qtd
SG 72, 73).

Fitzgerald came back to Princeton in September 1916 to repeat his junior
year; he contributed lyrics to the Triangle Club Christmas production,
Safety First, but was again forbidden to tour with it. In January 1917 his
relationship with Ginevra King finally ended. His academic performance
continued to be poor but he made 13 contributions to the *Nassau Lit*
between February and June of that year: four short stories, three poems, a
play and five book reviews. He would later incorporate one of the stories,
'Babes in the Wood' (May 1917), into his first novel, *This Side of Paradise*,
and another, 'Tarquin of Cheapside' (April 1917), would appear in his
second short-story collection, *Tales of the Jazz Age* (1922).

America entered the First World War on 17 April 1917 and, after
a brief return to Princeton in September 1917, Fitzgerald volunteered
for military service. He was commissioned as an infantry second lieutenant on 26 October and reported for training in November at Fort
Leavenworth, Kansas. There, in the officer's club, he started to write the
first version of a novel called 'The Romantic Egotist' which, from its
surviving chapters, seems to have been an early draft of *This Side of
Paradise*. In a letter to Edmund Wilson of 10 January 1918, he said that
'it purports to be the picaresque ramble of one Stephen Palms from the
San Francisco fire, thru school, Princeton to the end where at twenty
one he writes his autobiography at the Princeton aviation school' (qtd
SG 95). In February 1918, he went to Princeton on leave and completed
the novel at the Cottage Club. He sent it to Shane Leslie, who passed it
on to Scribner's on 6 May, with a letter which compared Fitzgerald to
Rupert Brooke and felt that Fitzgerald's likely death in the First World
War would boost sales: 'Though Scott Fitzgerald is still alive it has a
literary value. Of course when he is killed, it will also have a commercial
value' (qtd *SG* 97).

By June 1918, Fitzgerald was with the 67th Infantry Regiment at
Camp Sheridan near Montgomery, Alabama, where he was promoted
to first lieutenant. In July 1918, at the Montgomery Country Club,

he met Zelda Sayre, the 18-year-old daughter of a local judge, whose forename came from a fictional gypsy heroine. Scribner's rejected 'The Romantic Egotist' on 19 August 1918 but encouraged Fitzgerald to revise and resubmit it. In September, Ginevra King married Ensign William Hamilton and Fitzgerald noted in his scrapbook: 'THE END OF A ONCE POIGNANT STORY' (*RE* 27). In October, Scribner's turned down the revised version of 'The Romantic Egotist', prompting Fitzgerald to make another elegiac scrapbook entry: 'The end of a dream' (*RE* 35). His ledger recorded a third ending for 1917–18: it was his '[l]ast year as a Catholic' (qtd *SG* 101).

First Lieutenant Fitzgerald was sent to Camp Mills, Long Island, in November 1918 where he expected to embark for France. But the war ended before he could do so, ranking him among those who would thereafter always have to say, regretfully and apologetically, 'I didn't get over' (the title of one of his 1936 short stories). In this he contrasts with Amory Blaine in *This Side of Paradise*, with Gatsby and Nick Carraway in *Gatsby*, whose first conversation, before each knows the other's identity, concerns their wartime service in France, and with Dick Diver and Abe North in *Tender* – Dick does 'get over to Europe', although he sees no action, but Abe is a combat veteran of the trenches. On 10 January 1919, Father Sigourney Fay died of pneumonia, breaking a key link with Fitzgerald's past. He captioned the telegram informing him of Fay's death 'The end of a story' (*RE* 35). Fitzgerald was discharged from the army in February 1919 and looked to the future. He wanted to marry Zelda but she held him at bay while his prospects were uncertain. He went to New York to work as a copywriter for the Barron Collier advertising agency, producing a memorable motto for a laundry in Muscatine, Ohio: 'We Keep You Clean in Muscatine'. In his spare time, he wrote stories, sketches, film scripts, verses and jokes and submitted them for publication. Almost all were returned; he created a frieze of 122 rejection slips in his room at 200 Claremont Avenue. He did sell one story, 'Babes in the Wood', to the magazine *The Smart Set*, but was paid only $30 – hardly enough to convince Zelda of his earning power. She broke off their engagement in June 1919.

Fitzgerald then took a bold step. In July 1919, he quit his post at Barron Collier and returned to St Paul to live with his parents and to revise 'The Romantic Egotist' once more. On 16 August he wrote to Maxwell

Perkins at Scribner's to announce that the novel was now called *This Side of Paradise*. Perkins accepted the revised version on 16 September. In 'Early Success' (1937), Fitzgerald recalled how, while waiting for the novel to appear, 'the metamorphosis of amateur into professional began to take place – a sort of stitching together of your whole life into a pattern of work, so that the end of one job is automatically the beginning of another' (*CU* 86). In November, Harold Ober, then a partner in Reynolds's New York literary agency who would later strike out on his own, became Fitzgerald's agent and would remain so until July 1939, when Fitzgerald broke with him. Through Reynolds's, Fitzgerald sold a short story, 'Head and Shoulders', to the *Saturday Evening Post* for the first time. The *Post* was the best-known of the period's 'slicks' (magazines printed on coated paper), with a circulation in the 1920s that totalled 2,750,000 weekly copies. It paid well and would become a key source of income for Fitzgerald until the mid-1930s, when it felt Fitzgerald's stories were declining in quality. The *Post*'s fee for 'Head and Shoulders' was $400 ($360 after agent's commission), and it appeared there on 21 February 1920. Metro bought the film rights for this story for $2,250 and released a silent-movie version, 'The Chorus Girl's Romance', in 1920. The same studio paid $2,025 for another of Fitzgerald's 1920 *Post* stories, 'The Offshore Pirate' – the film of the same title appeared in 1921 – and took an option for $2,700 on Fitzgerald's future output. Fox purchased the rights to a third Fitzgerald *Post* story, 'Myra Meets His Family', for $900 and made it into the film *The Husband Hunter* (1920).

Fitzgerald was getting the money; now he would get the girl. In January 1920, he started to see Zelda again and they renewed their engagement. *This Side of Paradise* appeared on 26 March 1920 and made Fitzgerald famous. It is a very lively novel which draws on a wide range of storytelling techniques to portray the life of its protagonist, Amory Blaine, from boyhood to young manhood, taking him through school, Princeton, the army and several girlfriends. It caught the mood of the moment and presented an image of youth that was franker than ever before. The first print run of 3,000 copies sold out in three days. Six days after publication, on Saturday 3 April 1920, Fitzgerald married Zelda in St Patrick's Cathedral in New York and they spent their honeymoon at the Biltmore Hotel.

In the heady air of early 1920s New York, the Fitzgeralds ascended to the heights. They were a young, glamorous celebrity couple and they lived up to their role, going to parties, performing pranks, posing for photographs and granting interviews. Edmund Wilson observed: '[t]hey had a genius for imaginative improvisations' (qtd *SG* 157). But their lifestyle was expensive and the royalties from *This Side of Paradise* could not support it; the novel earned no more than $6,200 in 1920. Fitzgerald's main income came from short stories sold to the *Post* and *Metropolitan* and from film rights. His first short-story collection, *Flappers and Philosophers*, came out on 10 September 1920. It contained eight tales, including 'Head and Shoulders' and the memorable stories 'The Ice Palace' and 'Bernice Bobs Her Hair'. In May to July 1921, the Fitzgeralds went to Europe for the first time, returning to St Paul for the birth of their only child, Scottie, on 6 October 1921. As Zelda emerged from the anaesthetic, she remarked that she hoped her new daughter was 'beautiful and a fool – a beautiful little fool'; Fitzgerald later incorporated these comments into Daisy's account, in *Gatsby*, of her remarks after the birth of her baby (*GG*, 22).

Fitzgerald's second novel, *The Beautiful and Damned*, appeared on 4 March 1922. It was a novel of bulk and seriousness, influenced by the naturalist novelists Theodore Dreiser and Frank Norris. Longer and more sombre than *This Side of Paradise*, it followed the chaotic trail of Anthony Patch, whose life and marriage disintegrate as he waits to receive a large legacy. Its reviews and sales were reasonable, but it did not make his reputation as a major novelist or earn enough royalties to allow him to give up writing for magazines. His second short-story collection, *Tales of the Jazz Age*, came out on 22 September 1922. The most notable of its 11 stories were 'May Day' and 'The Diamond as Big as the Ritz'.

Fitzgerald seems to have begun to think about his third novel in June 1922, when he and Zelda were staying at the Yacht Club at White Bear Lake in Minnesota; he wrote to Maxwell Perkins that it would be set in the Midwest and New York in 1885, cover a shorter time span than his two previous novels, and include 'a Catholic element'. He wanted 'to write something *new* – something extraordinary and beautiful and simple + intricately patterned' (qtd *SG* 198). In August 1922, the Fitzgeralds were asked to leave the Yacht Club because of their wild parties and in October 1922, they rented a house at Great Neck, Long Island. *Nouveau-riche* show-business people lived in the area, in contrast to the old-money families who dwelt in Manhasset

Neck across the bay. Fitzgerald turned Great Neck and Manhasset Neck into West and East Egg in *Gatsby*. Fitzgerald's satirical play *The Vegetable: From President to Postman* was published by Scribner's on 27 April 1923 and quite well reviewed, but its stage production, premiered in Atlantic City on 19 November, bombed.

Scott and Zelda took ship again for France in April 1924. In the summer and autumn of that year they rented the Villa Marie at Valescure, near St Raphaël. Here Fitzgerald completed the version of *Gatsby* he would send to Maxwell Perkins. In July Zelda became entangled with a striking French naval aviator, Edouard Jozan. How far the relationship went is uncertain; but Fitzgerald saw it as a 'Big crisis' which caused irreparable damage (qtd *SG* 232). His sense that Zelda had betrayed him may well have fed into *Gatsby*. In the summer of 1924, the Fitzgeralds became friends with Gerald and Sara Murphy, a wealthy couple with three children who had settled in France and cultivated artistic interests and the art of good living. Fitzgerald used them to some extent as the models for Dick and Nicole Diver in *Tender* and dedicated the novel to them.

Fitzgerald mailed *Gatsby* to Maxwell Perkins at Scribner's on 27 October 1924. He and Zelda then drove to Rome, where they stayed at a hotel. Fitzgerald was unhappy in Italy, drank heavily, and got into a fight with some taxi drivers which ended with the police beating him up – an incident later used in *Tender*. But he also gave attention to revising *Gatsby*. On 20 November, Maxwell Perkins sent him a long letter which called the novel 'magnificent' but made three key criticisms: as a character, Gatsby was 'somewhat vague'; there was a '*total* lack of explanation of Gatsby's wealth' when there should be some hints of its source; and the story of Gatsby's earlier life came out all at once, when he told it to Nick on the night after Myrtle's death, rather than emerging in a piecemeal way, like the rest of the narrative. Fitzgerald revised the novel extensively on the galley proofs. The final version was published on 10 April 1925.

Near the end of his life, Fitzgerald would see the novel as showing the way he should have gone: in a letter of 1940 to Scottie, he wrote: 'I wished now I'd *never* relaxed or looked back – but said at the end of *The Great Gatsby*: "I've found my line – from now on this comes first. This is my immediate duty – without this I am nothing"' (*CU* 294).

If *Gatsby* had been instantly recognized as a masterpiece, this might have signposted Fitzgerald's future more clearly; but it was not. Its reviews were mixed and its sales relatively modest. But Fitzgerald made money from subsidiary rights. On 2 February 1926, a stage version of *Gatsby*, written by Owen Davies and starring James Rennie in the title role, opened on Broadway. It ran for 112 performances and later went on a successful tour. Fitzgerald estimated that it earned him around $17,000 or $18,000. Famous Players–Lasky-Paramount pictures bought the film rights for $45,000 and the silent-movie version, with Warner Baxter as Gatsby, premiered in 1926.

Fitzgerald kept in touch with the fortunes of *Gatsby* from a distance; he was staying in Capri when it came out and late in April 1925 he moved to Paris. In that month, he had his first face-to-face meeting with a young and then obscure American writer whom he had recommended to Perkins: Ernest Hemingway. Thirty-two years later, in the posthumously published *A Moveable Feast* (1964), Hemingway would produce a vivid but questionable account of this event and its aftermath. Fitzgerald had high ambitions for the novel which would follow *Gatsby*. On 1 May, he wrote to Maxwell Perkins that it was his 'happiest thought' and would be 'something really NEW in form, idea, structure – the model for the age that Joyce and Stein are searching for, that Conrad didn't find' (qtd *SG*, 268). His first plan was to write about matricide: a young movie technician, Francis Melarky, is travelling in Europe with his mother and eventually kills her.

His main literary project for the year, however, was the 17,000-word story 'The Rich Boy', which *Redbook Magazine* published over two issues in January and February 1926, and which contained a claim which would become famous and lead later to tension with Hemingway: that 'the very rich … are different from you and me'. Hemingway's 'The Snows of Kilimanjaro' (1936) satirized this by mocking Fitzgerald's 'romantic awe of the rich' and suggesting that the thing which makes the rich different is that 'they have more money' (*FS* 66). 'The Rich Boy' featured as the first tale in Fitzgerald's third short-story collection, *All the Sad Young Men*, which came out on 26 February 1926. This volume contained, among its nine stories, the three tales of the *Gatsby* group – tales on which Fitzgerald worked during the gestation of *Gatsby* and which bear some relation to its themes: 'Winter Dreams', 'Absolution' (which contains the 'Catholic element' mentioned in Fitzgerald's letter to Perkins of June 1922) and '"The Sensible Thing"'.

In early March 1926 the Fitzgeralds went back to the Riviera and lived in Juan-les-Pins, renting the Villa Paquita in May and then the Villa St Louis until December, when they returned to America. It was in the summer of 1926 that Fitzgerald probably began work on the matricide version of his fourth novel. The Fitzgeralds set off for Hollywood in January 1927, leaving Scottie with Fitzgerald's parents. United Artists had hired Fitzgerald to script a flapper comedy for the actress Constance Talmadge, but the result, called 'Lipstick', was never produced. The Hollywood visit, however, led to two important meetings. One was with the 17-year-old actress Lois Moran, who had already scored a success in the 1925 silent version of *Stella Dallas*. Fitzgerald, then 30, found her attractive, though they did not have an affair; she would be the original of Rosemary Hoyt in *Tender*. The second important encounter was with the young and famous MGM producer, Irving Thalberg, who would be the model for Monroe Stahr in Fitzgerald's final, unfinished novel, *The Last Tycoon*. After United Artists rejected 'Lipstick', Scott and Zelda went back east, renting a large house in Delaware, 'Ellerslie', where they would live until March 1928. Fitzgerald worked in a desultory way on his next novel but financial pressures drove him to take up writing short stories again in June 1927. Zelda began taking ballet lessons and had three articles published in magazines.

The Fitzgeralds went back to Paris once more in April 1928. In the same month, the short story 'The Scandal Detectives' appeared in the *Saturday Evening Post*, the first of a series about Basil Duke Lee, which drew on Fitzgerald's memories of his childhood and adolescence in St Paul. The *Post* would publish seven more Basil Duke Lee stories between July 1928 and April 1929. Zelda resumed ballet training again in Paris, this time with Madame Lubov Egorova. Scott and Zelda sailed back to America in September 1928 and lived at Ellerslie again until March 1929. Early that year Zelda started to write a series of stories about different types of girls in order to earn money to contribute to the cost of her ballet lessons. The magazine *College Humor* published five of these between July 1929 and February 1931, attributing them to 'F. Scott and Zelda Fitzgerald', and the *Post* featured a sixth, 'A Millionaire's Girl', in 1930, credited only to Scott. The Fitzgeralds returned to Europe in

March 1929, journeying from Genoa along the Riviera to Paris, then going to Cannes in June where they rented the Villa Fleur des Bois. In summer 1929, Fitzgerald appears to have resumed work on his fourth novel but jettisoned the matricide theme to focus on the European experiences of Lew Kelly, a young American film director, and his wife Nicole. In October 1929, the Fitzgeralds came back to Paris. The Wall Street Crash on 29 October had no direct impact on Fitzgerald since he owned no shares; but it did decisively mark the end of the decade which his life and work had seemed to symbolize and helped to make him look like yesterday's man, no longer at the cutting edge.

In 1930, Fitzgerald returned to his novel and took up the matricide theme once more. He made little progress on this but did write 'First Blood', the opening tale in a series about the young and wealthy Josephine Perry. The *Post* would publish the five 'Josephine' stories between April 1930 and August 1931. In April 1930, Zelda suffered her first mental breakdown and began the series of stays in sanatoria which would continue for the rest her life and whose emotional effect on Fitzgerald is poignantly summed up in his remark: 'I left my capacity for hoping on the little roads that led to Zelda's sanitarium' (qtd *SG* ix). On 23 April 1930 she went into the Malmaison clinic outside Paris, discharged herself against medical advice on 11 May, and then, after hallucinations and a suicide attempt, entered the Valmont clinic in Switzerland on 22 May. Dr Oscar Forel diagnosed her as schizophrenic and on 5 June she went into his clinic, Les Rives de Prangins, at Nyon on Lake Geneva, where she would stay for 15 months. Fitzgerald travelled between Paris and Switzerland to keep in touch with her.

Fitzgerald's father, Edward, died in late January 1931, and Fitzgerald returned to the USA for the burial. He wrote about this in the short story 'On Your Own' (1931) (*PH* 323–38) and later wove the account of the burial into Dick's return home for his father's interment in *Tender*. On 15 September 1931, Zelda was discharged from Prangins and returned to America on 19 September. The Fitzgeralds rented a house in Montgomery but Fitzgerald went to Hollywood on his own to work on the script of *Red-Headed Woman* for MGM (Metro-Goldwyn-Mayer). Zelda's own father died on 17 November 1931. Her mental condition declined again and in February 1932 she had a second breakdown and went into the Phipps Psychiatric Clinic of Johns Hopkins Hospital in Baltimore. In March, while still at Phipps, she drafted, with remarkable speed, a novel which she sent to Maxwell Perkins. Early in the year, Fitzgerald had drafted a plan for another version of his next novel, which would focus this time on the figure of Dick Diver. When he saw Zelda's draft of her novel, he reacted angrily, feeling she had stolen some of his material. Zelda agreed to make certain changes in response to his objections. In May, Fitzgerald rented a house called 'La Paix' at Towson, outside Baltimore and Zelda joined him and Scottie there after her discharge from Phipps on 26 June. In the summer of 1932, Fitzgerald set out a general plan for his novel, stating that it should show 'a man who is a natural idealist, a spoiled priest, giving in for various causes to the ideas of the haute bourgeoisie, and in his rise to the top of the social world losing his idealism, his talent, and turning to drink and dissipation' (qtd *SG* 393). Scribner's published Zelda's novel, *Save Me The Waltz*, on 7 October 1932 but it received poor reviews, sold no more than 1,400 copies, and earned only $120.73 in that year.

The Vagabond Junior Players in Baltimore staged a production of Zelda's play, *Scandalabra*, from 26 June to 1 July 1933. Near the end of October 1933, Fitzgerald gave the completed typescript of *Tender is the Night* to Scribner's for serial publication in their magazine. He then moved, in December 1933, to a rented house in Park Avenue, Baltimore. In January 1934, Zelda suffered her third mental breakdown and went into Sheppard-Pratt Hospital outside Baltimore; she was transferred in March to Craig House, Beacon, New York and an exhibition of her paintings was held in New York City from 29 March to 30 April. She re-entered Sheppard-Pratt on 19 May. *Scribner's Magazine* published *Tender* in four episodes from January to April 1934 and the novel came out in book form on 12 April. As with *Gatsby*, reviews were mixed and sales disappointing. In February 1935, Fitzgerald stayed at the Oak Hall Hotel in Tryon, North Carolina. His fourth and longest short-story collection, *Taps at Reveille*, containing 18 previously published tales, appeared on 20 March 1935. It includes five 'Basil' stories', three 'Josephine' stories and other impressive tales such as 'Crazy Sunday', set in Hollywood, 'The Last of the Belles', set in the American south, and 'Babylon Revisited', set in Paris and showing the human consequences of the 1920s economic boom.

Fitzgerald spent the summer of 1935 at the Grove Park Inn, Asheville, North Carolina and then, in September, he rented an apartment at the Cambridge Arms in Baltimore. In November he stayed at the Skyland Hotel in Hendersonville, North Carolina, where he started to write the 'Crack-Up' essays for the magazine *Esquire*. Zelda remained in Sheppard-Pratt but made repeated suicide attempts and on 8 April 1936, Fitzgerald transferred her to the Highland Hospital in Asheville. She would alternate between her mother's home and the Highland for the rest of her life and eventually die, aged 47, in a fire at the hospital in March 1948. In the summer of 1936, Fitzgerald himself returned to the Grove Park Inn. His 76-year-old mother died in August 1936. His 'The Crack-Up' essays appeared in *Esquire* in 1936; his friend and fellow-writer John Dos Passos deplored them for their self-absorption at a time of political crisis, but they now seem part of a tradition which links Renaissance anatomies of melancholy, most notably by Robert Burton, with modern writings on breakdown by Robert Lowell, Sylvia Plath, William Styron and Elizabeth Wurtzel.

In July 1937, Fitzgerald went to Hollywood for the third and final time. On the 14th of that month, he met Sheilah Graham, a Hollywood columnist of English origin who had led a remarkable life and with whom he would form the most important relationship of his last years. He worked on various scripts for MGM: *Three Comrades*; a projected Joan Crawford film called 'Infidelity' which was killed off by censorship; an adaptation of Claire Boothe Luce's play *The Women*; and a movie for Greta Garbo, *Madame Curie*. But he never really succeeded as a movie scriptwriter and MGM did not renew his contract after it expired on 27 January 1939. Walter Wanger of United Artists hired him to work with Budd Schulberg on a screenplay of a film called *Winter Carnival* but soon fired them for drunkenness. Schulberg later fictionalized the experience in his novel *The Disenchanted* (1950).

In January 1940, *Esquire* featured Fitzgerald's 'Pat Hobby's Christmas Wish', the first of 17 stories about a hack screenwriter. *Esquire* would publish 11 more Pat Hobby stories up to December 1940, and the final five, posthumously, from January to May 1941. (They would appear in one volume in 1962.) Between March and October 1940 Fitzgerald worked as a freelance screenwriter for Paramount, Universal, Twentieth Century-Fox and Columbia. A particularly important project between

May and August of that year was 'Cosmopolitan', a film adaptation of his own 1931 story, 'Babylon Revisited'; Leslie Cowan, an independent producer, hired him to write this, but it never reached the screen (Cowan later sold the rights to MGM and an adaptation by other writers appeared as *The Last Time I Saw Paris* in 1954).

Above all, however, Fitzgerald was working on his Hollywood novel; his protagonist, Monroe Stahr, was based on Irving Thalberg. But he did not complete it. In November 1940, he had a heart attack at Schwab's drugstore on Sunset Boulevard, and moved into Sheilah Graham's apartment to avoid climbing stairs. On 21 December 1940, aged 44, he died suddenly in her apartment of a coronary occlusion. The obituaries portrayed him as a failed and superseded figure, a symbol of the Jazz Age who had never really transcended it. But Stephen Vincent Benét saw matters more clearly in the conclusion to his review of Fitzgerald's unfinished novel which came out under the title of *The Last Tycoon* in 1941: 'You can take off your hats now, gentlemen, and I think perhaps you had better. This is not a legend, this is a reputation – and seen in perspective, it may well be one of the most secure reputations of our time' (*FR* 375–6). If the deaths of his sisters shadowed his birth, his own death foreshadowed his rebirth; his literary reputation would burgeon after the Second World War and make him a major literary presence to this day.

8

The Historical, Cultural and Literary Context

The Historical Context

Fitzgerald published his first novel in 1920 and his last completed one in 1934. In that time, the USA went from prosperity through catastrophe to slow recovery and the literary and cultural focus shifted from pleasure to politics. The historical context of *Gatsby* and *Tender* includes a rich mixture of elements: the aftermath of the First World War; the spectacular unintended results of Prohibition in the shape of organized crime and the rise of the gangster as a figure of folk myth; the spectre of government corruption in the Teapot Dome scandal; the presidential pursuit of pro-business policies; immense economic growth culminating in a boom followed by a bust; technological and organizational innovations which transformed the fields of transport, communications and popular entertainment; changes in the rights and roles of women; and the anxiety aroused by immigration and the restrictive legislation that resulted. All these elements play their parts in a range of ways in *Gatsby* and *Tender*.

In April 1917, the USA, under President Woodrow Wilson, entered its first-ever large-scale European war, breaking with its policy of neutrality after German submarines started to sink American merchant ships even if they were not carrying arms. The American Expeditionary

Force (AEF) of over 1,200,000 men, led by General Pershing, went to the Western Front in September 1918 and participated in some key battles – for example, the Meuse–Argonne offensive, in which Jay Gatsby was involved. The war took young Americans to Europe and plunged them into mortal combat; many died, including some of Fitzgerald's Princeton contemporaries; others were wounded or maimed – one of Gatsby's party guests, 'young Brewer who had his nose shot off in the war' (*GG* 62), is a fictional example of this; while still others – like Nick in *Gatsby*, or Krebs in Hemingway's short story 'Soldier's Home' (1925) – came back to the USA physically unharmed but psychologically dislocated, unable to settle back into the community they had left behind. There were also those, like Fitzgerald himself, who did not get overseas during the conflict but felt that they ought to have done.

The year 1919, the year after the war ended, was marked in the USA by labour unrest, strikes, race riots and bombings. Fitzgerald's short story 'May Day' evokes the 1 May 1919 riot in New York and, in 'Echoes of the Jazz Age' (1931), he identifies this as about the time the 'Jazz Age' started. There were fears, largely unfounded, that communists had fomented the unrest and a 'Red Scare' spread; civil liberties were curtailed and sometimes blameless immigrants deported. But the unrest and Red Scare subsided; Fitzgerald recalled that the 'events of 1919 left us cynical rather than revolutionary … It was characteristic of the Jazz Age that it had no interest in politics at all' (*CU* 14).

The year 1920 saw the start of nationwide Prohibition which was intended to produce a more sober and better-behaved nation but would have spectacular unintended results. In 1917 the US Congress had voted by the necessary two-thirds majority to submit the Eighteenth Amendment to the US Constitution, which prohibited the manufacture, sale, transportation, import and export of intoxicating liquors, for ratification by the states of the Union. The amendment was duly ratified on 16 January 1919 and on 28 October 1919, the National Prohibition Act, often known as the Volstead Act after the senator who promoted it, was passed. Prohibition went into force on a national scale on 17 January 1920; by this time it was already in effect in 33 American states. Prohibition seemed to work at first: arrests for drunkenness fell, liquor consumption dropped 30 per cent and the incidence of illnesses and deaths linked to alcohol lessened. But Prohibition was weakly enforced and as time went on it had several unintended consequences: it criminalized an activity which many people had previously thought of as a right, part of the 'pursuit of happiness' enshrined in the US Constitution, and effectively turned them into lawbreakers – it is worth stressing that all the alcohol consumed in *Gatsby* is illegal; it generated networks of organized bootlegging – the making and selling of illegal alcoholic drinks; and it aggrandized the gangster as a rich, influential and romantic figure who – like Gatsby – also engaged in other kinds of crime, such as gambling and bond fraud, and who sometimes aspired to respectable social status. Examples of big-time gangsters included Al Capone (1899–1947) in Chicago and Arnold Rothstein (1882–1928) in New York; the latter was partly Fitzgerald's model for Wolfsheim in *Gatsby*.

In 1920, the Republican Warren G. Harding won the US presidential election by a landslide and took up office in January 1921. He was the first of three Republicans to occupy the White House over the next 12 years: his successors were Calvin Coolidge, from 1923 to 1929; and Herbert Hoover, from 1929 to 1933. Harding was a popular president but his term was marred by 'Teapot Dome', the largest US government scandal prior to Watergate, when Albert B. Fall, the Secretary of the Interior, was accused of covertly granting Harry F. Sinclair of the Mammoth Oil Company exclusive leases to the naval oil reserve lands in Teapot Dome in Wyoming and in Elk Hills and Buena Vista in California, in return for large cash payments and interest-free loans. Though Harding himself was not directly involved, the resultant Senate investigation may have contributed to his premature death from a heart attack or stroke on 2 August 1923; his term of office became associated with corruption and it is notable that Harding's forename becomes the surname of the wealthy and corrupt Warren family in *Tender*. But his successor Calvin Coolidge restored a sense of probity to the presidency. Harding, Coolidge and Hoover all pursued policies, such as cutting taxes and reducing federal spending, which favoured business and the well-off. But these did not generate unrest because a steady growth in prosperity marked the decade. The total of national wealth expanded from about $187 million in 1912 to

$350 million in 1929. Labour costs fell by around 10 per cent due to technological and production innovations but wages rose by 33 per cent and prices stayed fairly stable. Share values quadrupled between 1919 and 1929 (though this would eventually contribute to the Wall Street Crash). Industrial productivity, which had risen only 12 per cent between 1910 and 1920, grew by 64 per cent between 1920 and 1930; factories were electrified and assembly-line working promoted. New industries fuelled economic growth. The automobile industry was especially important. In 1895, only four trucks and passenger cars had been made; by 1919, this had risen to 7,565,446, and it went on rising throughout the decade. Automobile production stimulated growth in associated industries, such as road-building, petroleum, and iron, steel, rubber and glass.

Mergers and consolidations concentrated this prosperity into relatively few hands. In 1929, 200 companies owned about 20 per cent of the national wealth and 1 per cent of banks controlled 46 per cent of the USA's banking resources. While some industries prospered, others were depressed, such as textiles and coal mining, and construction declined after 1926. But the sense of economic well-being was widespread and not confined to the rich. New consumer goods burgeoned: electric toasters and irons, refrigerators, coloured plumbing fixtures, phonographs and radios, sporting clothes and equipment. The introduction of the instalment plan put consumer goods within the reach of more people, though it increased the risk of debt. Industries concerned with communication, entertainment and leisure expanded, selling more telephones, radios, magazines and movie tickets. This expansion of production was matched by a growth in advertising, where Fitzgerald had found his first job.

The expansion of industry, technological innovation and the greater, though still limited, availability of consumer goods contributed to the important changes in the 1920s in the position and role of women in the USA. The Nineteenth Amendment to the US constitution, passed by Congress on 4 June 1919 and ratified on 18 August 1920, affirmed that the 'right of citizens of the United States to vote shall not be denied or abridged by the United States or by any State on account of sex [i.e. gender]' and thus effectively gave American women the right to vote for the first time. Outside the home, employment prospects for women widened. More office and sales jobs became available for middle-class white women, though domestic work remained the only resource for most women of colour. In the home, for those able to afford them, technological innovations and new consumer goods reduced the household labour which women had traditionally performed, such as clothes washing and carpet cleaning, while the mass production of food – bread, for example – lessened the time and effort of food preparation. In advertisements and magazines, a new female image appeared which Fitzgerald, and his fiction, had helped to define and publicize: the flapper. The flapper was characterised partly by appearance – bobbed hair (i.e. hair cut short to hang evenly all round the head), the use of make-up, short skirts, no corsets – and partly by startling and provocative behaviour: smoking, drinking, dancing to jazz, and sexual licence. All these changes in the position, role and image of women created challenges for both genders. The key female characters of *Gatsby* – Daisy, Jordan and Myrtle – and of *Tender* – Nicole and Rosemary – are all placed in complex and difficult situations and all, in their respective ways, present challenges to the major male characters – Gatsby, Tom, Nick and Wilson, and Dick Diver and Tommy Barban.

If attitudes to women were relaxing in the 1920s, attitudes to immigrants were hardening. Before the First World War, a larger number of immigrants had come to the USA than ever before, reaching a record high of 1,285,349 in 1907. But after the war, and the Russian Revolution of 1917, immigrants fell under suspicion because they were sometimes seen as responsible for the war and as engaged in subversion. In 1921, the Quota Law limited the number of yearly immigrants to about 300,000 and stipulated that the annual immigration from any one nation should be no more than 3 per cent of the number of foreign-born persons from that country resident in the USA in 1910. This effectively discriminated against those from southern and eastern Europe. The National Origins Act of 1924 increased this discrimination; it set the yearly quota for immigrants entering the USA at 2 per cent of the total of any given nation's residents in the USA as recorded in the 1890 census (before the large influxes of Italian and Slavic immigrants) and declared that, after 1 July 1927, annual immigration to the USA would be reduced so that by the end of the decade it would be permanently restricted to about 130,000 people whose ethnic composition would be proportionate to the ethnic composition of America in the 1920 census. The Act banned Asian immigration absolutely. The anxieties about immigration which led to the passing of these laws is echoed in *Gatsby* in Tom's concern about 'the rise of the colored races' and Nick's attitudes to Wolfshiem, the African Americans and south-eastern Europeans he sees on the Queensboro bridge and his Finnish servant. In *Tender*, US racist attitudes towards people of colour are transported to Europe and emerge in Dick Diver's dismissal of the 'nigger scrap' that results in the death of Jules Peterson (*TN* 123) and in the way in which the African Swede's death figures as little more than a means to advance the psychodrama of the white characters.

The 1920s, then, saw a range of changes in America, some emancipatory, some restrictive. While it is too simple to say that the decade came to an end with the Wall Street Crash, that cataclysmic financial catastrophe did serve as a fitting symbolic finale to the 1920s. Until early 1928 the rise in stock prices which had continued throughout the decade had matched the likely rewards which investors could expect. Increasing speculation, however, led to a situation in which some investors were buying stocks on credit through brokers who held what were called margin accounts; this involved borrowing from banks to buy stocks using those stocks themselves as collateral, on the assumption that the prices of those stocks would continue to rise and could be sold at some future point for a sum which would enable investors and brokers to repay the loans from the banks and take a tidy profit for themselves. But an economic recession began in summer 1929, corporate earnings fell and in October of that year a panic rush to sell stocks started. On 29 October a record number of over 16 million shares were traded and the Dow Jones Industrial Average fell 12 per cent, closing at 198; it had lost 183 points in under two months.

While the Crash was not the sole cause of the Great Depression of the 1930s, it did contribute to it and served as its most sensational precursor. Writing in 1931, Fitzgerald saw it as precipitating the end, not only of the 1920s economic boom, but of the Jazz Age as a whole: 'the most expensive orgy in history ... ended two years ago, because the utter confidence which was its essential prop received an enormous jolt [from the Wall Street Crash], and it didn't take long for the flimsy structure to settle earthwards' (*CU* 21). The orgy was followed by the Great Depression of the 1930s which brought high unemployment, and, in the USA, the election in November 1932 of the Democrat Franklin D. Roosevelt as President, who, once in office, initiated the 'New Deal', a programme of government intervention to tackle the economic crisis which marked a clear departure from the laissez-faire economic policies of Harding, Coolidge and Hoover. A further sign of the end of the Jazz Age was the ratification on 5 December 1933 of the Twenty-First Amendment to the US Constitution which repealed the Eighteenth Amendment and thus effectively spelled the beginning of the end for Prohibition.

These were the key historical aspects of the period of American history in which Fitzgerald emerged as a novelist and wrote *Gatsby* and *Tender*. In surveying these, we have touched on some of the key features of popular culture at this time: advertising, the automobile, the gangster as figure of folk myth, the movies. We shall now turn to other significant cultural developments.

The Cultural and Literary Context

Some of the significant intellectual, cultural and literary developments in this era originated in Europe but impinged on the USA, and some emerged in America itself. In atomic physics, the theory of relativity which Albert Einstein had outlined in 1905 was verified by Eddington's experimental observations in 1919 and challenged the concepts of time and space which Isaac Newton had developed in the seventeenth century. In popularized forms, the idea of relativity spread into the arts and humanities. The psychoanalytical ideas promulgated from the start of the twentieth century by Sigmund Freud, while scientifically unverifiable, suggested that human beings were much less rational than they had liked to imagine, and that the sexual drive was far more important than the nineteenth century had been prepared publicly to acknowledge. In the USA itself, William James, elder brother of the novelist Henry James and an able expository writer and lecturer, had explored the human mind, from a non-Freudian angle, in *The Principles of Psychology* (1890), where he had claimed that consciousness could not be called a 'chain' or 'train' but flowed like a river or stream, and that it would thus best be described as 'the stream of thought, of consciousness, or of subjective life'. Literary critics would adopt the phrase 'stream of consciousness' to describe a way of writing which tried to portray the flux of thought, sensations and emotion, most famously in James Joyce's novel *Ulysses* (1922). In his lectures and the books such as *The Will to Believe* (1897), *Pragmatism* (1907) and *The Meaning of Truth* (1909), James developed the philosophy of pragmatism, which held that the truth of a proposition depended not on its correspondence to some absolute reality, but on whether or not it worked in terms of its practical, social or psychological results. As he put it in *Pragmatism*: 'The true is the name of whatever proves itself to be good in the way of belief.' This justified holding beliefs which could not be decisively proven – religious beliefs, for example – if they seemed to produce good feelings and behaviour, but it also disturbingly implied that truth was always relative and provisional.

The challenge that the ideas of Einstein, Freud and William James posed to traditional structures of scientific, psychological and philosophical thought was matched in the artistic spheres by those innovations grouped under the rubric of 'Modernism' – although the mid- to late-twentieth century idea that there was only one, monolithic kind of Modernism has given way to the view that it is more accurate to think in plural terms of Moder*nisms* which vary in relation to gender, ethnicity, class, cultural location, geography and in the degree of their departure from more traditional or mainstream cultural forms. The best-known Modernist works are probably Pablo Picasso's painting known as *Les Demoiselles d'Avignon* (*The Maids of Avignon*, 1906–7); Igor Stravinsky's ballet score *Le sacré du printemps* (*The Rite of Spring*, 1913); James Joyce's *Ulysses* and T. S. Eliot's *The Waste Land* (both 1922). All these vividly and vigorously disrupted traditional forms in ways that shocked some of their original audience and excited others and which remain controversial today, though many of their modes have passed into popular culture (for example, pop videos or TV advertisements), where they are often unquestioningly accepted. Of course, 'traditional forms' were hardly static themselves: painting, music, fiction and poetry had changed throughout the nineteenth century; European painting, for instance, had seen the development of Impressionism, in the painting of artists such as Manet and Monet, and of what the English art critic Roger Fry called Post-Impressionism, in the work of Van Gogh, Gauguin and Cézanne. But nonetheless Modernist works of the kind mentioned above did represent a more radical break with what had gone before than anything which had appeared in the nineteenth century.

Modernist disruption of traditional forms was driven by a sense that such forms were no longer adequate to express human experience, certainly not in the modern world. As the examples above show, Modernist innovations spread across the traditional arts (and also included architecture and the new form of film) and were international, often produced by expatriates who had left their place of origin: Picasso, a Spaniard, was working in France; Stravinsky, a Russian, was working in Paris; Joyce, an Irishman, was working in Paris, Trieste and Zurich; and Eliot, an American, was working in London. Both the lives and the works of major Modernist artists were marked by dislocation and disruption, by displacements from traditional social as well as artistic communities, though these might take the form of temporary expatriation (as with Fitzgerald and Hemingway) rather than permanent relocation, as with Eliot and Pound.

In the USA, Modernism involved a complex negotiation between European and American cultural forms and with American life itself, which, in the 1920s, was the apogee of modernity. After the First World War, the USA was not only, as Fitzgerald claimed in 'Echoes the Jazz Age', 'the most powerful nation' (*CU* 14), but the most modern; in a way, Modernism was the texture of everyday life, especially in the big cities, as well as a set of new artistic practices. Some key Modernist American writers (including US expatriates such as Gertrude Stein) wanted to innovate in a way that would equal or surpass the Europeans, but also wished to call upon distinctively American resources of art and experience. Thus, for example, the poet Hart Crane aimed to write, in *The Bridge* (1930), a modern epic poem that would rival *The Waste Land* in its formal boldness and its literary-historical resonance but that would affirm American modernity, updating Milton and Shelley for the twentieth-century USA. The short-story writer and novelist

Ernest Hemingway worked to produce an unsparing prose which, for instance in the *In Our Time* (1925) stories, evoked moment-by-moment experience stripped of the veils of literary sensibility imported from Europe. John Dos Passos used collage and stream of consciousness in *Manhattan Transfer* (1925) to represent the thrust and criss-cross of modern urban life in the USA.

In America, however, as elsewhere, Modernism was not the only significant form of fictional writing. Naturalism, the detailed rendering of characters struggling, and often failing, to satisfy their desires in a constricting environment, remained a powerful mode in the 1920s and would enjoy something of a revival in the 1930s as writers became politically engaged with the effects of the Great Depression. Its most substantial American exponent in the 1920s was Theodore Dreiser, who had influenced Fitzgerald's second novel *The Beautiful and Damned* and whose *An American Tragedy*, published in the same year as *Gatsby*, remorselessly traced the life of Clyde Darrow from impoverished boyhood through murder to the electric chair.

One especially important aspect of American culture in the 1920s, which has received scant attention from most literary critics until recently, is the Harlem Renaissance, a movement of African American writers, artists and musicians based in and around the district of Harlem in Upper Manhattan in New York. The key manifesto of this movement is the anthology *The New Negro* (1925), edited by Alain Locke, a Professor at Howard University who had been the first African American to win a Rhodes scholarship to Oxford. Significant writers associated with the movement include Jean Toomer, whose novel *Cane* came out in 1923; Countee Cullen, whose first poetry volume, *Color*, was published in 1925; Langston Hughes, whose first poetry collection, *Weary Blues*, appeared in 1926; Nella Larsen, whose first novel, *Quicksand*, went on sale in 1928; Claude McKay, whose novel *Home to Harlem* was issued in 1928; and Zora Neale Hurston, who would later write the classic novel *Their Eyes Were Watching God* (1937). Figures from other artistic fields associated with the Harlem Renaissance include the actor Paul Robeson, the painter Aaron Douglas (who provided illustrations for *The New Negro*), the sculptor Archibald Motley, the tenor Roland Hayes, the jazz musician Duke Ellington and the blues singer Bessie Smith. Among Harlem Renaissance writers, attitudes to Modernism varied; for example, Jean Toomer used a fragmented Modernist technique in *Cane* while Countee Cullen produced accomplished poems in traditional verse forms.

Harlem is notably absent from *Gatsby* and Fitzgerald does not engage with its artistic movement directly, though he must have had some awareness of the cultural excitement there in the 1920s, since he was a friend of the white writer Carl Van Vechten, who knew Harlem well and portrayed it controversially in his best-selling novel *Nigger Heaven* (1926). But the Harlem Renaissance was a significant part of the cultural context in which *Gatsby* emerged, and critics have recently shown some interest in the relationship of *Gatsby* to narratives which show light-skinned African Americans trying to 'pass' as white, such as Nella Larsen's second novel *Passing* (1929); such narratives can be linked to Gatsby's attempt to 'pass' as socially acceptable in Daisy's eyes.

The relationship of *Gatsby* and *Tender* to the historical, intellectual, literary and cultural contexts outlined above is complex. Both novels engage with key aspects of the 1920s: the aftermath of war; the eruption of violence; the unintended consequences of Prohibition; the frantic pursuit of pleasure; the ending of illusion symbolized by the Wall Street Crash. In their style and structure, both novels employ discontinuity, fragmentation and perceptual ambiguity but do so within narratives which achieve a certain overall coherence. Although *Gatsby* is often seen as a more coherent novel than *Tender*, it is also more evidently allied to Modernism than the later novel. In terms of time, its nearest Modernist intertext is Eliot's *The Waste Land:* both works show the city, the modern world, as a place of vacuum and vision, opening on the void but sometimes vouchsafing hints of transcendence; both can look like broken epics punctuated by lyrical epiphanies; both invoke traces of ancient myth, ritual and religion to set their fragments in larger perspectives. But while Eliot departs sharply from traditional narrative verse, Fitzgerald retains key elements of the traditional novel; *Gatsby* has a plot and a story, a denouement and a conclusion, and consistent characters and settings. This makes *Gatsby* both Modernist and accessible.

Perhaps the strongest influence on Fitzgerald's third novel was not the Eliot of *The Waste Land* but the slightly more distant one of Joseph Conrad. From Conrad, Fitzgerald learnt a lot about how to use a first-person narrator who is both participant and observer and how to achieve the aim Conrad affirmed in his preface to *The Nigger of the Narcissus* (1897), which Fitzgerald reread just before he wrote *Gatsby*: 'My task is … by the power of the written word, to make you hear, to make you feel – it is, before all, to make you *see*.' The 'scenic method' employed by Henry James and Edith Wharton, which involved reducing intrusive authorial narration and offering a series of scenes from which readers could make their own inferences, also showed Fitzgerald how to make the reader see. A further significant model was the symbolic prose of Willa Cather in *My Ántonia* (1918) and *A Lost Lady* (1923). Fitzgerald's letters demonstrate his familiarity with these novels and both resonate in *Gatsby*.

In contrast to *Gatsby*, *Tender* seems in some ways a return to a more traditional narrative form. It has a third-person narrator who enters the points of view of different characters, who sometimes tells us things those characters do not know themselves, who comments on the action, and who offers general reflections about life. But the novel still shows much ambiguity and uncertainty, dissolves into many gaps and absences, and focuses, perhaps more than *Gatsby*, on specific moments which are so intense that they disrupt the desire to subdue them to an overall narrative plan. In other words, *Tender* still has many Modernist elements but these are combined with more traditional narrative features in a way that enables the reader to move between Modernist and traditional-realist perspectives or even to entertain them simultaneously. In 'The Crack-Up', Fitzgerald famously remarked that 'the test of a first-rate intelligence is the ability to hold two opposed ideas in the mind at the same time, and still retain the ability to function' (*CU* 69). There is a sense in which *Tender* asks us to hold two ideas in the mind at the same time and to continue to function: the Modernist idea of relativity and the traditional realist idea of secure knowledge; but *Tender* does not present these as abstract ideas but rather embodies them in the very process of its prose. In this respect, *Tender* goes beyond Modernism and anticipates novels of the later twentieth and early twenty-first centuries which employ both Modernist and traditionally realist techniques to explore modern experience in its full complexity, which involves both an awareness of relativity and a desire for certainty in dynamic combination.

9

A Sample of Critical Views

Both *Gatsby* and *Tender* received mixed reviews on their first appearance. Ruth Snyder, in the *New York Evening World*, concluded that *Gatsby* convinces us that 'Mr. Fitzgerald is not one of the great American writers of to-day', but in the *Saturday Review of Literature*, William Rose Benét praised *Gatsby*'s 'thoroughly matured craftsmanship' and its 'concision and precision and mastery of material'. In the *St Paul Dispatch*, James Gray called *Tender* 'a big, sprawling, undisciplined, badly coordinated book' while in the *New York Evening Journal*, Gilbert Seldes saw *Tender* as the great novel promised by the control Fitzgerald had demonstrated in *Gatsby*. His 'triumph' in *Tender* was that, 'without a trace of symbolism or allegory, he makes this special story universally interesting' (*FR* 196, 220, 221, 289, 293).

Once the initial review response had subsided, *Gatsby* and *Tender* received little critical attention until the 1940s, after Fitzgerald's death, when important essays and introductions by William Troy, Arthur Mizener, Lionel Trilling, John Dos Passos and Glenway Wescott appeared. Maxwell Geismar's *The Last of the Provincials: The American Novel, 1915–1925* (1943) contained a substantial chapter on Fitzgerald, 'Orestes at the Ritz', but the first book wholly devoted to him was Arthur Mizener's 1951 biography, which included perceptive critical observations and provided a major stimulus to further interest in his life and work. It was not until 1957, however, that the first full-length critical study appeared, James E. Miller Jr's *The Art and Technique of*

F. Scott Fitzgerald. This focused on Fitzgerald's first three novels, *This Side of Paradise*, *The Beautiful and Damned* and *Gatsby*. An expanded edition with an extra chapter on *Tender* and *The Last Tycoon* came out as *F. Scott Fitzgerald: His Art and His Technique* in 1964. Miller's analyses remain lucid and insightful and he is the first critic we shall sample.

James E. Miller, Jr.

In *F. Scott Fitzgerald: His Art and Technique*, Miller seeks to show that Fitzgerald was a far more conscious craftsman than had previously been acknowledged. He sets Fitzgerald's work from *Paradise* to *Gatsby* in the context of the dispute between Henry James and H.G. Wells, in the early twentieth century, about the nature of the novel. Wells advocated the novel of 'saturation' which can encompass whatever interests the author at the time of writing, even if it departs from a main theme or disrupts the fictional illusion; James endorsed the novel of 'selection' which chooses only salient details and incidents that enrich a main theme and enhance the fictional illusion. Anglo-American literary criticism in the mid-twentieth century favoured the Jamesian rather than Wellsian aesthetic and Miller shares this preference. He sees Fitzgerald's fictional craft as pursuing an upward curve of development from the novel of saturation, exemplified by *This Side of Paradise*, through a transition represented by *The Beautiful and Damned*, to the novel of selection in *Gatsby*, 'his masterpiece' (Miller xiii).

Miller suggests, however, that it was the fiction of Joseph Conrad rather than the ideas of Henry James which influenced Fitzgerald in *Gatsby*. In particular, Miller argues, Fitzgerald learnt from Conrad the device of the 'modified first person' in which the narrator effectively effaces the author and performs his functions, supplementing his own eyewitness accounts with material supposedly gleaned from other sources and vivified by his imagination. Miller contends that another important technique in *Gatsby*, its reshuffling of conventional chronological order, derives partly from Conrad and partly from Conrad's sometime collaborator, Ford Madox Ford. By Ford's own account, he and Conrad thought that the novel should not go 'straight forward' in presenting a character but should do so in the piecemeal way in which one gets to know a person in actual life; you should first 'get [a character] in with a strong impression, and then work backwards and forwards over his past' (qtd Miller 112). Fitzgerald gets in his strong impression of Gatsby at the end of chapter 1, when Nick sees him on his dark lawn, reaching out his arms and trembling, and then, as the novel proceeds, working back and forth over his past and scrambling chronology. As Miller observes:

> Just how much Fitzgerald has rearranged the events of Gatsby's life can be seen by tracing events through the book chronologically; the only glimpse of Gatsby's boyhood is in the last chapter; the account of Gatsby, at the age of seventeen, joining Dan Cody's yacht comes in Chapter 6; the important love affair between Gatsby and Daisy, which took place five years before the action in the book when Gatsby, then in the army, first met Daisy, is related three separate times (Chapters 4, 6, and 7), but from various points of view and with various degrees of fullness; the account of Gatsby's war experiences and his trip, after discharge, back to Louisville to Daisy's home, is given in Chapter 8; and Gatsby's entry into his present mysterious occupation through Wolfshiem is presented, briefly, in Chapter 9. The summer of 1922, the last summer of Gatsby's life, acts as a string on to which these varicolored 'beads' of his past have been 'haphazardly' strung. (Miller 113–14; chapter numbers in Roman numerals in original)

Miller sees *Gatsby* as the crown of Fitzgerald's achievement but acknowledges that his technique in *Tender*, especially his use of point of view, is 'highly varied and sophisticated'. This could seem to produce, however, 'an embarrassment of riches'. *Tender* is as varied in technique as *This Side of Paradise*, but lacks that novel's 'exuberant experimentation'. Though 'more complex in conception' than *Gatsby*, it lacks *Gatsby*'s absolute control. In *Tender*, Fitzgerald seems always about to bring its 'disparate materials' into 'clear, thematic focus' but never quite does so (Miller 139). Miller makes some interesting suggestions, however, about how to interpret the 'disparate materials', especially in his idea that several of the characters around Dick reflect his weaknesses and make the novel a kind of allegory:

> In his quest for identity, Dick is confronted at every turn with reflections of the self, and it is here that the novel seems to achieve

much of its rich and complex texture. The book may be said to have a
mirror or echo structure: a number of the characters who revolve about
Dick Diver reflect one or another of his weaknesses in isolation. As he
looks about him, he can see not the self he is in process of dissipating,
but the several selves warring like vultures to take over the carcass of
his soul. In a way, the book with its mirror structure may be read as
an allegory, with Everyman (or at least American Everyman) Diver
journeying through a multitude of temptations – and succumbing to all
of them: Money, Liquor, Anarchy, Self-Betrayal, Sex. These abstractions
take carnal embodiment in Baby Warren, Abe North, Tommy Barban,
Albert McKisco, and Rosemary Hoyt. But each of these characters is
supplemented with additional figures who echo and re-echo the vice set
to trap the selfhood of the unwary wayfarer.   (Miller 142–3)

This interpretation might seem to focus too much on Dick and to
turn the novel into the equivalent of an Expressionist drama, in which
different characters represent aspects of a single mind. But Miller is
aware of the cultural and social dimensions of *Tender*, arguing that it
'tends in its thematic complexity to move rhythmically both inward
and outward, inward to an exploration in depth of the spiritual malaise
of Dick Diver, outward to an examination in breadth of the sickness of
a society and a culture'. As a 'brilliant example of the novel's outward
movement', Miller cites the passage starting 'Nicole was the product of
much ingenuity and toil' which we analysed in chapter 3 of this book.
Miller is concerned to maintain the sense that Dick's downfall should
be understood in both an inner and outward sense. The world which
Nicole represents creates him to serve its own ends and destroys him
when he is no longer useful to it. 'He is a victim – but he is victim
not only of these outside forces but also of his inner weaknesses and
compulsions' (Miller 146, 147).

Miller's 1957 book established the idea that Fitzgerald could be seen
as a conscious craftsman whose work culminated in the achievement of
Gatsby. His expanded version of his book in 1964 suggested that *Tender*,
even if not quite *Gatsby*'s equal in its technical control, was a richly
resourceful and interesting work. Two years later, Richard D. Lehan's
F. Scott Fitzgerald and the Craft of Fiction (1966) would provide further
explorations of Fitzgerald's novels which emphasized their complexity.

Richard D. Lehan

In his account of *Gatsby* in *F. Scott Fitzgerald and the Craft of Fiction*, Richard Lehan focuses on the ambivalence of Nick's attitudes towards Gatsby and the Buchanans which produces the irony of the novel:

> Nick Carraway is repulsed by and attracted to Gatsby. He is repulsed by the man's vulgar taste and gaudy display; he is attracted by the sincerity of Gatsby and his fidelity of commitment. He is repulsed by the Buchanans' *droit de seigneur* [lord's right] and their moral carelessness; he is attracted by their mobility and their heightened life … We see through Nick what is shoddy and glamorous in both Gatsby and the Buchanans, and this antithetical juxtaposition is the source of the novel's irony. Nick as ironic narrator is constantly tugged at – attracted and repelled by the same experience. The only character in the novel who puts experience to the scrutiny of an active conscience, Nick can say at one and the same time that 'there was something gorgeous about' Gatsby and that Gatsby 'represented everything for which I have an unaffected scorn'.   (Lehan 109, 110)

Working through these ambivalences teaches Nick that 'illusions have moral consequences' and that youthful dreams must be re-examined in the sober light of experience. Nick's sadness at Gatsby's fate is partly due to 'the sadness he feels for his own lost youth' (Lehan 111).

Lehan sees Fitzgerald's emphatic opposition of the worlds represented by Gatsby and the Buchanans as both weakening and strengthening his novel. By stressing the difference between those worlds, 'making the Buchanans the quintessence of snobbery, Gatsby the epitome of social unacceptability', he weakens the novel's credibility in realistic terms, so that it seems unlikely that, after five years of marriage to Tom, Daisy would encourage Gatsby's attentions. But he does give the novel another dimension, that of the romance, and moves 'the American novel toward mythical meaning'. With the theme of '[i]dealism in conflict with materialism', he approached 'the story of America itself'. Lehan argues, however, that Fitzgerald, in *Gatsby*, did not stop at the story of America, but went further: he 'extended his novel beyond history to the realm of metaphysics, to the story of man's fight against the process of time'.

rel. disagree, boxed, reverse for T's affair

Three realms are interrelated in *Gatsby* so that it is 'thematically and structurally like a series of ever-widening ripples' which 'move from a personal sphere (a story of unrequited love), to a historical level (the hope and idealism of the frontier and of democracy in conflict with a rapacious and destructive materialism), to a metaphysical sphere (man's desire to preserve and relive the idyllic moment)' (Lehan 113–14, 116, 118). Lehan valuably deepens our sense of *Gatsby*'s complexity, even if we may feel that his oppositions and his definitions of the three spheres of the novel are too neat.

Like Miller, Lehan feels that *Tender* lacks the 'control' of *Gatsby* and suggests that he may have 'brought too many disparate elements to the novel and extended the theme too broadly beyond the story of Dick Diver to include American history and [Oswald] Spengler's theory of the declining West'. He contends that, in *Tender*, 'Fitzgerald never really succeeded in working out a coherent and sustained point of view; was never satisfied with the inverted time sequence; and inserted a number of implausible episodes' (Lehan 146, 147). Despite these problems, however, the novel has sufficient thematic focus for him to compare and contrast it with *Gatsby*:

> Whereas *Gatsby* was a novel about what could never be, *Tender* is a novel about what could have been. Dick Diver had the talent and genius to succeed; he also had in his youth the necessary vision and sense of commitment. He was sidetracked by the very rich and by his own weakness, which was to feel needed and be the center of attention. Both Gatsby and Dick Diver believed that they could make time stand still; Gatsby thought he could recapture the lost past, and Dick Diver thought that his future would wait for him. Fitzgerald suggests that both were not aware of the nature of time.   (Lehan 148)

Tender may be less technically accomplished than *Gatsby*, but it still has much to offer.

Lehan's book, like Miller's, was crucial in establishing that Fitzgerald's work was worthy of sustained attention and that *Gatsby* and *Tender*, while not necessarily of equal stature, were especially interesting in terms of theme and technique. Like other Fitzgerald critics of this period, however, they were very male-centred in their approach, tending to see the women characters as little more than adjuncts to the men. With the growth of feminist criticism from the 1970s, Fitzgerald's female characters began to be revalued in ways that cast new light on his fiction. The next critic we shall consider, Sarah Beebe Fryer, provides rich examples of this revaluation in regard to Daisy in *Gatsby* and Nicole in *Tender*.

Sarah Beebe Fryer

In her 1984 essay on *Gatsby* and her 1985 essay on *Tender* and *Save Me the Waltz*, later assimilated into her full-length study *Fitzgerald's New Women: Harbingers of Change* (1988), Sarah Beebe Fryer sees Fitzgerald's women characters as exemplifying the difficulties American women faced in the 1920s when confronted with mixed messages about their roles and identities. As suggested in chapter 8 of this book, American women gained the vote in 1920 and to a limited extent enjoyed wider employment opportunities and greater sexual freedom, but they experienced no thoroughgoing emancipation. Fryer argues that Fitzgerald's women characters dramatize in various ways the confusion this could produce.

In her analysis of *Gatsby*, Fryer is concerned to defend Daisy against what Fryer regards as Nick's limiting judgements, which critics have often echoed and sometimes amplified. Fryer points out that Nick, except for his short one-to-one conversation with Daisy in the first chapter, only presents her external behaviour or the comments other people – Jordan and Gatsby – make about her. Nick perceives her affectation, her role-playing, but offers no analysis of what might lie beneath it. Fryer suggests, however, that we see enough of Daisy to infer her complex and conflicted feelings:

> In three key scenes – Nick's first visit to the Buchanans [chapter 1], Gatsby's reunion with Daisy [chapter 5], and the hot afternoon at the Plaza [chapter 7] – Nick's simple descriptions of Daisy reveal her genuine love for Gatsby, her intense fear of emotions in general, and her craving for stability. The juxtaposition of these forces suggests the severity of Daisy's conflict: her longing for personal freedom is brought out by her deep-rooted love of Gatsby, but her fear of emotions and her need for stability make her cling to her unsatisfactory marriage to Tom.   (Fryer [a] 157–8)

Fryer offers plausible interpretations of each of these scenes as revealing Daisy's mixed emotions and aspirations, and supports her readings by citing Jordan's account of Gatsby's wartime relationship with Daisy, her motives for marrying Tom and the early days of their wedded life. In conclusion, Fryer affirms that Daisy is 'a victim of complex needs and desires' who 'deserves more pity than blame' (Fryer [a] 145).

Like Daisy in *Gatsby*, Nicole in *Tender* and Alabama Beggs in *Save Me the Waltz* have been brought up to believe men must look after women – first their fathers, then their husbands. But in contrast to Daisy, Nicole and Alabama see changes in the world around them, encountering women who work alongside men and enjoy similar benefits in terms of self-esteem and income. This increases their feeling that they are inadequate and lack purpose. Fryer cites passages from Nicole's interior monologue, which we analysed in chapter 3 of this book: Nicole feels, for example, that she is 'tired of knowing nothing and being reminded of it all the time' (*TN* 178) and, believing Dick's view that 'work is everything', she is, Fryer contends, bound to feel inadequate when she has no work of her own. Fryer points out that Nicole has brains as well as beauty. When she is at Dohmler's clinic as a girl, Franz acknowledges her 'excellent mind' and tells Dick that Dohmler 'gave her a little Freud to read' (*TN* 146). She sometimes seems to understand people – including Dick himself – better than he, a trained psychiatrist, does; in the incident where Lanier complains that he has been bathed in dirty water, Dick sits on the bedside and gestures to Nicole to take over.

According to Fryer, Nicole 'struggles sadly with her internalized notion that she is virtually worthless except by association with men'. *Tender* does portray two career women but both of these suffer: one is Rosemary, who enjoys fame as a movie actress but does not find mutual romantic love; the other is Dick's patient, the 'American painter who had lived long in Paris' (*TN* 201), who suffers a possibly psychosomatic skin disease which has made her 'a living, agonizing sore' and who declares that she is 'sharing the fate of the women of my time who challenged men to battle' (*TN* 203). Lacking successful female role models, Nicole pursues romance, 'one of the few options traditionally available to women', and has an affair with Tommy Barban. This shows her increasing psychological health but also her continuing willingness to let 'her relationships with men' define her

(Fryer [b] 324). Nonetheless Tommy is better than Dick since he at least sees her as sane.

> In *Tender*, Nicole ... takes small but important steps toward her own personal freedom in a world dominated by men ... But because she continues to define herself in terms of her connections with men, her self-esteem remains shaky: men can destroy or affirm her sense of self-worth almost at will ... Nicole ..., presented under the cloak of schizophrenia, is a representative twentieth-century woman, embodying conflicting ideas of femininity (submissiveness) and independence.   (Fryer [b] 325)

Fryer put forward an important argument for a reconsideration of Fitzgerald's female characters as perceptive portraits of women torn by the wider conflicts over femininity current in their time, and valuably shifted the focus away from the male characters in ways that prompt a revaluation of Fitzgerald's achievement in *Gatsby* and *Tender*, and across the whole range of his fiction. But Fryer's critical approach remained a traditional one which treated characters as if they were real people and novels as if they were fairly direct reflections of social reality. In the 1980s and 1990s, under the influence of deconstruction and poststructuralism, the critical emphasis changed and fictional characters and their worlds were seen more as textual constructions than reflections of realities. This approach was sometimes more widely extended so that not only literary works but also societies and nations themselves were regarded as textual constructions, in the sense that their identities were shaped by discourses of race, class and gender. The next essay we shall consider is an example of twenty-first century criticism which takes this kind of approach to *Gatsby*, linking it with discourses about race and nation.

Barbara Will

In her essay '*The Great Gatsby* and the Obscene Word' (2005), Barbara Will begins with Nick's claim that 'Gatsby turned out all right at the end' (*GG* 8). The ending of the novel, in which Gatsby becomes a symbol of American aspiration, reinforces this claim; but its validity depends on forgetting that most of the novel has shown Gatsby as corrupt: a criminal and an adulterer. Will contends that *Gatsby* 'self-consciously inscribes this process of forgetting into its own narrative' and that this is 'the point of one of [its] most important yet least critically examined scenes', in which Nick erases the 'obscene word' scrawled on Gatsby's 'white steps' (*GG* 171). This erasure is required, Will suggests, in order that Gatsby should 'turn out all right at the end' and represent America. But by portraying this erasure, Fitzgerald also seems to raise questions about whether the ending of the novel is as inevitable as it can seem. 'Gatsby "turn[s] out all right" only if we forget, or repress, his obscenity.' Will points to the etymology of 'obscene', from the Latin 'obscenaeus' which means both 'against the presentable' and 'unrepresentable'. Thus 'obscene' incorporates the ideas of that which cannot be represented and that which works against representation, threatening 'the conventional language of narration or the normative discourses of a nation' (Will 125, 126).

Will points to the ways in which, in the text of the novel, Gatsby eludes representation, to the repeated vanishings with which he is associated. At key points in the text – when Nick first glimpses him on his lawn at the end of chapter 1 (*GG* 25), after he introduces him to Tom in chapter 4 (*GG* 72) – he vanishes; his smile, at the very moment that it assures that it has 'precisely the impression of you that, at your best, you hoped to convey', vanishes (*GG* 49); he is elusive at his parties, in his past, in his business affairs; when he relates his early encounters with Daisy, he reminds Nick of 'something – an elusive rhythm, a fragment of lost words', but what he has 'almost remembered' remains 'uncommunicable forever' (*GG* 107). The emphasis on Gatsby's dreaminess undermines the idea that he is the heir of Benjamin Franklin and of the heroes of Horatio Alger stories. Gatsby is always about to deliver meaning but never does so. Both Nick and Tom try to pin him down to a fixed meaning: for Nick, he is, ultimately, an American, indeed a universal hero; for Tom he is corrupt, threatening the rigid class and racial boundaries, the supremacy of the 'Nordic' race which Tom wants to uphold.

Gatsby's own ethnic origins are unclear, but he is linked with organized crime through the Jewish Wolfshiem, and his own original surname, 'Gatz', may or may not be Jewish; this uncertainty indicates how Gatsby is 'always "vanishing" into racial and hence social indeterminacy'. 'Neither identifiably black nor identifiably Jewish, the shifting, obscure, ever-vanishing figure of James Gatz/Jay Gatsby troubles the category of "whiteness"', at a time (as we saw in chapter 8 of this book) of intense anxiety about immigration as a source of social and political instability. Gatsby cannot be seen as definitely Other – like the African Americans in the limousine or the Greek Michaelis – but he is 'not quite white'. But 'being "not quite" is perhaps Gatsby's most troubling aspect ... Gatsby consistently eludes the terms of both national and textual belonging.' This elusiveness is epitomized in the 'obscene word' which could be a racial insult – it is presented as 'a defilement of whiteness' in that it is scrawled on 'the white steps' – but which is finally unknowable (Will 133, 135, 136).

In the passages which follow Nick's erasure of 'the obscene word', Gatsby is presented as knowable and indeed inscribed in not merely an individual but a national narrative, that of America. Setting him in a lineage that links him with the early Dutch settlers and establishes his racial credentials displaces the possibility that Gatsby may be of 'alien' extraction and his links with those, like Wolfshiem, who are. This is one of the ways in which he 'turn[s] out all right at the end'. But Nick's prior erasure of 'the obscene word' undermines his affirmation of Gatsby as a representative of a racially exclusive idea of America, since it enacts the same process of dissolving fixed meaning that made Gatsby so troubling earlier:

> If the threat of Gatsby in the text lies precisely in the way in which he 'vanishes' from categorization and social or racial signification, then Nick's erasure of the obscene word stages a similar process, making the obscene word 'vanish' in order to cancel out the obscenity of vanishing. Gatsby is purified by this gesture, but the gesture itself reasserts the primacy of indeterminacy in the text. Put 'under erasure' in the Derridean sense, Gatsby's obscenity becomes the absence that allows the text's ultimate presence to emerge: the presence of generations of Nordic American settlers, mythically united for a moment in Nick's transitional vision of national essence. (Will 139)

The incident of the erasure of the obscene word, Will suggests, prevents the end of *Gatsby* from becoming a mystifying affirmation of national identity and indicates how any such identity depends on erasure and indeterminacy: how it is defined not only by its positive terms but also by what it excludes, both in terms of ethnic others and in terms of a more general indeterminacy on which all signification depends. Will's interpretation fruitfully combines deconstructive ideas derived from the thought of Jacques Derrida, an awareness of the novel's relation to contemporary debates, in Fitzgerald's time and in our own, about national and ethnic identity, and close attention to specific textual detail (particularly the often-overlooked scene of 'the obscene word'), in relation to more general aspects of the text. Our next sample of criticism, also published in 2005, considers how the narrative structure of *Tender* relates to one of its explicit key concerns, psychoanalysis, which is seen here as offering not so much psychological truths as narratives which can bridge traumatic ruptures and, ultimately, traverse the storyless void beneath signification.

Susann Cokal

In 'Caught in the Wrong Story: Psychoanalysis and Narrative Structure in *Tender is the Night*' (2005), Susann Cokal investigates 'the ways Freud's storytelling form and structure influenced Fitzgerald's attempt to *express*' the content of *Tender*. Cokal contends that *Tender* 'centres on incest as a site of narrative reorganization'. The stories Nicole tells herself, and that others tell themselves, about her father's incestuous violation 'represent ruptures in psyche and life-story'. 'Repairing or bridging those ruptures', according to Cokal, 'gave Fitzgerald the opportunity to offer comment on psychoanalysis and its theories of incest and mental disorder while experimenting with narrative form in ways that he hoped would prove revolutionary.' Cokal cites Fitzgerald's claim in a letter to Maxwell Perkins, quoted in chapter 7 of this book, that his fourth novel would be 'something really NEW in form, idea, structure – the model for the age that Joyce and Stein are searching for, that Conrad didn't find' (qtd *SG* 268). This ambition allies him with Modernist writers who aimed to generate new styles to represent psychological and social processes. Cokal acknowledges that *Tender*, while Fitzgerald's 'most experimental' text, is not as deeply innovative as, for example, Gertrude Stein's *Tender Buttons* (1914). She asserts, however, that *Tender* 'does weave back and forth in time and point of view' and calls its 'architecture' a 'Freudian triptych, with each section offering not only a major plot movement but also a shift in principal point of view' (Cokal 75, 76). But, Cokal argues, these point-of-view shifts are not merely arbitrary:

> Points of view [in *Tender*] tend to change because one character's narrative fantasy no longer works and must be replaced by another. For example, Rosemary's fantasy of the perfect Diver family breaks down when she finds Nicole raving in the bathroom; it is then necessary to shift to an alternative fantasy, the slightly more realistic one entertained by Dick, who knows Nicole is sick but believes that their intersecting transference-loves are actually her cure. Dick's fantasy disintegrates in turn, leading to his disastrous imprisonment in Rome and the strange avowal that he has raped an infant; then we shift to Nicole's doctors, and gradually to Nicole herself, all of whom have other fantasies about her cure. (Cokal 91)

When Nicole observes Dick with their children, he is emphatically seen as a father for the first time. It is Dick as her surrogate father whom she moves away from, shedding the part of 'Daddy's Girl' to assume the role of the adulteress – or rather, of the daughter who leaves Daddy to assert her own desire; but she does so 'with another dominant male'. In Book 3 of *Tender*, Nicole's worldview comes to seem the only viable one in a situation in which all the characters are in the grip of 'illusion, delusion, and some form of psychosis'. Her point of view increasingly commands the narrative. In Cokal's words, it is 'as if [Nicole] takes over the writing of the story, making it about her rather than Dick (usually considered the novel's hero or antihero) or Rosemary' and turning it into a more linear narrative (Cokal 91).

Insofar as *Tender* does start to turn into a more linear narrative as Nicole's point of view becomes uppermost, it does not necessarily achieve a conclusion that satisfies readers. Dick fades out with a 'dying fall' and Nicole's marriage to Tommy can look like a submission to another and more oppressive figure who resembles her father more closely than Dick. Cokal suggests that this possibly unsatisfying ending is Fitzgerald's recognition that a case history never really ends, never achieves closure. While this deferral of closure could seem another sort of repression, it might not be wholly negative but 'a kind of unconscious editing of a story, eliminating undesirable events' which 'also creates a story, calling it into being by means of symptoms that escape repression's boundaries and express what is individual in a life'. In this perspective, *Tender* demonstrates, and implicitly celebrates, 'the psychoanalytic model as a source of plot and an affirmation of the power of the right words to create good stories', provided that we also acknowledge that 'the "good" story, the interesting tale, is also the "wrong" one', in the sense that it works to mask, not a trauma, but the void which lies beneath all stories (Cokal 95).

Conclusions

This sample of critical views suggests how *Gatsby* and *Tender* are open to a range of critical approaches. Each of these five interpretations is interesting, illuminating, plausibly argued, and supported by specific examples from the texts of the novels it discusses – and each is also questionable and partial. Many other readings of *Gatsby* and *Tender* have been offered and more will continue to appear, and this is an index of the fertility of the two novels. Both have that capacity to generate multiple and constantly multiplying interpretations which has been seen as the defining feature of the classic literary work.

Further Reading

Other Works by Fitzgerald

There are several works by Fitzgerald which are interesting in themselves and which will help to enrich your understanding and enjoyment of *Gatsby* and *Tender*. His two other completed novels, *This Side of Paradise* (1920) and *The Beautiful and Damned* (1922), and his unfinished *The Last Tycoon* (1941), give a broader and deeper sense of his themes and his constant experimentation with fictional form. The galley-proof version of *Gatsby*, which Fitzgerald altered significantly in the light of Maxwell Perkins's feedback, has now been published as *Trimalchio* (2000), and is a substantial work in its own right which also enables us to see how Fitzgerald's revisions created the final version of the novel, for example by inserting the famous description of Gatsby's smile in chapter 3 (*GG* 49). The version of *Tender* first published in 1951, in which Malcolm Cowley, supposedly acting in accordance with Fitzgerald's own second thoughts, reversed the positions of Books 1 and 2 in the original edition to make the narrative run more chronologically is well worth reading and comparing with the original version.

There is a range of short stories particularly associated with *Gatsby* and *Tender* in terms of theme: the *Gatsby* group, consisting of 'Absolution', '"The Sensible Thing"' and 'Winter Dreams' and a rather larger and more diffuse *Tender* group, the most relevant of which are 'One Trip Abroad'; 'Jacob's Ladder'; 'Magnetism'; 'A Short Trip Home'; 'On Your Own'; 'Indecision'; and 'Babylon Revisited'. There are also four vivid essays by Fitzgerald which bear on *Gatsby* and *Tender*: 'Echoes of the Jazz Age'; 'My Lost City'; 'The Crack-Up'; and 'Early Success'. Zelda Fitzgerald's *Save Me The Waltz* (1932) is a vivid, stylistically inventive novel which (as Fitzgerald complained) draws on some similar material to *Tender*.

Key Novels of the Period by Other Writers

The 1920s was a very productive period in American literature. Key novels which provide fascinating comparisons and contrasts with *Gatsby* and *Tender* are Sinclair Lewis's *Main Street: The Story of Carol Kennicott* (1920), a satire on the American Midwest from which Fitzgerald, and Nick Carraway, came; Theodore Dreiser's *An American Tragedy* (1925), a very powerful naturalistic tale in which Clyde Darrow's desire to marry a wealthy young woman leads him to murder and the electric chair; John Dos Passos's *Manhattan Transfer* (1925), an innovative, multi-faceted novel of New York life; and Ernest Hemingway's masterly *The Sun Also Rises* (1926) (UK title: *Fiesta* (1927)), set among American and British expatriates in Paris.

Biography

Both Arthur Mizener's *The Far Side of Paradise* (1951), the first Fitzgerald biography, and Andrew Turnbull's *Scott Fitzgerald* (1962), by an author who was 11 when he first met Fitzgerald, remain readable and reliable. Matthew J. Bruccoli's *Some Sort of Epic Grandeur* (1981) is the most detailed biography yet. André Le Vot's *Scott Fitzgerald* (1983), trans. William Byron, is an accomplished biography which includes an insightful interpretation of *Gatsby*. Jeffrey Meyers's *Scott Fitzgerald* (1994) has been strongly criticized by some Fitzgerald scholars but is lively and informative. *The Romantic Egoists* (1974), edited by Matthew J. Bruccoli, Scottie Fitzgerald Smith and Joan P. Kerr is a superb compilation which reproduces excerpts from Fitzgerald's scrapbooks, photographs and newspaper and magazine articles, and provides an incomparable impression of Scott and Zelda's life and work.

Criticism

General books on Fitzgerald

There are several important critical studies of Fitzgerald which include substantial discussions of *Gatsby* and *Tender*: James E. Miller, Jr, *F. Scott*

Fitzgerald: His Art and Technique (1964) and Richard Lehan, *F. Scott Fitzgerald and the Craft of Fiction* (1966), both sampled in chapter 9 of this book; Milton R. Stern, *The Golden Moment: The Novels of F. Scott Fitzgerald* (1970); John F. Callahan, *The Illusions of a Nation: Myth and History in the Novels of F. Scott Fitzgerald* (1972); Brian Way, *F. Scott Fitzgerald and the Art of Social Fiction* (1980); Sarah Beebe Fryer, *Fitzgerald's New Women: Harbingers of Change* (1988); and Andrew Hook, *F. Scott Fitzgerald: A Literary Life* (2002). Two significant critical anthologies with key essays on *Gatsby* and *Tender* are Arthur Mizener (ed.), *Scott Fitzgerald: A Collection of Critical Essays* (1963) and Ruth Prigozy (ed.), *The Cambridge Companion to F. Scott Fitzgerald* (2002).

The references in the section on Sarah Beebe Fryer in chapter 9 of this book are from her essays 'Beneath the Mask: The Plight of Daisy Buchanan' in Donaldson (1984 – details below), 154–66 (cited as Fryer [a]) and 'Nicole Warren Diver and Alabama Beggs: Women on the Threshold of Freedom', *MFS* 31:2 (Summer 1985), 318–25), cited as Fryer [b].

Books, critical anthologies and essays about *Gatsby*

Richard Lehan's *The Great Gatsby: The Limits of Wonder* (1990) is a very good study from a traditional critical perspective. Ronald Berman's *The Great Gatsby and Modern Times* (1994) and *The Great Gatsby and Fitzgerald's World of Ideas* (1997) are absorbing and original contextual studies. Nicolas Tredell's *Fitzgerald's The Great Gatsby: A Reader's Guide* (2007) covers the novel's style and structure, its critical reception and publishing history, its play, film and opera versions and its literary influence. Key critical anthologies are Ernest H. Lockridge (ed.), *Twentieth Century Interpretations of The Great Gatsby* (1963) and Scott Donaldson's *Critical Essays on F. Scott Fitzgerald's The Great Gatsby* (1984). Nicolas Tredell (ed.), *F. Scott Fitzgerald: The Great Gatsby: A Reader's Guide to Essential Criticism* (1997) traces the critical history of *Gatsby* from 1925 to the 1990s, with copious extracts from relevant critics. Important and as yet uncollected essays on *Gatsby* (possibly accessible from school and university databases) include Meredith Goldsmith, 'White Skin, White Mask: Passing, Posing and Performing in *The Great Gatsby* (*MFS*, 49:3 (Fall 2003), 443–68); the essay sampled in chapter 9 of this book, Barbara Will, '*The Great Gatsby* and the Obscene Word' (*College Literature*, 32:4 (Fall 2005), 125 –44); and Benjamin Schreier, 'Desire's Second Act: "Race" and *The Great Gatsby*'s Cynical Americanism' (*Twentieth Century Literature*, 53:2 (Summer 2007), 153–84).

Books, critical anthologies and essays about *Tender*

Milton R. Stern's *Tender is the Night: The Broken Universe* (1994) focuses on *Tender's* engagement with American history. Matthew J. Bruccoli's *The Composition of Tender is the Night: A Study of the Manuscripts* (1963) is a fascinating account of the 17 extant compositional stages of the novel, while Bruccoli and Judith S. Baughman's *Reader's Companion to Tender is the Night* (1996) provides much valuable data, including full details of the passages from 37 of Fitzgerald's short stories which he incorporated into *Tender*. Key critical anthologies are Marvin J. Lahood's *Tender is the Night: Essays in Criticism* (1969) and William Blazek and Laura Rattray (eds), *Twenty-First Century Readings of Tender is the Night* (2007). Important and as yet uncollected essays on *Tender* (possibly accessible from school and university databases) include Robert Wexelblatt, 'F. Scott Fitzgerald and D. H. Lawrence: Bicycles and Incest' (*American Literature*, 59:3 (October 1987), 378–88); John Haegert, 'Repression and Counter-memory in *Tender is the Night*' (*Essays in Literature*, 21:1 (March 1994), 97–116); and the essay sampled in chapter 9 of this book, Susann Cokal, 'Caught in the Wrong Story: Psychoanalysis and Narrative Structure in *Tender is the Night*' (*Texas Studies in Language and Literature*, 47:1 (Spring 2005), 75–100).

Index

Alger, Horatio, 204
Allen, Louisa (FSF's grandmother), 168
America (USA)
  American Dream, 27, 159, 161
  American Expeditionary Force (AEF), 54,
    183–4
  California, 65, 67, 185
  Chicago, 65, 67, 185
  economic growth, 183, 185–6
  Eighteenth Amendment (1919), 184, 189
  flappers, 187
  gangsters, 183, 185
  Great Depression, 188, 189, 192
  immigration, 183, 187–8, 205
  Midwest, 9, 144, 153, 175, 210
  national identity, 27, 161, 168, 205–6
  National Origins Act (1924), 187–8
  National Prohibition (Volstead) Act
    (1919), 184
  New York City, 9, 30, 32, 41, 44, 47, 59,
    60, 62, 70, 74, 83, 103, 114, 116,
    143–4, 146, 153, 154, 173, 174, 175,
    180, 184, 185, 192, 210
  New York State, 159, 169, 180
  Nineteenth Amendment (1920), 186
  Prohibition, 57, 183, 184–5, 189, 193
  Quota Law (1921), 187
  Teapot Dome scandal, 183, 185
  Twenty-First Amendment (1933), 189
  Wall Street Crash, 83–4, 162, 186, 188–9,
    193
  women's role, 186–7, 201
  World War One (First World War), 172,
    173, 183–4, 187, 191
Arbuckle, Roscoe ('Fatty'), 119, 121

Barron Collier advertising agency, 173
Baughman, Judith S., 212
Baxter, Warner, 1, 177
Belasco, David, 44
Benét, Stephen Vincent, 182
Benét, William Rose, 195
Berman, Ronald
  *The Great Gatsby and Fitzgerald's World
    of Ideas* (1997), 211
  The Great Gatsby and Modern Times
    (1994), 211
Bible
  Genesis, 23
  Luke, 19
Bishop, John Peale, 171
Blazek, William
  *Twenty-First Century Readings of Tender is
    the Night* (2007), 212
Book of Common Prayer (1662), 116, 140
Brooke, Rupert, 170, 172

Bruccoli, Matthew J., 77
  The Composition of Tender is the Night (1963), 212
  Reader's Companion to Tender is the Night (1996), 212
  The Romantic Egoists (1974), 210
  Some Sort of Epic Grandeur (1981), 210
Bunyan, John
  The Pilgrim's Progress (1678–84), 131
Burnett, Frances Hodgson, 34, 37
  Little Lord Fauntleroy (1886), 37
  The Secret Garden (1911), 37
Burton, Robert, 181

Callahan, John F., *The Illusions of a Nation* (1972), 211
Capone, Al, 185
Carlyle, Thomas, 164
Cather, Willa
  A Lost Lady (1923), 194
  My Ántonia (1918), 194
Cézanne, Paul, 191
Chicago University, 85
Cokal, Susann, 'Caught in the Wrong Story' (2005), 206–8, 212
College Humor, 178
Conrad, Joseph
  Heart of Darkness (1902), 19
  'Preface', *The Nigger of the Narcissus* (1897), 194
Coolidge, Calvin, 185, 189
Cowan, Leslie, 182
Cowley, Malcolm, 25, 209
Crane, Hart, *The Bridge* (1930), 191
Crawford, Joan, 181
Cullen, Countee, *Color* (1925), 192, 193

Davies, Owen, 177
deconstruction, 203, 205, 206
Derrida, Jacques, 205, 206
DiCaprio, Leonardo, 1
Donaldson, Scott, *Critical Essays on F. Scott Fitzgerald's The Great Gatsby* (1984), 211
Donne, John, 'A Valediction: Forbidding Mourning', 131, 140
Dos Passos, John, 67, 181, 195
  Manhattan Transfer (1925), 210

Douglas, Aaron, 192
Dreiser, Theodore, 175
  An American Tragedy (1925), 192, 210

Eddington, Sir Arthur Stanley, 189
Einstein, Albert, 189, 190
Eliot, Dr Charles W., 149
Eliot, George, *Middlemarch* (1871–2), 159
Eliot, T. S., 1, 191
  The Waste Land (1922), 33, 57, 190, 191, 193
Ellington, Duke, 192
Esquire (magazine), 181
Etty, William, 45
Europe, 21, 22, 35, 38, 54, 57, 64, 77, 153, 157, 159, 173, 175, 177, 178, 179, 183, 184, 187, 188, 189, 191, 192
existentialism, 130

Fadiman, Clifton, 59
Fall, Albert B., 185
Fay, Father Sigourney, 170, 173
Fitzgerald, Annabel (FSF's sister), 169
Fitzgerald, Edward (FSF's father), 168–9
Fitzgerald, F. Scott, life
  and Ernest Hemingway, 177
      Ginevra King, 171, 172, 173
      Harold Ober, 174
      Irving Thalberg, 178, 182
      Lois Moran, 178
      Maxwell Perkins, 173–4, 176, 177
      Shane Leslie, 170, 172
      Sheilah Graham, 168, 181, 182
      Sigourney Fay, 170, 173
      Zelda Fitzgerald (*née* Sayre), 167, 173, 174–6, 178–81, 209–10, 210
  at Barron Collier advertising agency, 173
      Newman School, 169–70
      Princeton University, 170–2
      St Paul Academy, 169
  in Asheville, North Carolina, 181
      Baltimore, 180, 181
      Capri, 177
      Delaware, 178
      France, 176, 177, 178, 179
      Great Neck, Long Island, 175–6
      Hollywood, 178, 179, 181–2
      Italy, 176

St Paul, Minnesota, 168, 169, 170, 173, 175, 178
birth, 168
daughter, 167, 175, 176, 178, 181
death, 182
family origins, 168
finances, 167, 173, 174, 175, 177, 178, 180
illnesses, 171, 172, 182
marriage, 167, 174
parents, 168–9
physique, 168
Roman Catholicism, 73, 169, 170, 173, 175, 178
US Army service, 172–3
Fitzgerald, F. Scott, movies of his fiction
The Chorus Girl's Romance (1920), 174
The Great Gatsby (1926), 1, 177
The Great Gatsby (1949), 1
The Great Gatsby (1974), 1
The Husband Hunter (1920), 174
The Last Time I Saw Paris (1954), 182
The Offshore Pirate (1921), 174
Fitzgerald, F. Scott, movie-writing jobs
'Cosmopolitan' (1940), 182
'Lipstick' (1927), 178
Madame Curie (1938–9), 181
Three Comrades (1937–8), 181
Winter Carnival (1939), 181
The Women (1938), 181
Fitzgerald, F. Scott, nonfiction
'Author's House' (1936), 168
'The Crack-Up' (1936), 181, 194, 209
'Early Success' (1937), 174, 209
'Echoes of the Jazz Age' (1931), 184, 209
'Handle with Care' (1936), 164
'My Lost City' (1932), 159, 209
'Pasting it Together' (1936), 171
'Princeton' (1927), 170–1
Fitzgerald, F. Scott, novels (except *Gatsby* and *Tender*)
The Beautiful and Damned (1922), 44, 170, 175, 192, 196, 209
The Last Tycoon (1941), 178, 182, 196, 209
'The Romantic Egotist' (written 1918), 170, 172, 173
This Side of Paradise (1920), 123, 168, 170, 172, 173, 174, 175, 196, 197, 209
Trimalchio (2000), 209

Fitzgerald, F. Scott, plays, poems and shows
The Captured Shadow (1912), 170
The Coward (1913), 170
Fie! Fie! Fi-Fi! (1914), 171
'Football' (1911), 170
The Girl from Lazy J. (1911), 169
The Vegetable: From President to Postman (1923), 176
Fitzgerald, F. Scott, short stories
'Absolution' (1924), 177–8
'Babes in the Wood' (1917), 172, 173
'Babylon Revisited' (1931), 84, 180, 182, 209
'Bernice Bobs Her Hair' (1920), 175
'The Captured Shadow' (1928), 170
'Crazy Sunday' (1932), 180
'The Diamond as Big as the Ritz' (1922), 175
'First Blood' (1930), 179
'Head and Shoulders' (1920), 174, 175
'The Ice Palace' (1920), 175
'I Didn't Get Over' (1936), 173
'Indecision' (1931), 209
'Jacob's Ladder' (1927), 209
'The Last of the Belles' (1929), 180
'Magnetism' (1928), 209
'May Day' (1920), 175, 184
'Myra Meets His Family' (1920), 174
'The Mystery of the Raymond Mortgage' (1909), 169
'The Offshore Pirate' (1920), 174
'One Trip Abroad' (1930), 209
'On Your Own' (wr. 1931; pub. 1979), 179, 209
'Pat Hobby's Christmas Wish' (1940), 181
'The Rich Boy' (1926), 73, 83, 177
'The Scandal Detectives' (1928), 178
'"The Sensible Thing"' (1924), 178, 209
'A Short Trip Home' (1927), 123, 209
'Tarquin of Cheapside' (1917), 172
'Winter Dreams' (1922), 177, 209
Fitzgerald, F. Scott, short-story collections
All the Sad Young Men (1926), 177
Flappers and Philosophers (1920), 175
Tales of the Jazz Age (1922), 172, 175
Taps at Reveille (1935), 180
The Pat Hobby Stories (1962), 181

Fitzgerald, Mary (*née* MacQuillan) (FSF's mother), 168
Fitzgerald, Michael (FSF's grandfather), 168
Fitzgerald, Scottie (FSF's daughter), 167, 175, 176, 178, 180, 210
Fitzgerald (*née* Sayre), Zelda, 167, 173, 174–5, 176, 178–80, 181
  'A Millionaire's Girl' (1930), 178
  Save Me the Waltz (1932), 180, 201, 202, 209–10
  'Scandalabra' (1933), 180
Ford, Ford Madox, 196–7
Franklin, Benjamin, 204
Freud, Sigmund, 189, 190, 202, 206–7
Fryer, Sarah Beebe
  'Beneath the Mask: The Plight of Daisy Buchanan' (1984), 201–2, 211
  Fitzgerald's New Women: Harbingers of Change (1988), 201, 211
  'Nicole Warren Diver and Alabama Beggs: Women on the Threshold of Freedom' (1985), 201, 202–3, 211

Garbo, Greta, 181
Gauguin, Paul, 191
Geismar, Maxwell, *The Last of the Provincials* (1943), 195
Girard, René, 71
Gogh, Vincent van, 191
Goldberg, Rube, 50, 53
Goldsmith, Meredith J., 'White Skin, White Mask: Passing, Posing and Performing in *The Great Gatsby*' (2003), 211
Graham, Sheilah, 168, 181, 182
Grant, General Ulysses S., 19, 21, 24–5, 28, 45, 54, 158, 159–60
Gray, James, 195
The Great Gatsby, textual features
  adjectives, 7, 17, 18, 57, 62, 71, 90–1, 101–2, 110, 116, 129, 130, 144
  adverbs, 31–2, 62, 72, 84, 130
  aposiopesis, 56, 156
  beginning, 5–11, 13–19, 25–8, 160–1
  circumlocution, 9–10, 25, 27–8
  dashes, 16–17, 27, 31, 55, 56
  dialogue, 31, 55, 56, 62–3, 103, 143, 144

diction, 2, 8. 17, 25, 27, 28, 32, 56, 84, 101–2, 103, 110, 140
ending, 2, 142–6, 152–7, 163–4
euphemism, 9–10, 25, 27–8, 61, 73
guest list, 40–8, 54, 56, 57, 63
imagery, 2, 8, 9, 10, 17–18, 27, 28, 32–3, 57, 62, 63, 84, 92, 98–9, 106, 111, 128, 130, 131, 140, 155, 156, 157
indirection, 5, 7, 25, 130, 139, 140, 160–1
intertextual links, 2, 18–19, 28, 33, 45, 57, 85, 93, 111, 116, 131, 140, 193
intratextual links, 2, 10, 27–8, 42, 57, 84, 91, 111, 140
irony, 32, 61, 74, 81, 92, 118, 131, 156, 199
lists, 22, 55, 62, 81, 84
metaphor, 8, 9, 18, 19, 53, 54, 57, 90, 92, 93, 103, 108, 128, 145, 151, 155–6, 157
metonymy, 33, 57, 116, 153
mythical references, 42, 47, 54, 57, 72, 79, 129, 193, 199, 205
narrator, 1, 5, 7–10, 25, 26–7, 55, 60–1, 101, 115, 117, 127, 130, 134, 193–4, 196, 197
nouns, 15, 45, 63, 71, 90–1, 102, 103, 111, 116, 140
Owl-Eyed Man, 44, 47, 63, 79, 129, 145
oxymoron, 32
parallelism, 16
personification, 33, 55, 57
point of view, 197
religious references, 16–17, 28, 72, 73, 81–2, 108, 116, 124, 128
romantic modernism, 1, 71, 139
romantic vocabulary, 8, 9, 10, 93
sentences, 7, 8, 9, 16–17, 27, 28, 31, 38, 56, 60, 61, 72, 73, 84, 90, 93–4, 99, 110, 117–18, 127, 129, 130–1, 140, 155, 156
simile, 18, 70, 73, 92, 93, 117–18, 131, 145
tenses, 61
timescales/signals, 16, 26, 27, 28, 31, 42–3, 57, 90, 94, 127, 153, 154, 156, 196–7
verbs, 18, 31, 61, 72, 81, 84, 90, 102, 103, 108, 116, 117, 128–9, 154, 155, 157
zeugma, 153

The Great Gatsby, themes and topics
  aesthetics, 18, 56, 62, 71, 82, 90, 93, 152,
    155, 162
  automobiles (cars), 41, 45, 46, 69, 71, 84,
    92, 100, 102–3, 108, 111, 113, 114,
    115–16, 124, 126, 127, 140, 143,
    145, 152, 153, 154
  class, 42, 62–3, 204
  commodity, 17, 62, 71, 81, 145, 146
  consumerism, 2, 59, 62, 64, 66, 71, 81,
    84, 144
  ethnicity, 188, 193, 204–6
  gender, 2, 7, 62, 87–94, 100–4, 109–12,
    110, 111, 162, 187
  identity, 7, 10, 16, 27, 59, 61, 62, 101,
    161, 173, 205–6
  innocence, 154, 155
  liminality, 91–2
  mimetic desire, 71
  money, 2, 43, 59–64, 68–74, 80–6
  nature, 47, 85
  parties, 2, 29–33, 40–8, 54–8, 87–94, 161
  society, 2, 29–33, 40–8, 54–8, 63, 81, 85,
    110, 111, 145, 161
  trauma, 2, 55, 84, 113–18, 126–32,
    138–41, 162–3
  value, 17, 69, 71, 74, 82, 83, 85, 145
  war, 2, 19, 47, 131
  World War One (First World War), 42,
    44, 46, 74, 109, 113, 153, 183, 184,
    193, 197

Haegert, John, 'Repression and counter-
    memory in *Tender is the Night*'
    (1994), 212
Harding, Warren G., 185, 189
Harlem Renaissance, 192–3
Harvard University, 22, 35, 79, 106, 149
Hayes, Roland, 192
Hemingway, Ernest, 177, 191
  In Our Time (1925), 192
  A Moveable Feast (1964), 177
  'The Snows of Kilimanjaro' (1936), 73,
    177
  'Soldier's Home' (1925), 184
  The Sun Also Rises (*Fiesta*) (1927), 210
Hollywood, 38, 48, 50, 160, 178, 179, 180,
    181, 182

Homer, 92
  The Illiad, 42
  The Odyssey, 54, 57
Hoover, Herbert, 185, 189
Howard University, 192
Hughes, Langston, *Weary Blues* (1926), 192
Hurston, Zora Neale, *Their Eyes Were
    Watching God* (1937), 192

Impressionism, 191

James, Henry, 189, 194, 196
James, William, 189–90
  The Meaning of Truth (1909), 190
  Pragmatism (1907), 190
  The Principles of Psychology (1890), 190
  The Will to Believe (1897), 190
Johns Hopkins University, 21
Jonson, Ben, *Volpone* (1607), 47
Joyce, James, 1, 177, 191, 206
  Ulysses (1922), 190
Jozan, Édouard, 176

Keats, John, 1
  'Ode on a Grecian Urn', 80, 85, 164
Kerr, Joan P., 210
Key, Francis Scott, 'The Star-Spangled
    Banner' (1814), 168
King, Ginevra, 171, 172, 173

Ladd, Alan, 1
Lahood, Marvin J., *Tender is the Night: Essays
    in Criticism* (1969), 212
Larsen, Nella
  Passing (1929), 193
  Quicksand (1928), 192
Lee, Robert E., 24
Lehan, Richard D.
  F. Scott Fitzgerald and the Craft of Fiction
    (1966), 198–201, 211
  The Great Gatsby: The Limits of Wonder
    (1990), 211
Leslie, Shane, 170, 172
Le Vot, André, *Scott Fitzgerald* (1983), 210
Lewis, Sinclair, *Main Street: The Story of Carol
    Kennicott* (1920), 210
Lincoln, Abraham, 163
Locke, Alain, *The New Negro* (1925), 192

Lockridge, Ernest H., *Twentieth Century Interpretations of The Great Gatsby* (1963), 211
Lowell, Robert, 181
Luce, Claire Boothe, 181
Luhrmann, Baz, 1

Magoffin, Elizabeth, 169
Manet, Édouard, 191
McClennan, Howard (Dean of Princeton), 172
McKay, Claude, *Home to Harlem* (1928), 192
McQuillan, Louisa (FSF's grandmother), 169
McQuillan, Philip F. (FSF's grandfather), 168
Meyers, Jeffrey, *Scott Fitzgerald* (1994), 210
Miller, James E., Jr., *F. Scott Fitzgerald His Art and Technique* (1964), 195–8, 200–1, 210–11
Milton, John, 191
Minerva, 47, 79 *see also* Pallas Athene
Mizener, Arthur, 195
    The Far Side of Paradise (1951), 210
    Scott Fitzgerald: A Collection of Critical Essays (1963), 211
Modernism, 1, 37, 71, 190–4
Monet, Claude, 191
Moran, Lois, 178
Motley, Archibald, 192
Mulready, William, 45
Murphy, Gerald, 176
Murphy, Sara, 176

Nassau Literary Magazine, 171
New Testament, 19, 28
Newton, Sir Isaac, 189
Norris, Frank, 175

Ober, Harold, 174
O'Hara, John, 164

Pallas Athene, 76, 79, 85 *see also* Minerva
Perkins, Maxwell, 173–4, 175, 176, 177, 178, 180, 206
Pershing, General John J., 49, 50, 54, 184
Picasso, Pablo, 77, 191
    Les Demoiselles d'Avignon (*The Maids of Avignon*, 1906–7), 190
Plath, Sylvia, 181

poststructuralism, 203
Pound, Ezra, 191
pragmatism, 190
Prigozy, Ruth, *The Cambridge Companion to F. Scott Fitzgerald* (2002), 211
Princeton Tiger, 171
Princeton University, 45, 170–2, 174, 184
Prohibition, 57, 183, 184–5, 189, 193
psychoanalysis, 163, 206, 212

Rappe, Virginia, 121
Rattray, Laura, Twenty-First Century Readings of Tender is the Night (2007), 212
Redbook Magazine, 177
Rennie, James, 177
Robeson, Paul, 192
Rockefeller, John D., 60, 63, 81
Roosevelt, Franklin D., 189
Rothstein, Arnold, 185

Sartre, Jean-Paul
    Being and Nothingness (1943), 97
    Nausea (1938), 129
Saturday Evening Post, 174, 178
Schreier, Benjamin, 'Desire's Second Act: "Race" and *The Great Gatsby*'s Cynical Americanism' (2007), 211
Schulberg, Budd, *The Disenchanted* (1950), 181
Scott, Cecilia Ashton (FSF's grandmother), 168
Scribner's (FSF's publisher), 172, 173, 174, 176, 180
Scribner's Magazine, 180
Seldes, Gilbert, 195
Shah of Persia, 49, 50, 51, 52
Shakespeare, William, 1, 163
    Hamlet, 154
    Henry IV 1, 45
    A Midsummer Night's Dream, 19
    Sonnet: 'When my love swears that she is made of truth', 135
    Twelfth Night, 158
Shelley, Percy Bysshe, 1, 191
    'Ode to the West Wind', 68
Sinclair, Harry F., 185
The Smart Set, 173

Smith, Bessie, 192
Snyder, Ruth, 195
Spengler, Oswald, 200
Stein, Gertrude, 177, 191, 206
    Tender Buttons (1914), 206
Steinbeck, John, 67, 164
Stella Dallas (1925 movie), 178
Stephens, Toby, 1
Stern, Milton R.
    The Golden Moment: The Novels of F. Scott
        Fitzgerald (1970), 211
    Tender is the Night: The Broken Universe
        (1994), 212
Stravinsky, Igor, 191, *Le sacré du printemps*
    (*The Rite of Spring*, 1913), 190
Styron, William, 181
Swinburne, Algernon Charles, 93, 111
    Atalanta in Calydon, 93
    'Faustine', 45

Talmadge, Constance, 178
Tender is the Night, textual features
    adjectives, 12, 13, 36, 50, 65, 66–7, 123,
        150
    adverbs, 13, 68, 150
    aposiopesis, 40, 56, 99
    beginning, 11–13, 19–25, 25–8
    dialogue, 36, 39–40, 56, 97, 98, 99,
        124–5, 136, 149
    diction, 2, 12, 27, 28, 36, 52, 56, 84, 110,
        123, 140
    direct discourse, 135
    ellipses, 135, 150
    ending, 2, 142, 146–52, 157–60, 163–4
    enigma, 39, 125, 140
    free indirect discourse, 135–6
    gothic mode, 79, 123, 126
    hyperbole, 122
    imagery, 2, 12, 26, 27, 28, 37, 50, 53, 54,
        55, 57, 66, 68, 70, 71–2, 78–9, 84,
        90, 98–9, 106, 111, 134, 135, 136,
        137, 140, 151
    irony, 21, 22, 54, 67, 97, 122, 136, 138,
        149, 150, 151, 159, 160
    indirect discourse, 50, 135–6
    indirection, 25, 140, 160–1
    interior monologue, 21, 27, 77, 82, 84,
        99, 135, 160, 202

intertextual links, 2, 23, 28, 37, 54, 57,
    85, 111, 135
intratextual links, 2, 27–8, 84, 111, 140
lists, 22, 39, 57, 64–5, 66, 81, 84,
    136–7
metaphor, 12, 23, 53, 54, 65, 67, 79, 106,
    108, 137, 140, 151
mythical references, 23–4, 28, 54, 79–80
narrative description, 36, 97
narrator, 1–2, 5, 21, 23–4, 25, 26, 38, 39,
    40, 50, 65, 66, 68, 96, 108, 121, 122,
    123, 134–5, 136, 158–9, 160, 194
nouns, 12, 36, 66, 123
oxymoron, 97, 134
parallelism, 51, 56, 136
personification, 79
point of view, 2, 36, 50, 55, 97, 108, 121,
    123, 125, 135, 136, 137, 149, 158,
    197, 200, 206–7
realist mode, 126, 194
religious references, 12, 13, 53–4, 68, 84,
    108, 123, 124, 151–2
romantic modernism, 1, 37, 139
semi-dialogue, 77–8, 84
sentences, 2, 12, 13, 21, 24, 27, 28, 40,
    50, 51–2, 56, 65, 66, 67–8, 79, 84,
    96, 97, 99, 110, 123, 135–6, 136–7,
    138, 140, 148, 150
simile, 12, 13, 27, 50, 52, 53, 57, 78, 79,
    108, 149–50
tenses, 31, 51, 78, 84, 158
thriller mode, 125
time signals, 2, 12, 26, 27, 28, 31, 51, 57,
    77, 200, 206–7
verbs, 12, 13, 36, 51, 52, 53, 66, 67, 68,
    80, 97, 106, 107, 108, 123, 135,
    150, 151
Tender is the Night, themes and topics
    aesthetics, 23, 56, 68, 84, 96, 106, 162
    automobiles (cars), 50, 52
    class, 64, 66, 68, 81
    consumerism, 2, 39, 57, 59, 64, 66, 67,
        78, 84, 85
    ethnicity, 121, 188
    gender, 2, 87, 94–100, 104–9, 109–12,
        150, 162, 187
    identity, 26, 53, 57, 59, 66, 138, 161,
        197–8

Tender is the Night, themes and topics –
   continued
  incest, 2, 56, 97, 113, 118, 124, 125, 138,
    206, 212
  innocence, 12, 13, 26, 37, 150,
  intactness, 20, 22, 23, 132, 134, 140
  money, 2, 59, 64–8, 74–80, 80–6, 95,
    99, 133, 137, 139, 158, 160, 161–2,
    198
  nature, 53
  parties, 2, 29, 33–40, 48–58, 124, 151
  pregnancy, 67, 78
  role-reversal, 135
  romantic modernism, 1, 37
  society, 2, 29, 33–40, 48–54, 54–8, 110,
    111, 161, 198
  trauma, 1, 2, 23, 55, 84, 113,
    118–26, 132–8, 138–41, 162–3,
    206–8
  value, 74, 83, 85
  war, 1, 2, 12, 13, 24, 79, 110
  World War One (First World War), 49, 53,
    54, 113, 183, 193
Tennyson, Alfred Lord
  'The Eagle', 150
  Locksley Hall, 156–7
Thalberg, Irving, 178, 182
Tolstoy, Leo, 170
Toomer, Jean, *Cane* (1923), 192, 193
trauma studies, 163
Tredell, Nicolas
  Fitzgerald's The Great Gatsby: A Reader's
    Guide (2007), 211

F. Scott Fitzgerald: The Great Gatsby: A
   Reader's Guide to Essential Criticism
   (1997), 211
Triangle Club, 171, 172
Trilling, Lionel, 195
Troy, William, 195
Turnbull, Andrew, *Scott Fitzgerald* (1962),
   210

USA *see* America

Van Vechten, Carl, *Nigger Heaven* (1926),
   193
Vassar College, 167
Voltaire, 45

Wanger, Walter, 181
Way, Brian, *F. Scott Fitzgerald and the Art of*
   Social Fiction (1980), 211
Wells, H. G., 196
Westcott, Glenway, 195
Wexelblatt, Robert, 'F. Scott Fitzgerald and
   D. H. Lawrence: Bicycles and Incest'
   (1987), 212
Wharton, Edith, 194
Will, Barbara, '*The Great Gatsby* and the
   Obscene Word' (2005), 203–6, 211
Wilson, Edmund, 171, 172, 175,
Wilson, Woodrow, 183
Wurtzel, Elizabeth, 181

Yale University (New Haven), 19, 20, 21, 22,
   41, 88, 90, 159